Offenders for a Word

Offenders for a Word

DANIEL C. PETERSON
STEPHEN D. RICKS

ASPEN BOOKS

Offenders for a Word:
How Anti-Mormons Play Word Games
to Attack the Latter-day Saints

No portion of this book may be reproduced in any form without written
permission from the publisher, Aspen Books, 6211 South 380 West,
Salt Lake City, UT 84107

Library of Congress Cataloging-in-Publication Data

Peterson, Daniel C.
　　Offenders for a word : how anti-Mormons play word games to attack
　　the Latter-Day Saints / Daniel C. Peterson and Stephen D. Ricks.
　　　　p.　cm.
　　Includes bibliographical references and index.
　　ISBN 1-56236-208-9 : $9.95
　　　　1. Church of Jesus Christ of Latter-Day Saints—Apologetic works.
　　2. Mormon Church—Apologetic works.　3. Church of Jesus Christ of
　　Latter-Day Saints—Controversial literature—History and criticism.
　　4. Mormon Church—Controversial literature—History and criticism.
　　I. Ricks, Stephen David.　II. Title.
　　BX8635.P48　1992
　　289.3—dc20　　　　　　　　　　　　　　　　　　　92-32724
　　　　　　　　　　　　　　　　　　　　　　　　　　　　　CIP

Printed in the United States of America

10　9　8　7　6　5　4　3　2　1

Cover design: Brian Bean

About F.A.R.M.S.

Publication of this volume has been made possible in part by the Foundation for Ancient Research and Mormon Studies (F.A.R.M.S.), a non-profit educational and research organization dedicated to the study of ancient scripture, especially the Book of Mormon. F.A.R.M.S. encourages and supports such research and makes its results available as inexpensively as possible through journals, books, and a newsletter. (For further information about the Foundation and the services it offers, write F.A.R.M.S., P.O. Box 7113, University Station, Provo, UT 84602 or call toll free 1-800-327-6715).

And the multitude of all the nations that fight against Ariel, even all that fight against her and her munition, and that distress her, shall be as a dream of a night vision.

It shall even be as when an hungry man dreameth, and, behold, he eateth; but he awaketh, and his soul is empty: or as when a thirsty man dreameth, and, behold, he drinketh; but he awaketh, and, behold, he is faint, and his soul hath appetite: so shall the multitude of all the nations be, that fight against mount Zion. . . .

Wherefore the Lord said, Forasmuch as this people draw near me with their mouth, and with their lips do honour me, but have removed their heart far from me, and their fear toward me is taught by the precept of men:

Therefore, behold, I will proceed to do a marvellous work among this people, even a marvellous work and a wonder. . . .

Surely your turning of things upside down shall be esteemed as the potter's clay. . . .

And in that day shall the deaf hear the words of the book, and the eyes of the blind shall see out of obscurity, and out of darkness.

The meek also shall increase their joy in the Lord, and the poor among men shall rejoice in the Holy One of Israel.

For the terrible one is brought to nought, and the scorner is consumed, and all that watch for iniquity are cut off:

That make a man *an offender for a word*, and lay a snare for him that reproveth in the gate, and turn aside the just for a thing of nought. . . .

They also that erred in spirit shall come to understanding, and they that murmured shall learn doctrine.

Isaiah 29:7-8, 13-14, 16, 18-21, 24 (emphasis ours)

Contents

Abbreviations Used in Notes

JD   Watt, G. D., et al., eds. *Journal of Discourses*. 26 vols. London: Latter-day Saints Book Depot, 1855-86.

HC   Roberts B. H., ed. *History of the Church*. 2d ed., rev. 7 vols. Salt Lake City: Deseret Book, 1978.

TPJS *Teachings of the Prophet Joseph Smith*, selected and arranged by Joseph Fielding Smith. Salt Lake City: Deseret Book, 1984.

▲

Introduction

▲

The somewhat cryptic title of this work—*Offenders for a Word*—comes from the twenty-ninth chapter of the book of Isaiah, a chapter that is not only replete with prophecies of the restoration of the gospel and the coming forth of the Book of Mormon, but with predictions of the kind of opposition that would greet the latter-day work. Much of this opposition, as we are convinced and attempt to show in the pages that follow, rests upon the manipulation of language, upon illegitimate semantic games that truly make innocent people "offenders for a word."

While we are confident that our conclusions are fully justified by the evidence as well as by reason, we are aware that these conclusions may seem controversial to some of our readers. In order to avoid the possible suggestion of tendentiousness in our renderings of early Christian materials, we have generally followed standard English translations of these sources, rather than providing our own. To the best of our ability, we have followed the plain sense of these, as well as other sources that we cite, although we are aware that other interpretations are possible. Given the very large number of references that we cite in the course of this work, it is inevitable that some unintentional errors may have crept in. We feel confident, however, that such errors as there might be have had no effect on the argument.

This book has taken many years, moving by fits and starts, to reach publication. Many people have helped us along the way. We wish to thank Ronald E. Taylor and our colleague Prof. Dilworth B. Parkinson, who stepped in to save an early version of the book from a disastrous computer failure. Robert L. Durocher, John Gee, and Matthew Roper supplied useful information. Adam Lamoreaux and Gaye Strathern did yeoman service in reading portions of the text and in checking many of the references. Deborah D. Peterson was supportive in many ways, direct and indirect. Shirley S. Ricks helped in getting the material into a publishable format, as did Melvin J. Thorne. Curtis Taylor and Stan Zenk, of Aspen Books, were a pleasure to work with. We also express our gratitude to Reverend Stephen Hoekstra, of Vail, Colorado, and Reverend Henry F. Fingerlin, of Littleton, Colorado, who—doubtless unintentionally—provided some of the inspiration for our writing. Though unsympathetic to our position, Reverend H. Jeffrey Silliman, of Salt Lake City, offered useful comments on an early draft.

We dedicate this volume to our wives, Deborah and Shirley.

▲

Is Mormonism Christian?
An Investigation of Definitions

▲

"When *I* use a word," Humpty Dumpty said, in rather a scornful tone, "it means just what I choose it to mean—neither more nor less."

"The question is," said Alice, "whether you *can* make words mean so many different things."

"The question is," said Humpty Dumpty, "which is to be master—that's all."[1]

THEOLOGIANS DO NOT, generally, ask other theologians if they are heretics. Most people are too well aware of the subjective nature of such designations to rely on a person's self-description in this manner. Very few men and women, we all realize, would choose to describe themselves as "heretics" or "heterodox," except perhaps in an ironic vein. On the other hand, we routinely ask—certainly we can at least imagine ourselves asking—whether some living or

---

1 Carroll (1963): 269.

historical person is a Christian, or a Jew, or a Buddhist, or a Muslim. Hospital admission forms and military induction papers, to choose two illustrations from among many, commonly ask for precisely such information, just as they inquire about weight and home address and full name. Furthermore, we seem to expect that the answer given to this question—"Of what religion are you?"— conveys objective truth, that it depends not on the position and preferences of some other individual or group of individuals empowered to accept or reject it, but on the simple, straightforward facts of the case. If the patient in Room 3458 has identified herself as Catholic, a priest will be called in when necessary. If Private Roth says he is a Jew, that fact will be noted on his dog tags. We do not see these matters as subject to debate or prey to controversy, any more than we would normally consider weight, home address, or full name questions for dispute. That Isaac Newton was a Christian seems as objectively valid a judgment, and as universally acceptable a claim, as that he formulated the laws of gravity or lived in early eighteenth-century England.

There are voices today, however—insistent and often loud voices—who would make of the designation "Christian" a judgment no more objective, no more universally acceptable and agreed upon, than the verdict of "heresy." Indeed, these accusing voices would apply the terms "heretic" and "non-Christian" according to rules of their own choosing, making them virtual synonyms. This is strikingly evident in the recent fashion, among certain circles, of denying that Mormonism is Christian.[2] There are probably few

---

2 A few examples might include Coe and Coe (1985): 188; Gruss (1980): 17-18; *The Utah Evangel* 33 (July/August 1986): 1; van Baalen (1983): 159; Whalen (1963): 173; Molland (1959): 355; Decker and Hunt (1984): 82, 246 (cf. on this Scharffs [1986]: 123-24, 353-55); Geer, "Who Is This Man . . . ?"; Martin (1955): 7, 51; Martin (1976): 3; disappointingly, Brauer (1971): 575; Spittler (1962): 11-18; Decker (1979): 23, 27-28; Decker, "To Moroni with Love"; Lanczkowski (1972): 208-13. This is to be distinguished from the (much more sophisticated) view, held by some scholars, that Mormonism is somehow post-Christian, that—as the view's foremost contemporary exponent, Jan Shipps, would put it—Mormonism is to Christianity as Christianity is to Judaism. Such a notion is beyond the scope of this study; anyway, its adherents are able simultaneously to hold opinions on the

Latter-day Saints who have not, at one time or another, been told—usually to their considerable surprise—that they are not Christians. Indeed, a large and well financed campaign has been underway for several years to convince the general public that The Church of Jesus Christ of Latter-day Saints, despite its unwavering identification of itself as Christian, does not deserve and cannot lay claim to that title. Hundreds and perhaps thousands of fundamentalist and other conservative Protestants in the United States and abroad are working desperately to alert mankind to the dangerous "Satanic nature of the Christ-denying cult of Mormonism."[3] Of course, these critics would not gladly admit that their denial of Mormon Christianity rests upon subjective grounds; they claim instead to issue their judgment on the basis of cold, hard, objective facts, submitted to rigorous, value-neutral analysis.

The campaign of which we speak is a literal one and not merely our own sensationalistic metaphor. It has its rallies, its enthusiastic volunteers, and its professional organizers and cheerleaders. It uses all the media of print, radio, and television to publicize its point, and has produced a flood of newspapers, pamphlets, newsletters, and books. Some few years ago, for example, a Houston-based organization seeking contributions to fund a "Christian" radio station in Provo, Utah, published a pamphlet entitled "KEYY: A Missionary Opportunity." Attempting to arouse its audience to the magnitude of the challenge posed by Mormonism, the pamphlet announced that "there are seven . . . counties in Utah with *no known Christians!* (There are more Christians per capita in India

---

question at issue here, which is whether or not Mormonism is Christian. Significantly, they contradict one another: Shipps (1985) affirms that it is, while Utter (1897): 13-23 (hesitantly), Molland (1959): 348, and Lanczkowski (1972) deny. (It is interesting to note that, in the English edition of Lanczkowski's work, the section dealing with the Mormons has been altogether deleted. Did he have second thoughts about the appropriateness of including the Mormons between Mongols and Muisca religion, or was it the simple fact of the size and relative power of Latter-day Saints in English-speaking countries that daunted the publishers?)

3 *The Utah Evangel* 33 (May 1986): 3; cf. *The Utah Evangel* 31 (May 1984): 1. Mormonism is "one of the more virulent strains of American cults"; Martin (1985): 173.

than in the State of Utah.) . . . This is an amazing opportunity to penetrate the darkness!"[4]

On 25 July 1986, the vocal anti-Mormon J. Edward Decker and a contingent of his followers even attempted to present a petition to leaders of The Church of Jesus Christ of Latter-day Saints, demanding that Mormons cease calling themselves Christians. (Unfortunately for the Deckerites, Church offices were closed for the long Pioneer Day weekend. Richard Baer, one of Decker's lieutenants, was finally able to deliver the petition on 8 August 1986.) Nearly 21,000 people had signed the petition by that date, and the drive was intended to continue.

Ed Decker and his friends do not, of course, seriously expect the Latter-day Saints or their leaders to "concede" that they are not Christians. (Church spokesman Jerry Cahill, asked what would be done with the petition and its accompanying documents, replied rather cryptically: "They will receive the attention they deserve, I suppose.") The effort, therefore, seems to have had one or both of the following goals: (a) to generate publicity for the accusation that Latter-day Saints are not Christians, or (b) simply to embarrass the Mormon Church.[5] The latter aim would not be out of character. Decker also actively fomented hostility toward Mormons in connection with construction of Brigham Young University's Jerusalem Center for Near Eastern Studies. He made at least one lengthy visit to Israel for that purpose, and the co-author of his book *The God Makers*, Dave Hunt, was the centerpiece of a Jerusalem press conference where representatives of eight denominations denounced Mormons as non-Christians. Of this latter episode, the long-time Israeli Jewish mayor of Jerusalem, Teddy Kollek, has tellingly observed that the anti-Mormon "attitude . . . was less than Christian."[6] And, indeed, the claim that The Church

---

4 "KEYY: A Missionary Opportunity," 5 (italics in the original), 8.

5 Salt Lake *Tribune* (26 July 1986); Salt Lake *Deseret News* (9 August 1986). Alert readers will recall the Nazi technique of "the Big Lie."

6 Kollek (1990): 78; cf. also "Leader of Anti-Mormon Group Admits He Helped Stir Jews' Furor over Center," Salt Lake *Tribune* (10 August 1985); "Christian

of Jesus Christ of Latter-day Saints is not Christian is frequently advanced with a passion and a vehemence that can shock unsuspecting Mormons hearing it for the first time. Speaking of what he calls "this sinister subject," William C. Irvine, for example, does not mince words: Mormonism is "a fountain of slime."[7]

While, in the view of these religious enthusiasts, Mormonism is a positive evil, its sinister nature is well concealed. Kenneth Boa, an active crusader against dissenters from mainstream Protestantism, declares Mormonism to be "one of the most effective counterfeits of biblical Christianity ever devised."[8] In *The Utah Evangel*, Mormonism is described as a "vicious imitation."[9] It is "devious" and "dishonest,"[10] and Mormons are "dupes."[11] "Dr." Walter Martin, the indefatigable "cult"-watcher, wrote of the Latter-day Saints that "they have not in the past hesitated to employ deception

---

Groups Join in Protest of Mormon Center," Denver *Intermountain Jewish News* (19 August 1985). This issue resulted in bomb threats against Mormon chapels and death threats against individual members of the Church. We have unpublished documentation on file, covering further anti-Mormon efforts to sow discord in Jerusalem.

7 Irvine (1921): 128, 133.

8 Boa (1984): 64; cf. P. B. Smith (1970): 52; J. O. Sanders (1962): 111-13.

9 *The Utah Evangel* 31 (March 1984): 2.

10 *The Utah Evangel* 31 (January 1984): 12, and 31 (March 1984): 6; cf. Decker and Hunt (1984): 246 (vs. Scharffs [1986]: 353). The Book of Mormon is a "sham," declares Martin (1955): 50, "cloaked in the finery of saintly language and masqueraded as divine revelation." The book of Abraham, according to Decker (1979): 46, is "pure fraud." Mormon belief in the restoration of the priesthood, says Fraser (1977): 91, rests on "chicanery." (Boettner [1986]: 266, no amateur in the language of religious disrespect, terms Catholic penances and indulgences "clever frauds.") *The Utah Evangel* 33(July/August 1986): 6, relates an anecdote to illustrate the fact that Mormon missionaries are generally liars, and suggests that their church trains them thus.

11 See Decker, "To Moroni with Love," 46, and virtually any issue of *The Utah Evangel*. The Book of Mormon is a "rank fake" (van Baalen [1983]: 162). Mormonism is "a religion built on patent fraud" (Whalen [1963]: 173). These facts are self-evident to all but the benighted Mormons.

in their effort to mimic orthodox Christianity."[12] More recently, "Dr." Martin revealed to his disciples that "Mormonism strives with great effort to masquerade as the Christian church."[13] Its army of missionaries is a vital concomitant of this vast lie: they merely "pose as Christians."[14] But the deception does not restrict itself to missionaries: Even a former Secretary of Education, Latter-day Saint Terrell H. Bell, in an invited presentation to the student body of Rev. Jerry Falwell's Liberty Baptist College, was only "posing as an exponent of the Christian faith."[15]

What is it, according to their adversaries, that Mormons have to hide? Why would they be so careful to dissimulate and mislead? Harold Lindsell is far from alone in reporting that the Latter-day Saints are actually pagans.[16] "When the Mormons opened their new temple . . . in Dallas," reported Kenneth L. Woodward in *Newsweek*, "visitors were hounded by fundamentalists . . . who waved placards proclaiming, 'Welcome to America's Newest Pagan Temple.' "[17]

Confronted with such hostility, and with charges that seem to come from out of nowhere, most Latter-day Saints, understandably, are at a loss for a reply. One sometimes suspects, in fact, that certain militant fundamentalist mindsets tend to see paganism

---

12 Martin (1976): 29; cf. *The Utah Evangel* 31 (December 1984): 1, 3. "Dr." Martin was something of an authority on misrepresentation; cf. the discussion of him in Brown and Brown (1984), which gives a certain ironic tang to his accusation, in Martin (1955): 17, that the "cults" project "deceptive veneers of pseudo-scholarship."

13 Martin (1985): 226; cf. Whalen (1963): 157. Theosophy also "masquerades," says Martin (1955): 41. Rather similar charges are made against the Roman Catholics; cf., for example, Whealon (1986): 16-17.

14 Fraser (1977): 10.

15 *The Utah Evangel* 30 (June 1983): 1.

16 Lindsell (1987): 115.

17 Woodward (1985): 65. This is, on the whole, a disappointing article, written with Mr. Woodward's usual incomprehension of what Mormonism is about; cf. A. L. Sanders (1986): 68.

everywhere—reflecting, perhaps, a deep-seated psychological alienation from the world and from society that goes beyond what any Christian ought to feel as "a stranger and a pilgrim." Bob Mc-Curry, for example, calls upon Christians to shun the "demonic" institution of Halloween.[18] Other examples could be provided without difficulty, but two will serve: Early in 1992, many newspapers carried a wire service story that offers a particularly extreme illustration of such attitudes, telling of a man whom an Indianapolis Municipal Court convicted of criminal mischief, a misdemeanor, for toppling and smashing a limestone monument on the statehouse lawn. The monument had been inscribed with the Ten Commandments. But, not, it would seem, with the Ten Commandments in precisely the form to which this gentleman was accustomed. To quote the newspaper account, the man's "defense was civil disobedience. He argued that the monument in question amounted to state endorsement of a pagan religion. He said the version of the commandments inscribed on the monument was a heretical one that lacked the Second Commandment's forbiddance [sic] to make graven images. He has said Indianapolis is loaded with graven images that depict ancient gods and goddesses."[19] And Ellen Goodman, in a nationally syndicated 1986 newspaper column, reported on a lawsuit in Greenville, Tennessee, brought by twelve "Christian" parents against the public schools: "The parents object to the tale of 'Goldilocks.'. . . They object to the dance around the burning wolf in 'The Three Little Pigs' because it promotes witchcraft. . . . A seventh-grade reader called on children to use their imagination, 'the powerful and magical eye inside your head.' This, said [one parent], was an 'occult practice.' " "The objections these parents raise," wrote Ms. Goodman, "are easily the stuff of parodies." Unfortunately, however, they represent very much the

---

18 See McCurry, "The Truth about Halloween."

19 As given in the Salt Lake City *Deseret News* (29 February 1992), on the basis of a UPI story. The article does not explain, but it seems probable that the monument on the statehouse lawn contained a Catholic version of the Ten Commandments.

mentality of many anti-Mormons. "In a chilling piece of testimony, [the mother who is the leader of the parental group] said that her religious belief did not allow for religious tolerance. 'We can not be tolerant of religious views on the basis of accepting other religions as equal to our own.' "[20]

Most non-fundamentalists, though, including many who profess to be Christians, have somehow managed to miss the occultism of "The Three Little Pigs." Even among fundamentalists, probably only a minority recognize in Halloween a demonic threat to their children, or fear imagination as a form of sorcery. More to the point, the Latter-day Saints have generally seemed to their neighbors to be decent, moral, religious people. Few Christians, even, have seen through the quiet, clean, religious Mormon exterior to the horrendous evil that, their critics declare, lies at Mormonism's heart. Hence the pressing need for the current campaign against The Church of Jesus Christ of Latter-day Saints. The public must be warned.

How have the Mormons managed to succeed in their fiendish ruse thus far? For many fundamentalist critics, the answer is quite simple. They are deceivers, says Dave Breese.[21] Mormonism "use[s] the language of the Holy Scripture to hide its true character."[22] It projects a deliberately confusing and "filmy coat of

---

20 Salt Lake City *Deseret News* (21 July 1986).

21 See Breese et al. (1985); cf. Decker (1979): 26, 29; *The Utah Evangel* 33(July/August 1986): 4; van Baalen (1983): 148, 151; Whalen (1963): 168; at Martin (1955): 53, Mormons are seen as blasphemers. They are out to "deceive the unwary"; *The Utah Evangel* 33 (May/June 1986): 4. According to Martin (1955): 46 (cf. 74), Mormonism "ensnares" souls; cf. also Decker and Hunt (1984): 157, 208, 230-31, 236-37, 252 (vs. Scharffs [1986]: 213, 270, 331, 341-42, 361-62). Compare the anti-Christian polemicists of the second and third centuries A.D., who were agreed, in the words of Gonzales (1970): 1:99-100, that "Christians approach only those who are ignorant—that is, women, children, and slaves—for they know that their 'science' would not resist solid refutation." (This is precisely the charge that Decker and Hunt [1984] make against Mormonism; cf. Scharffs's reply [1986]: 341.)

22 Irvine (1921): 128; cf. Fraser (1977): 8, 32. This is typical of "cultists"; cf. Martin (1955): 5, 74.

pseudo-Christian testimony."[23] Even the Articles of Faith are "deceptive," "hid[ing] heretical Mormon doctrines behind Christian terminology."[24]

But what is the purpose of such a "cleverly designed counterfeit of the Christian religion"? What is the goal of "the Mormon masquerade"?[25] Predictably, "Dr." Walter Martin knows. It is "cult infiltration."[26] The Latter-day Saints are attempting to insinuate themselves into Christianity in order to destroy it. For Mormonism is not merely non-Christian, it is "anti-Christian."[27] The relationship between Mormonism and Christianity is adversarial.[28]

---

23 Martin (1976): 30; cf. J. O. Sanders (1962): 109. Yount, "Black Brother, Black Sister," identifies one Mormon tool as "their slick publications." The deception is, of course, deliberate—certainly on the part of Mormon leaders; cf. Decker, "To Moroni with Love," 46. Cultists are just generally tricky devils. A favorite technique of Jehovah's Witnesses, says Martin (1955): 18, is "bluffing Christians into silence." They deal in "deliberate falsehood" (p. 32).

24 *The Utah Evangel* 33 (May 1986): 6; cf. *The Utah Evangel* 33 (July/August 1986): 6; *The Utah Evangel* 34 (May-June 1987): 6; Whalen (1963): 167. Martin (1955): 52, says that the Articles of Faith are "a clever and, I believe, a deliberate attempt to deceive the naive into believing that Mormonism is a Christian religion." Mormons have, says Rowe (1985): 28, a "heretical hidden agenda."

25 Martin (1976): 30, 20.

26 Martin (1976): 31. Decker and Hunt (1984) see Mormonism as, in the first instance, a subversive, theocratic movement. This is, of course, the view of classical American anti-Catholicism, which is well-represented by the work of Boettner (1986). Boettner's book is, however, much more competently written than is *The God Makers*.

27 Martin (1985): 213; so, too, *The Evangel* 37 (October 1990): 12; J. O. Sanders (1962): 109; van Baalen (1983): 170; Decker and Hunt (1984): 143 (vs. Scharffs [1986]: 203). Martin (1955) is generous with this accusation: Jehovah's Witnesses are "anti-Christian" (p. 18) and Charles T. Russell of Jehovah's Witnesses was "a sworn enemy of historical Christianity" (p. 24), Theosophy is "anti-Christian" (p. 44) and "anti-Biblical" (p. 39), Christian Science is "one of the most dedicated enemies of the evangelical Christian faith" (p. 58).

28 Scott (1979): passim; cf. too, Decker and Hunt (1984): 125 (vs. Scharffs [1986]: 181-82).

"To trust in Mormonism is to reject Christ."[29] Thus, there is a "deadly poison behind the honeyed words"[30] which Mormons use to conceal their deep "contempt for Christians."[31] John Henry Yount, in a pamphlet addressed to blacks, sounds this chilling alarm: "After a century-and-a-half of ripping-off white people and sending them to a Christless eternity, Mormonism is coming after you."[32] In the view of these anti-Mormons, it is likely that the Antichrist will be a Mormon.[33] "If Christianity is the thesis," writes Rick Branch, "then Mormonism must be its antithesis."[34]

After enduring hundreds of pages of our "experts" in the course of our research for this book, however, we wonder who has contempt for whom. Walter Martin, for example, alludes to the "blatant chicanery" of the Unity School of Christianity and calls it "a monstrous farce." Those who accept the claims of Mary Baker Eddy are, he says, "her zealous lackeys." Jehovah's Witnesses are "arrogant." Martin is also extremely sarcastic about the story of

---

29 *The Evangel* 37 (November 1990): 12.

30 J. O. Sanders (1962): 111.

31 *The Utah Evangel* 31 (March 1984): 6. The charge that Mormon temple ritual mocks Christian clergy was long a favorite among anti-Mormons, sparking, for example, considerable controversy in connection with the dedicatory services for the Denver Temple; cf. Decker and Hunt (1984): 246; but see also Scharffs (1986): 353.

32 Yount, "Black Brother, Black Sister" (emphasis ours). Mr. Yount denounces "the white-racist Mormon leadership" and attempts to align himself with the civil rights movement of the 60s. However, the pamphlet's short sentences and gigantic print would seem to imply a rather different attitude toward his intended audience.

33 See *The Utah Evangel* 31 (December 1984) and 33 (April 1986); also Decker and Hunt (1984): 229, 250 (vs. Scharffs [1986]: 15, 329, 358). (Do Mormons even come *close* to fulfilling the criterion of 1 John 2:22 and 2 John 7? Usually, they are accused of viewing the advent of Christ in too-fleshly terms! See below.) Martin Luther's eminent biographer Ronald Bainton notes with great regret the tendency in the Protestant Reformation to identify the Catholic Church and its leaders with Antichrist; cf. Bainton (1950): 330.

34 In *The Utah Evangel* 31 (January 1984): 12. (Rick Branch is the only Hegelian anti-Mormon we have ever encountered.)

Mormonism. "The general story of how Smith received his 'revelation' is a most amusing piece of fantasy," he writes, "and would be occasion for genuine laughter were it not for the tragic fact" that so many people believe it. And, he says, in order to believe it Mormons have to be egomaniacs. Likewise, Martin's treatment of Christian Science displays deep sexism, and his chapter on Father Divine is appallingly racist. He ridicules "cultists" generally, speaking, for instance, of "their manifestly feeble powers of logical thought." In fact, when he says of Jehovah's Witnesses that they "vilify and condemn all religious opponents as 'enemies of God' and perpetrators of what they term 'a racket,' " Walter Martin is very accurately describing what was, until his death in 1989, his own operation. He could seldom bring himself to grant the sincerity of those whom he attacked, and he could never grant their intelligence.[35]

G. H. Fraser adopts much the same tone. He caricatures Mormon beliefs on the afterlife, and then cites his own caricature to show that Mormons "have never been able to visualize a heavenly scene where the blessed are more than heavenly unemployed in a land of eternal sex." The Latter-day Saints hold their ludicrous, unscriptural beliefs because they don't understand English grammar. Elsewhere, approvingly citing earlier writers, he remarks that "Mormons, as a people, have never possessed . . . a modicum of common sense." Fraser is unwilling even to grant the legitimacy of Latter-day Saint religious impulses, declaring that "the Mormons have never displayed any of the graces of religion in their migrations and settlements." At still another place, he denies that there was any religious persecution of the Mormons, and points to

---

35 In order of citation, the references are to Martin (1955): 78, 80, 64, 18, 49-50, 55, 34, 37, 84-102, 16, 24. Loraine Boettner, whose book is described by Spittler (1962): 117, as "a veritable encyclopedia of evangelical criticism of Romanism," shows his characteristic tone when he says, on p. 253: "To Protestants the whole *ex cathedra* business appears, on the one hand, as particularly monstrous and vicious, and on the other, as just a big joke—a joke perpetrated on the Roman Catholic people who are so docile and unthinking and so poorly informed as to believe in and submit to such sophistry." We are proud that there exists no comparable literature in Mormonism.

their own obnoxious behavior as justification for what bad treatment they did receive.[36] He thus whitewashes one of the great blots on American history, in what must rank as a classic illustration of blaming the victim. (Those who make similar arguments with regard to Hitler's attempted extermination of the Jews are generally termed anti-Semites. Yet Fraser's book is highly thought of among anti-Mormons.)

But we must leave such quibbles, and return to the alleged duplicity of the Latter-day Saints. We have remarked that most Christians seem to have been taken in by Mormon attempts to disguise the paganism of their religious beliefs. Fortunately, the "experts" are not fooled by such Mormon craftiness. "Orthodox Christianity," reports James Spencer, "agree[s] unanimously that the Mormon Church [is] a non-Christian cult."[37] Certain strains of anti-Mormonism (perhaps in an effort to forestall the obvious and important question of what Mormons are if they are not Christian) have pronounced them to be "the Islam of America."[38] J. R. van

---

36 In order of citation, the references are to Fraser (1977): 14, 84, 183, 175-88.

37 Spencer (1984): 138. We have tried to show in our essay "Is Mormonism a Cult?" in this volume, that the term "cult" is so vague, and has been so abused, as to be virtually useless.

38 The Decker petition denying Mormons the name "Christian" asks them to use "New World religion" as a self-designation in its place—whatever *that* may mean! For recent equations of Mormonism with Islam, see *The Utah Evangel* 31 (February 1984): 1; Molland (1959): 348; Whalen (1963): 167. The supposed "Islamic connection" was especially popular in the nineteenth and early twentieth centuries, and deserves a separate study. In many cases, the accusation that Mormons are not Christian seems to reflect the accuser's ignorance of non-Christian religions, which leads him to overstate the differences between Mormonism and traditional Christianity while undervaluing the considerable areas of commonality. To cite an example, one of the authors, in writing to a leader of the southern California Ex-Mormons for Jesus about their denial of his Christianity, suggested that she talk with a Muslim if she wanted to meet a *real* non-Christian. He was immediately accused of holding a double standard: "How," came the reply, "can you be offended when we call you non-Christian, and then turn right around and call *Muslims* non-Christian?!?" Of course, the crucial difference, recognized even by Molland (1959): 348, is that Mormons claim to be Christian, whereas Muslims do not. More on this below.

Pelt, on the other hand, imagines that "the Mormon conception of deity rather resembles that of Buddhists"[39]—although, given the utter absurdity of the comparison, it does not surprise us that he provides no support for his assertion. More recently, it has become fashionable among anti-Mormons to call the object of their attacks Hindus, or even Satanists.[40] The wild variety which characterizes these comparisons—is an Islamic Hindu Buddhism even remotely

---

39 J. R. van Pelt, "Mormons," in Jackson (1977): 8:18; cf. Decker and Hunt (1984): 254 (vs. Scharffs [1986]: 364). It will become apparent that Decker and Hunt (1984) seem willing to say almost anything, however inconsistent, if it will damage Mormonism. In recent years, Decker has come under attack from fellow anti-Mormons like Wally Tope and the Tanners for apparently untrue claims that he was poisoned by agents of the Latter-day Saints during a trip to Great Britain.

40 Decker and Hunt are the foremost proponents of the Hindu theory. They are also among the chief advocates of the Satanist theory—which says something about their view of non-Christian religions! (For them, Hinduism equals Satanism; cf. Decker and Hunt [1984]: 60, 137, 251; contrast Scharffs [1986]: 197; cf. Scharffs [1986]: 256.) Of course, it is always difficult to tell how serious Mr. Decker is. On purported Mormon Hinduism, see Decker and Hunt (1984): 28, 32, 60, 250-51, 254, 258 (vs. Scharffs [1986]: 10, 81-83, 101, 358-59, 364, 371). On alleged Mormon Satanism, see Decker and Hunt (1984): 71-78; 105-09; 127-31; 134-35; 138-39; 160-61; 170; 188-92; 208-10; 216, 248-49; 251 (vs. Scharffs [1986]: 31, 48, 97, 109-18; 122-23; 133; 145; 148; 155-59; 170; 172; 183-84; 187-91; 196-99; 209; 219; 228; 249-51; 271-72; 276; 296; 356; 359); cf. also the tract, "Questions for Your Temple Tour." Compare Ed Decker's "The Question of Freemasonry," 7-8; *The Utah Evangel* 33 (July/August 1986): 4; Fraser (1977): 41, 74. *The Utah Evangel* 33 (May/June 1986): 2, contains a handy list of etymologies linking Mormonism with Satan-worship. A Deckerite tract entitled "Temple Marriage: Eternal Commitment or Eternal Damnation?" alleges that Mormon temple rituals are really Baal worship; cf. W. Thompson, "What We Should Know about Roman Catholicism." The *Prayer Bulletin* of Saints Alive in Jesus (December 1984) contains a "Prayer Map" of Utah which presupposes many of Mr. Decker's views on this subject. (These Prayer Bulletins are an excellent—and often amusing—source for Deckerite ideology.) "It has been wisely observed," says Martin (1955): 11, "that the field of apologetics has the depth of the oceans and the breadth of the celestial galaxies." However, one will search in vain in his writings for any evidence of such broad sympathy and deep erudition. In a discussion of Unity's denial of trinitarianism, for example (Martin [1955]:75), he characterizes their position as one of "abject pantheism." To use such an adjective to describe one of the most venerable and philosophically significant of theological viewpoints speaks eloquently of Martin's provincialism.

conceivable?—reminds one strongly of the tale of the blind men and the elephant.[41]

Tiring of the attempt to place Mormonism in the context of world religions—an attempt for which they have no real competence, and which is, anyway, intended only to stamp Mormonism as non-Christian—a vocal faction of anti-Mormons has come to prefer the "Satanist" identification advanced most loudly in recent times by J. Edward Decker.[42] This view of The Church of Jesus Christ of Latter-day Saints represents perhaps one of the first real innovations in anti-Mormon writing since Eber D. Howe's 1834 *Mormonism Unvailed*. Not content to repeat the standard claims that Mormonism is false, adherents of this school of anti-Mormonism assert that at least some of the leaders of The Church of Jesus Christ of Latter-day Saints know full well that it is false, and that they are conscious worshipers of Lucifer. Rather than denying the reality of supernatural events in the founding of Mormonism, these anti-Mormons admit them—but declare them to have been Satanic. Of the Mormon priesthood, Decker writes: "Its origin is a lie and its power is the power of priestcraft, and its author is Satan."[43]

---

41 Van Baalen (1983): 151, sees in Mormonism a pastiche of "Christianity, Judaism, Mohammedanism, Fetishism, Communism, Manichaeism, Campbellism, and others." Whalen (1963): 157, recognizes "paganism, Judaism, Christianity, Swedenborgianism, Spiritism, and Campbellism." (Alas for the Campbellites!) Whalen (1963): 158: "That the hodgepodge of heresies which is Mormonism can produce such results is a continual source of amazement." Indeed. Yet, as J. L. Smith admits in *The Utah Evangel* 33 (July/August 1986): 8, "this untenable, inconsistent, groundless, illusive hodgepodge of tenets . . . has enslaved millions since its inception more than 150 years ago."

42 Not all anti-Mormons accept Decker's "Satanist" theories. Jerald and Sandra Tanner (1988) sharply attack Decker and his sidekick Bill Schnoebelen on this issue, and the Tanners continue to raise serious questions about Decker's integrity. The "New Age anti-Mormonism" of Ed Decker and his associates is discussed by Peterson (1991): 231-60, in his critique of Loftes Tryk's *The Best Kept Secrets in the Book of Mormon*.

43 Decker, "To Moroni with Love," 47. Decker and Hunt recognize Mormonism as a spiritual movement, albeit one with demonic roots. Of course, one of their major subtheses also has it that the Latter-day Saint Church is a Satan-led political

Some Mormons have responded to such accusations by declaring their own deep feelings about Jesus, and by pointing to beliefs and practices that, they feel, demonstrate that they are Christians.[44] This response has left their detractors generally unmoved.[45] "The Mormon and the Christian worship at entirely different altars," asserts Ed Decker, "with doctrines and 'gospels' that fully separate the one from the other."[46]

Perhaps the charge that Latter-day Saints are non-Christians requires a different approach. By struggling to justify themselves to their detractors, Mormons have sometimes come dangerously close to recognizing the claim implicit in much anti-Mormon literature—that the title of "Christian" somehow belongs to fundamentalist Protestants, and that it is theirs to bestow or withhold. Yet, as will be shown in what follows, this is at best a dubious claim. Latter-day Saints are not the only people who are surprised and puzzled by it. Lloyd J. Averill, for instance, the author of a useful volume entitled *Religious Right, Religious Wrong*, explains that he wrote his book for mainstream Christians who are "especially troubled" by fundamentalism's "claim of exclusive rights to the Christian name."[47] Further, the assertion that they alone are Christians is rendered even more doubtful by the fundamentalists' refusal to recognize the flimsy—indeed, often paradoxical—grounds upon which that claim is based.

---

conspiracy. For a close parallel to their view of Mormonism, compare the N.I.C.E. in C. S. Lewis's novel *That Hideous Strength*.

44 The book by Wells (1985), for example, and the article by Weyland (1985), are largely of this character. On the other hand, the approach taken by Forrest, "Are Mormons Christian?" resembles our own, although on a smaller scale. Eugene England's essay, "What It Means to Be a Mormon Christian," found in England (1984): 173-90, is superb and even moving.

45 After all, as *The Utah Evangel* 31 (March 1984): 2, points out, Mormons are "wolves in sheep's clothing."

46 Decker, "To Moroni with Love," 4. Carver (1983) is a fairly effective reply to Mr. Decker's pamphlet.

47 Averill (1989): xiii.

We reject in the strongest possible way the false declaration that The Church of Jesus Christ of Latter-day Saints is non-Christian. We declare, in the strongest words that we can find to do so, that Mormons are Christian, and that Mormonism is a Christian faith. The words of the ancient Book of Mormon prophet Nephi express the feelings of today's Latter-day Saints, both leaders and ordinary members of the Church: "We talk of Christ, we rejoice in Christ, we preach of Christ, we prophesy of Christ, and we write according to our prophecies, that our children may know to what source they may look for a remission of their sins."[48]

In debating the contention of our critics that we are really not Christian at all, we rely upon the social nature of words and of language, according to which meanings and usages are rarely if ever dictated by a single person or even by a single faction. A couple of illustrations should serve to make clear what we mean.

In order to determine the semantic range of a given term, to understand its meaning, compilers of dictionaries do not engage in solitary meditations in their studies. They do not ponder the etymology of the term and then decide what it *ought* to mean. Instead, they survey as exhaustively as possible the way the term is actually used. They realize that it is a linguistic community as a whole which determines the character of a language and the meanings of the words within that language.

Every human baby born into a human community inherits a language that has existed before his or her birth and will presumably exist after his or her death. Much of that baby's education, from infancy through maturity (or even through graduate school), will consist in learning the language of its culture (and of its subculture). This is not an entirely passive process, for the growing child will be able to produce its own sentences and to produce its own thoughts—perhaps even to frame sentences and think thoughts that the world has never before known. But its liberty is set within limits, constrained by the social character of language. The child may limit itself to purely conventional use of language—e.g. "Hand

---

48 2 Nephi 25:26.

me the sugar, please"—or may come to write poetry, like that of Gerard Manley Hopkins, in which the conventional rules of usage and meaning are stretched and refreshed. But individual human beings can never wholly liberate themselves from conventional grammar and meaning except at the cost of becoming unintelligible to those around them. To say "Globe he chair the" is to use ordinary English words in such a bizarre way and, apparently, at such a distance from recognized signification, as to speak mere gibberish. To use "book" for "boat," or to mean "amoeba" by "symphony," is to put an end to communication—at least until someone manages to decode the speaker's private language.

It is our contention that there exists a fairly coherent basic meaning to the term "Christian" and its lexical equivalents in other languages, a meaning that can be traced throughout, and illustrated by, a long and richly documented history. Since this meaning is well established, latecomers have only a very limited ability to alter it, much in the same way that the new-born infant possesses only a constrained freedom in using its received language. To use the word "Christian" in a new and different sense is to limit communication—or even to mislead—until outsiders are able to decode and understand that new and different usage.

We shall survey the way the word "Christian" has historically been used, and shall argue that the historic meaning of the term is clearly broad enough to include The Church of Jesus Christ of Latter-day Saints, as well as fundamentalist anti-Mormons. We shall also contend that attempts to redefine the term have thus far failed to create a new definition that, in excluding Mormons, would not also exclude millions of people, past and present, commonly regarded as Christians.

Notably, we shall discover that the Roman Catholic Church—no insignificant part of what ordinary speakers and writers think of when they use the word "Christian"—is subject to many of the same arguments as are the Latter-day Saints, and prey to a very similar intolerance. Mainstream Protestant writer Lloyd Averill, for instance, who has listened to fundamentalist denunciations of Mormons and Roman Catholics, hears in them "frustration, outrage, desperation, and latent violence."[49] Let us note here just a few of the rhetorical similarities. Bob Witte has devoted an entire pamphlet, "Mormonism: The $3.00 Bill of Christianity," to the metaphor of other-people's-religion-as-counterfeit. It is not his metaphor alone, however, for anti-Catholics, too, offer deliverance "from the darkness of a counterfeit religious system."[50] Gleason Archer's description of Mormonism as a "dangerous counterfeit of the historic Christian faith" can easily be matched by Keith Green's similar intimations about Roman Catholicism.[51] Jimmy Swaggart terms the Church of Rome "a shimmering mirage that lures men to their deaths as they die of thirst . . . that delivers eternal torment instead of eternal life."[52] To pick up another common theme, G. H. Fraser seems occasionally to deny that Mormonism is really a religion at all. Rather, it is a giant business scam, hiding behind religion. "The presidents and prophets of the past several decades have been much more prone to receive their revelations from the spirit of Dow-Jones." Indeed, Fraser remarks that, "The names of the two priesthoods are the only element that lends a religious flavor to the structure of the priesthood."[53] This, too, can be paralleled in fundamentalist attacks on the Church of Rome: "Our American freedoms," cries Rev. Loraine Boettner, "are being threatened today by two totalitarian systems, Communism and Roman Catholicism. And of the two in our country, Romanism is

---

49 Averill (1989): 107. The Salt Lake City *Deseret News* for 7 August 1988 reported the case of a passenger on a Delta Air Lines flight from Atlanta to Greenville, South Carolina, who had to be subdued after he slammed a stewardess to the floor and threatened to "kill everyone who is not a born-again Christian."

50 Dunlap, "Alex Dunlap Answers Roman Catholic Priest," 2.

51 See Archer's "Translator's Preface" to the (historically worthless) Ahmanson (1984): 8; Green (1984b).

52 Swaggart (1985b): 35.

53 In order of citation, see Fraser (1977): 19, 88, 152, 87. In this position, too, Fraser has allies in Decker and Hunt (1984). With remarkable inconsistency, considering their claim that Joseph Smith was a Hindu, they describe him on p. 159 as "a classical humanist atheist"; contrast Scharffs (1986): 372.

growing faster than is Communism and is more dangerous since it covers its real nature with a cloak of religion."[54] Boettner's refusal to grant the religiousness of Roman Catholicism is paralleled by the refusal of certain other anti-Catholics even to refer to the Roman Catholic *Church*. To the Rev. Donald F. Maconaghie, as well as to the writers of Chick Publications, there is only "the Roman 'Church,' " or "the Roman Catholic Institution."[55] The charge of "paganism," too, is not restricted to Mormons, but is directed against Catholics as well.[56] The Church of Rome, according to one source, is "based on fetishism and sorcery."[57] And Jimmy Swaggart argues that the Catholic practice of auricular confession, along with many other elements of both doctrine and practice, "has its origins in heathenistic, pagan rituals."[58]

The question of whether the Church of Rome is even Christian at all is a big one among fundamentalists. "Catholicism," writes Karl Keating, summarizing the position taken by many of these fundamentalists, "is part Christian, part pagan, and wholly to be rejected."[59] And Jimmy Swaggart, at least, is less ambivalent than

---

54 Compare Boettner (1986): 3. Rev. Boettner further denies that Catholicism is really a religion at pp. 32, 64, and 460; but see p. 450. This book went into its 25th printing in March 1986. It is an Evangelical Book Club selection, and was specially highlighted in the big California "Christian" bookstore where we bought it. Keating (1988) terms it "the 'Bible' of the anti-Catholic movement within fundamentalism" (p. 28), and describes Loraine Boettner as "the intellectual godfather of modern fundamentalist anti-Catholicism" (p. 291). In other words, much as we wish it were otherwise, we are not citing a fringe figure.

55 See the newsletter of The Conversion Center (May/June 1990); Chick Publications February 1990 Retail Catalog, 28.

56 Against Catholics: Zacchello (1984): 14-16, 91; Ironside (1982): 23; W. Thompson, "What We Should Know about Roman Catholicism"; Boettner (1986): 10, 11, 13, 23-24, 53, 55, 90, 256, 272, 274, 286, 292-93, 455, 459-60. Martin (1955): 45, so views Theosophy—but it is not certain that Theosophy ever aspired to be called Christian.

57 Boettner (1986): 288-89.

58 Swaggart (1985a): 41; cf. 38.

59 Keating (1988): 154; cf. 16.

even Keating's summary would suggest: Catholicism, he says, "is a false religion. It is not a Christian religion."[60] "Rome fulfills the prophetic description of the 'Whore' [of Revelation 17] in every way!" scream the advertisements of Chick Publications. "There is nothing 'Christian' about her."[61]

In the course of this study, in fact, we shall see that the very people who want to run the Latter-day Saints out of Christendom don't have a great deal of affection for most of the rest of their fellow Christians, either. Lloyd Averill does not exaggerate when he speaks of the "refusal of fundamentalists to recognize that anything Christlike is happening outside of the fundamentalist movement," of their extreme and strident rhetoric. We shall see little reason, in the course of the present study, to reject Averill's description of fundamentalism as "ungenerous and unlovely."[62]

Those who deny that Mormonism is Christian usually imagine that they are doing so on the basis of a standard they find in the Bible. "In order to be a Christian," wrote "Dr." Walter Martin with all the air of a man asking something both simple and self-evident, "one must conform to the Scriptures."[63] (Martin's claim raises certain obvious questions from the start: Just how simple and unambiguous are the Scriptures? Must one conform absolutely and in every detail? How much deviance, if any, is allowed before one ceases to be a Christian? Is there only one possible scriptural position? If so, can both Quakers and Presbyterians be Christians? Methodists and Anglicans? Pre-millennialists and post-millennial-

---

60 Keating (1988): 90; cf. 93.

61 Chick Publications February 1990 Retail Catalog, 31.

62 Averill (1989): 77, xiv. On p. 52, Averill quotes evangelical Edward J. Carnell, former president of Fuller Theological Seminary, as lamenting that fundamentalism "sees the heresy in untruth but not in unloveliness." On fundamentalist rhetoric, see pp. 46-51.

63 Martin (1955): 41. Such a proposition is itself meta-scriptural. It is nowhere to be found in the canon. The New Testament never says what is required to be a Christian, and, as we shall see, does not define the term.

ists?[64] Charismatics and non-charismatics? Fundamentalists, notes Karl Keating, are "convinced . . . that the Bible is easy to understand, and convinced that all its parts admit but one interpretation and that anyone interpreting differently must be acting in bad faith."[65] But we will leave such questions for another place.) What such a rule would mean in practice—"if you do not conform to [my reading of] the scriptures, you are not a Christian"—is evident from the writings of Martin's fundamentalist ally, Loraine Boettner, who (somewhat incoherently and illogically) informs us that "if the Roman Church were reformed according to Scripture, it would have to be abandoned."[66] "The best book written against Romanism," says Joseph Zacchello, "was not written by a Protestant or by a former priest, but by God. It is the BIBLE."[67] We shall first examine whether Scripture provides us with a clear definition of what a Christian is, or what beliefs he or she must adhere to in order to retain the title. If it does not, the anti-Mormon case is unintelligible and should be dismissed as having no biblical authority.

Does the New Testament Define "Christianity"?

Several leading anti-Mormons cite as their mandate for a crusade against The Church of Jesus Christ of Latter-day Saints the two verses of Jude 3-4, wherein the New Testament admonishes them to "earnestly contend for the faith which was once delivered unto the saints. For there are certain men crept in unawares, who were before of old ordained to this condemnation, ungodly men, turning

---

64 Averill (1989): 140-41, offers examples of the varied interpretations of future prophecy offered by fundamentalists—each interpreter claiming to possess the absolute, indisputable truth.

65 Keating (1988): 102.

66 Boettner (1986): xii.

67 Zacchello (1984): vii. Emphasis his. He is (or, at least, claims to be) a former priest.

the grace of our God into lasciviousness, and denying the only Lord God, and our Lord Jesus Christ."[68]

But how does this apply to the Mormons? Do the Latter-day Saints somehow deny the Father and the Son? Not according to the first Article of Faith, which specifically affirms belief in both. Are the Latter-day Saints peculiarly prone to "lasciviousness"? Where is the evidence for a claim like that? It seems quite clear that the admonition of Jude 3-4 for followers of Christ to "earnestly contend for the faith" against "ungodly men" cannot refer specifically to Mormons or Mormonism. And, in fact, since the Mormons don't really fit Jude's description particularly well, it seems rather difficult to apply these verses to them at all.

So, having established the negative proposition that Jude 3-4 does not apply to the Latter-day Saints in any obvious way, we must ask ourselves what the occasion for Jude's exhortation actually was. The answer to that question is significant. A reading of the entire epistle makes it clear that Jude's concern was at least as much ethical as theological. The people he opposed were encouraging "lasciviousness" [*aselgeia*, or "sexual transgression"]. His target was a group of Christians, antinomians, who rejected authority and understood divine grace as sanctioning flagrant immorality.[69] This appears to be rather an odd analogy to use on the Mormons, whom our "experts" tend to consider too concerned with "works-righteousness" and too devoted to a priesthood.[70] After all, haven't the Latter-day Saints long insisted that sexual sin was

---

68 The passage is used, for example, by J. O. Sanders (1962): 5, and Martin (1955): title page.

69 Compare the interpretations of W. J. Dalton, "Jude," in Fuller, Johnston, and Kearns (1975): 959a-960e; Alexander and Alexander (1977): 644; D. F. Payne, "Jude," in Bruce (1986): 1590-92; Blair (1975): 339-42; T. W. Leahy, "The Epistle of Jude," in Brown, Fitzmyer, and Murphy (1968): 2:378-80.

70 See below. Mormons could plausibly argue that a better analogue for Jude's "filthy dreamers" would be their saved-by-grace-alone, no-need-of-church-or-priesthood fundamentalist Protestant critics. But no Mormons have, to our knowledge, made such an argument.

second only to murder or to the denial of the Holy Ghost in its seriousness? (See Alma 39:5.)

It is apparent, then, that Jude 3-4 does not legitimize a campaign against the Mormons. Instead, it calls upon believers in Christ to combat immorality and to condemn sin—the very position taken by The Church of Jesus Christ of Latter-day Saints. If anyone today stands in need of the kind of rebuke suggested by Jude 3-4, it would have to be someone who exaggerates the role of grace. And someone like that is more likely to be found among the critics of The Church of Jesus Christ of Latter-day Saints than among the Mormons.

Other prominent writers against the Latter-day Saints and others who diverge from conservative Protestant orthodoxy vaguely cite the Bible as a whole as the basis and justification for their efforts. P. B. Smith, a Canadian writer, will serve to illustrate this position.[71] "The Christian Bible," Smith writes, "is insistent upon the ground rules and the necessity of testing any group of people who call themselves Christians: 'Beloved, believe not every spirit, but try the spirits whether they are of God: because many false prophets are gone out into the world. Hereby know ye the Spirit of God: Every spirit that confesseth that Jesus Christ is come in the flesh is of God: And every spirit that confesseth not that Jesus Christ is come in the flesh is not of God: and this is that spirit of anti-Christ, whereof ye have heard that it should come; and even now already is it in the world. . . . Hereby know we the spirit of truth, and the spirit of error' (1 John 4:1-3, 6). Whatever else this passage says, it indicates that everybody who uses the name of Jesus Christ is not a Christian."[72]

But this is precisely what the passage in question does *not* say. The word "Christian" is neither defined in it nor even mentioned. Only one doctrinal standard is laid down: The spirit of truth will not teach gnosticism or docetism—early Christian heresies which

---

71 P. B. Smith (1970): 9-10.

72 P. B. Smith quotes all of 1 John 4:1-6. We have edited it for the sake of brevity. A glance at the original will show that the meaning has not been affected.

denied or downplayed the reality of Jesus' physical body—but will affirm the actual incarnation of Christ; it will not teach that Christ was only spiritually the Son of God, or that he did not have an actual body of flesh and blood. "Whosoever shall confess that Jesus is the Son of God, God dwelleth in him, and he in God" (1 John 4:15).

Do the Latter-day Saints deny that Jesus is the Son of God? No, for the first Article of Faith and literally hundreds of passages in their scriptural books teach his divine Sonship in the most explicit terms. Do they deny that he had a real body, a body of literal flesh and blood? Absolutely not. Indeed, fundamentalist critics of Mormonism have usually argued that it views the advent of Christ in *too* carnal terms.[73] Given their complaints on that score, anti-Mormons certainly cannot deny that Mormons regard Jesus as the Son of God. How, then, can they apply 1 John 4 to The Church of Jesus Christ of Latter-day Saints? They cannot. It is entirely irrelevant.

"Who is a Christian?" asks Frederick Sontag. "When one considers this question, the most interesting thing to note is that Jesus did not say much about it."[74] But, in fact, Professor Sontag understates the case. If one is looking for explicit treatment of the word "Christian," Jesus said absolutely *nothing* on the question. The striking thing about the New Testament's use of the word "Christian" is its infrequency. Indeed, the word appears only three times, and never in the mouth of Jesus.[75] (The term "Christianity" is completely absent.) And close examination of those three occurrences will easily show that they offer no grounds for expelling Mormons from Christendom.

---

73 See below. Spittler (1962): 24, describes the speculations of one or two early Mormon leaders on the subject as "a blasphemous stench." (For good measure, he throws in the adjective "deceptive," as well.)

74 Sontag (1986): 113.

75 It occurs four times in the Book of Mormon.

In Acts 11:26 we are told that "the disciples were called Christians first in Antioch."[76] Here, the use of the passive verb— they "*were called* Christians"—allows us to infer that the term was first used by non-Christians.[77] That is to say that the Christians did not, at first, call themselves by that name. In fact, as E. H. Trenchard notes of the biblical evidence, "In early times this name was mainly used by outsiders or by enemies."[78] It was "originally used as a pagan designation."[79] "It is a characteristically Gentile appellation," declares F. F. Bruce, "and would never have been devised by Jews."[80] Instead, the term "Christian" was modeled on such words as "Herodian" and "Caesarian," already in circulation, probably on the mistaken assumption that the title "Christ," a Greek translation of the Hebrew "Messiah," was a proper name like "Herod" and "Caesar."[81] "Christian" probably meant nothing more complicated, originally, than "Christ's people" or, perhaps,

---

76 The book of Acts is frequently dated to near the end of the first century (so H. Wansbrough, "Acts of the Apostles," in Fuller, Johnston, and Kearns [1975]: 822d). Dillon and Fitzmyer place it A.D. 80-85. ("Acts of the Apostles," in Brown, Fitzmyer, and Murphy [1968]: 2:165). Trenchard, "Acts," in Bruce (1986): 1266, prefers to puts its writing "before A.D. 64." J. A. T. Robinson (1977): 72, no hesitant controversialist, opts for "about 62."

77 See Dillon and Fitzmyer, "Acts of the Apostles," in Brown, Fitzmyer, and Murphy (1968): 2:190. They dismiss as "not cogent," however, evidence for the view that "this title was first used by Roman officials, who sought to distinguish Jesus' followers from Jews"; cf. W. Grundmann, "Christos," in Kittel and Friedrich (1974): 9:537; Trenchard, "Acts," in Bruce (1986): 1288.

78 Trenchard, "Acts," in Bruce (1986): 1288.

79 So F. D. Gealy, "Christian," in Buttrick (1962): 1:572. Gealy reports the theory that the Christians were deliberately named after Nero's *Augustaniani* youth gang, who were active in Antioch. *Christianos*, he notes, is an odd Greek form, and probably a Latinism.

80 Bruce (1972): 232, 267-68.

81 Bauer (1957): 865; W. Grundmann, "Christos," in Kittel and Friedrich (1974): 9:536; Dillon and Fitzmyer, "Acts of the Apostles," in Brown, Fitzmyer, and Murphy (1968): 2:190; Munch (1967): 106; Bruce (1972): 231-32, 267-68; J. P. Meier, "Part One: Antioch," in Brown and Meier (1983): 35 n. 81.

"partisans of Christ."[82] (In the United States, we have frequently called people "Jacksonian democrats," or "Freudian analysts," or "Marxists," or "Darwinians." The history of Christianity is amply supplied with "Augustinians," "Pelagians," "Lutherans," "Calvinists," "Mennonites," and the like. All of these titles occur on the same principle as "Christian.")

Who were these people who first were called "Christians"? What was the composition of the Church at Antioch, which drew that designation from outsiders? For one thing, it included "prophets" (Acts 13:1).[83] (This should give some critics of Mormonism food for thought, for they often claim that Jesus Christ is the final revelation of God, and that there can consequently be no prophets after him. Yet here, the first congregation of Jesus' followers to receive the title of "Christian" is characterized, precisely, by Christian prophets.)

Many of the congregants in the Antioch branch were Hellenistic; the group was deeply involved with the Gentile mission and heavily influenced by Pauline teachings.[84] Outsiders probably began to notice that Christians were not merely another sect of Jews because the church at Antioch did not require circumcision of converts.[85] But to leave it at that would be to commit a gross oversimplification. The careful presentation of John P. Meier on the subject shows clearly that there were, among the "Christians" of Antioch, believers along the whole spectrum of attitudes toward the Jewish law. Paul's was not only not the only influence at Antioch, it was

---

82 These translations are suggested respectively by Bruce (1972): 232, and Polkinghorne, "1 Peter," in Bruce (1986): 1561. Trenchard, "Acts," in Bruce (1986): 1288, has "Christ's men."

83 As did the congregation at Jerusalem (Acts 11:27).

84 Differing views of the mission of Jesus led to a dispute between certain Jerusalemite and Antiochene Christians on the subject of circumcision; cf. Acts 15:1; Munch (1967): 107; Bruce (1972): 231, 266, 282-85, 288.

85 So, among others, J. P. Meier, "Part One: Antioch," in Brown and Meier (1983): 35 n. 81.

not the dominant one.[86] Why is that fact important? Simply because Mormons are often expelled from Christendom because they do not accept the supposedly Pauline doctrine of salvation by grace alone. But neither, it seems, did members of that Antiochene congregation who were the very first in the Old World to receive the title of "Christian."

Amid the various theological strands that characterized Antiochene Christianity, loyalty to Jesus Christ was the unifying thread. This is of the utmost significance. Concluding his study on *Unity and Diversity in the New Testament,* James D. G. Dunn points out *"the surprising extent to which the different unifying factors in first-century Christianity focus again and again on Christ, on the unity between Jesus the man and Jesus the exalted one.* And when we ask in addition what both unifies *and* marks out the distinctiveness of first-century Christianity, the unifying strand narrows again and again to Christ alone. As soon as we move beyond it, as soon as we begin to attempt to fill it out in word or practice, diversity quickly becomes as prominent as unity. And the more we attempt to add to it, the more disagreement and controversy we find ourselves caught up in. In the final analysis then, the unity of first-century Christianity focuses (often exclusively) on Jesus the man now exalted, Christ crucified but risen."[87]

What made a person a Christian in the first century, and what makes a person a Christian today, is, simply, a commitment to Jesus Christ. Such commitment is central to the religion of the Latter-day Saints. It is evident in their hymns, their scriptures, their prayers, and their religious rituals. Clearly, then, there is nothing in Acts 11:26 that will justify a denial that Mormons are Christians.

In Acts 26:28, Agrippa II makes his famous reply to Paul: "A little more, and your arguments would make a Christian of me."[88]

---

86 See J. P. Meier, "Part One: Antioch," in Brown and Meier (1983): 24.

87 Dunn (1977): 371-72 (emphasis in original).

88 Following the Jerusalem Bible, which reproduces well the sense of the Greek. (The NEB here is periphrastic, and too wordy.) On this "slightly humorous retort," see H. Wansbrough, "Acts of the Apostles," in Fuller, Johnston, and Kearns

This statement occurs after a brief speech by Paul at Caesarea, in which the apostle relates to Agrippa and Festus the story of his conversion.[89] The doctrinal content of Paul's speech is slight, but that slightness is itself deeply significant: Paul bears witness that Jesus had been foretold by the Jewish prophets, that he suffered and rose from the dead, and that it is through Jesus that forgiveness may be obtained. Paul describes his mission as that of summoning people to "repent and turn to God, and do works meet for repentance" (Acts 26:20). There is no evidence that the apostle's speech at Caesarea mentioned original sin, or a metaphysical trinity, or salvation by grace alone, or *ex nihilo* creation, or any of the other doctrines for which, as we shall see, Mormons are expelled from Christendom by zealous critics. Yet Paul does not deny Agrippa's perception of his minimal theological statement as a summation of "Christianity" (Acts 26:29).

If Paul's statement to Agrippa and Festus is accepted as a scriptural test for the Christianity of The Church of Jesus Christ of Latter-day Saints, the Mormons pass easily. Do they believe that the Jewish prophets foretold the coming of Jesus Christ? Emphatically yes. Indeed, the three books of scripture revealed through the Prophet Joseph Smith offer prophecies of the advent of Christ that

---

(1975): 840i; Bruce (1972): 268; cf. Dillon and Fitzmyer, "Acts of the Apostles," in Brown, Fitzmyer, and Murphy (1968): 2:211. Trenchard, "Acts," in Bruce (1986): 1311, rejects the King James rendering of Agrippa's exclamation—"Almost thou persuadest me to be a Christian"—on "textual and exegetical grounds." Instead he follows the translation of F. F. Bruce—"In short you are trying to make me act the Christian!"—and characterizes it as a "slightly cynical evasion"; so, too, Alexander and Alexander (1977): 568; Munch (1967): 245.

89 As elsewhere in ancient writings, it is unlikely that the speeches of Acts are verbatim transcripts. Rather, they are likely to be the compositions of "Luke." But they probably conform quite well to the occasion and to the character of the speaker, and "reproduce an authentic picture of apostolic Christianity." See H. Wansbrough, "Acts of the Apostles," in Fuller, Johnston, and Kearns (1975): 822a-c; cf. J. A. T. Robinson (1977): 100. If the report of Agrippa's use of the term "Christian" is authentic—which cannot be demonstrated—the word was in circulation by A.D. 57-60. For chronological information on this incident, see J. A. Fitzmyer, "A Life of Paul," in Brown, Fitzmyer, and Murphy (1968): 2:221; H. H. Rowdon, "The Historical and Political Background and Chronology of the New Testament," in Bruce (1986): 1045; "Bible Dictionary" in Latter-day Saint edition of the Bible, s.v. "Chronology"; Alexander and Alexander (1977): 467.

are far clearer and more specific than anything found in the present text of the Hebrew Bible. Do Mormons believe that Jesus suffered and rose from the dead? Absolutely! "The fundamental principles of our religion," Joseph Smith said, "are the testimony of the Apostles and Prophets, concerning Jesus Christ, that He died, was buried, and rose again the third day, and ascended into heaven; and all other things which pertain to our religion are only appendages to it."[90] Do Mormons believe that it is through Jesus Christ that forgiveness may be obtained? The third Article of Faith should leave no doubt of that. Nor should literally scores if not hundreds of passages in the scriptures of the Latter-day Saints. Do Mormons believe it their duty to summon people to "repent and turn to God, and do works meet for repentance"? Without a doubt they do. (See, for example, D&C 6:9; 11:9; 14:8; 18:14, 41; 19:21, 31; 36:6; 44:3; etc.) Do Mormons call upon their hearers to do good works? Indeed they do, and this is one of the charges which their critics inconsistently bring against them, claiming that it shows them to be non-Christian. In fact, the Latter-day Saints meet Paul's minimum statement of Christianity remarkably well. If there is anyone who should be doing some soul-searching on this point, it might well be those who condemn The Church of Jesus Christ of Latter-day Saints for teaching that men and women must "do works meet for repentance." Acts 26:28 cannot plausibly be used to purge Mormons from Christianity.

It will be noted that in neither of the two instances discussed above is the term "Christian" found in the mouth of the Apostle Paul. Instead, it is found in the mouths of unbelieving outsiders. This is significant, since, as we have mentioned, it is often against the standard of allegedly Pauline teachings that Mormonism is weighed in the balance and found "non-Christian."[91] If Paul himself did use the word "Christian," there is no New Testament

---

90 *TPJS*, 121.

91 Citing Galatians 1:9, J. O. Sanders (1962): 20 alleges that "there is no identity whatever between Paul's Gospel and that of the Mormons. It is without doubt another gospel." Sanders is too sure of himself. Anderson (1983) is a fine Mormon interpretation of the Apostle to the Gentiles.

proof that he did, and no scriptural indication whatsoever as to *how* he might have used it. Thus, there is no Pauline definition of the term and no Pauline reason to deny that Mormons are Christians. Enemies of The Church of Jesus Christ of Latter-day Saints who seek biblical justification for banishing it from Christendom will have to look elsewhere for ammunition, and they have only one more chance:

1 Peter 4:16 represents the last relevant New Testament passage.[92] Yet it is virtually without theological content, merely assuring the believer that he need not worry if he suffer as a "Christian." Persecution is contrasted with suffering "as a murderer, or as a thief, or as an evildoer." And even here, perhaps, we are to think of "Christian" as an identification made by persecuting outsiders, just as "murderer," "thief," and "evildoer" might be judgments rendered by a Roman court.[93] It is, says F. F. Bruce, "by implication used by non-Christians."[94]

We might also note that being "Christian" here probably has a behavioral aspect. After all, suffering "as a murderer, or as a thief,

---

92 J. A. Fitzmyer, "The First Epistle of Peter," in Brown, Fitzmyer, and Murphy (1968): 2:362-63, assigns this letter to ca. A.D. 64. W. J. Dalton, "1 Peter," in Fuller, Johnston, and Kearns (1975): 950f, and F. J. Polkinghorne, "1 Peter," in Bruce (1986): 1551, place its composition A.D. 62-64. J. A. T. Robinson (1977): 66-67, argues that we can date 1 Peter "with a fair degree of accuracy in the spring of 65." Based on this approximate consensus, we have a reasonably clear *terminus ante quem*: The adjective "Christian" was being used by early A.D. 65. And perhaps, if Acts 11:26 is accurate, and if, therefore, Peter's use of the word is later, it was in use several years before that. Tacitus's *Annals* were written ca. A.D. 116. *Annals* XV, 44 puts the term *Christianos* in the mouth of the Roman mob during Nero's great fire. However, given ancient historiographical method, it would be reckless to assume—though it is not impossible—that Tacitus precisely reflects the linguistic usage of 19 July, A.D. 64.

93 A similar use may possibly occur in *The Martyrdom of Polycarp* 3:2; cf. Polkinghorne's brief discussion, "1 Peter," in Bruce (1986): 1561, of the list of offenses given in 1 Peter 4:15. As B. Reicke observes, the list seems to designate "unlawful and not simply immoral activity"; cf. Reicke (1964): 125. To Fitzmyer, "The First Epistle of Peter," in Brown, Fitzmyer, and Murphy (1968): 2:368, on the other hand, the term "Christian" in 1 Peter 4:16 "implies in this context a compatibility with Christ in suffering."

94 Bruce (1972): 268.

or as an evildoer" clearly would flow from something the sufferer *does*. A person is not punished merely for holding the theoretical belief that murder might be acceptable. (In an instance like this, faith without representative works is legally irrelevant.) A thief is not merely a believer in the abstract redistribution of wealth. Both of these are "evildoers," and it is as evildoers that they suffer or are punished by the law. If Peter really meant that suffering as a "Christian" was analogous to suffering "as a murderer, or as a thief, or as an evildoer," is it not logical to infer that he saw "Christianity" as expressing itself in behavior? So do the Latter-day Saints! It is Mormon insistence upon the necessity of repentance and good works which, as we shall see below, leads many anti-Mormons to deny that the Latter-day Saints are Christian. If, for this offense, they are thrust from the Christian fold, they may well find Peter already outside the wall. This is not bad company to keep.

Manifestly, the charge that Mormonism fails to meet the New Testament definition of "Christianity" is utterly groundless, for the simple reason that no such definition exists. The word "Christianity" does not even occur in the text. On the other hand, of course, the term "Christian" does occur, albeit rarely. It, too, remains undefined, although its context in the three places where it is to be found allows us perhaps to infer some very basic notions about how New Testament writers used it.

How does Mormonism fare, following an exhaustive survey—not hard to manage!—of the rather sparse biblical data on this question? The Latter-day Saints do extremely well. They meet every criterion. By every New Testament standard, Mormons are Christians.

A test case will make this completely clear: Robert McKay, a dedicated anti-Mormon who is based in Oklahoma, tells us that one must be "born again" in order to be a Christian. He bases his assertion upon John 3:7.[95] "The New Testament definition of a Christian is one who has been born again," he says.[96] But there is a problem here, as the alert reader can easily see by now. The

---

95 *The Utah Evangel* 34 (May-June 1987): 4.

96 *The Evangel* 38 (October 1991): 4.

problem is that John 3:7 does not mention the word "Christian"—
and, thus, can hardly be said to "define" it or to lay down conditions for its use. Indeed, the word "Christian" does not occur in the
gospel of John at all, nor, for that matter, in any of the four
gospels. Robert McKay's insistence that the New Testament defines
the word "Christian" leads us to wonder if he might have a
different New Testament than we have, one perhaps outfitted with
more verses, additional chapters, or extra books. For we can find
no definition of the term in any New Testament passage known to
us.

The claim of anti-Mormons that the New Testament itself clearly
excludes The Church of Jesus Christ of Latter-day Saints from
Christendom is hereby shown to be baseless, to be totally without
foundation. In a very real sense, the entire overall question of
whether Mormonism is Christian is already decided, and nothing
more need be said. But charity is an important biblical virtue, and
so we should, perhaps, permit the critics to have their say. Still, it
should never be forgotten amidst all the names and dates and details
which will follow that, by the (admittedly rather vague) standard of
the New Testament, the Latter-day Saints have been demonstrated
to fall within Christianity. No issue discussed below can call that
demonstration into question.

Do Denials That Latter-day Saints Are Christians Find Support in the Early Church?

As we have seen, the term "Christian" began its career among
outsiders, "more as an insult than as a title of honor."[97] The great
Roman historian, Tacitus (d. A.D. 120), for example, was able to
describe how Nero's persecuting zeal fell upon "a class of men,
loathed for their vices, whom the crowd styled Christians."[98]
Indeed, it is not until the second century that we can document use

---

97 Küng (1980): 135: "eher ein Schimpfname als ein Ehrenname."

98 Tacitus, *Annals* 15:44—*quos per flagitia invisos vulgus Christianos appellabat.*
English translation in Jackson (1969): 5:283.

of the designation among Christians themselves.[99] By February of 156, Polycarp of Smyrna could boldly declare to the Roman proconsul, just prior to his martyrdom, "I am a Christian."[100] (It is ironic that any attempt to define the term "Christian" based on noncanonical texts earlier than the second century must necessarily rely upon its use by pagans.)

Of course, it is not uncommon that nicknames are adopted by their targets. One thinks of "Yankee" or, for that matter, of "Mormon."[101] But what did the early Christians mean by their use of the term? It will be interesting to survey, briefly, some of the earliest writings we have from Christians outside of the New Testament. It is not, of course, that we think these early documents scriptural, or believe that they should be included in the canon. Still, they are extremely early—in a few cases, some scholars have argued, perhaps earlier than certain books in the New Testament itself—and they provide an extremely useful window for observing just how the earliest Christians viewed themselves and how they used words. (Furthermore, it should be recalled that these earliest writers knew the apostles. They *spoke* the language of the New Testament. There is good reason to believe, therefore, that they had at least some notion of what earliest Christian teaching was about. Twentieth-century Christians should dispute their views only with good reason.)

Of these early writers, Ignatius of Antioch is particularly important for our present purposes. He is the earliest writer who commonly uses the word "Christian." How does he use it? In a very interesting way. In his *Epistle to the Romans*, Ignatius

---

99 Bruce (1972): 268. Clearly, by the time of the correspondence between Pliny and Trajan, i.e., between A.D. 97 and A.D. 109, the term "Christian" was both well-known and punishable.

100 *The Martyrdom of Polycarp* 10:1. English translation in Lake (1970): 2:325; cf. 12:1-2. F. D. Gealy, "Christian," in Buttrick (1962): 1:562, agrees that it is in the second century that the term "Christian" came into "common use" among the followers of Jesus themselves.

101 Cf. Stewart (1975).

addresses his co-believers with regard to his own impending martyrdom: "Only pray for me for strength, both inward and outward, that I may not merely speak, but also have the will, that I may not only be *called* a Christian, but may also be found to *be* one."[102] He got his wish, and was thrown to the beasts at Rome under Trajan, ca. A.D. 108. Plainly, to Ignatius, who—significantly[103]—was the third bishop of Antioch, being a Christian depended at least partially upon behavioral criteria.[104] He wanted to really *be* one. "A Christian . . . gives his time to God," he writes to Polycarp. "This is the work of God."[105] On several occasions, he summons his readers to be "imitators of God."[106] On another occasion he exhorts the Magnesians, "Let us learn to lead Christian lives."[107] Ignatius is faithful, in other words, to an important part of the heritage of his church in Antioch, reiterating the ethical emphasis of the gospel of Matthew—which, many scholars think, was very likely written there only a few decades earlier.[108]

---

102 Ignatius of Antioch, *Epistle to the Romans* 3:2. English translation in Lake (1970): 1:229.

103 J. P. Meier, "Part One: Antioch," in Brown and Meier (1983): 35, thinks so; cf. also Gonzales (1970): 1:76 (n. 56); W. Grundmann, "Christos," in Kittel and Friedrich (1974): 9:576.

104 In a similar situation, *The Martyrdom of Polycarp* (3:2) speaks of "the nobility of the God-loving and God-fearing people of the Christians." English translation in Lake (1970): 2:317. Aristides, a Greek Christian apologist of the early second century A.D., emphasized the Christians' mutual love and "superior customs." "Because of this [public-relations-style]manner of presenting Christianity, Aristides says little about the beliefs" of the Church; cf. Gonzales (1970): 1:102. A virtually identical charge is routinely made against the Mormons. The great German theologians and historians of doctrine, Albrecht Ritschl and his student Adolf von Harnack, held that ethics and morals were the essence of Christianity—not dogma.

105 Ignatius of Antioch, *Epistle to Polycarp* 7:3. English translation in Lake (1970): 1:275-76.

106 As at Ignatius of Antioch's *Epistle to the Ephesians* 1:1, *Epistle to the Trallians* 1:1, *Epistle to the Philadelphians* 7:2, *Epistle to the Romans* 6:3.

107 Ignatius of Antioch, *Epistle to the Magnesians* 10:1.

108 See J. P. Meier, "Part One: Antioch," in Brown and Meier (1983).

Outsiders, too, sometimes noticed the great emphasis given by Christians to moral behavior. Writing sometime between A.D. 97 and A.D. 109, Pliny the Younger describes a regular "ceremony" practiced in the early church: Christians, he tells the Emperor Trajan, "bind themselves by oath . . . to abstain from theft, robbery, and adultery, to commit no breach of trust and not to deny a deposit when called upon to restore it."[109] (It is frequently alleged against Mormon temple worship, by the way, that oaths are forbidden by the New Testament. Apparently, either the earliest Christians did not understand this or else the anti-Mormons are wrong.)

In his *Epistle to the Ephesians*, Ignatius appears to presume yet another sense of the term "Christian," an ecclesiastical one, when he writes of "the Christians of Ephesus, who . . . were ever of one mind with the Apostles."[110] This is consistent with his *Epistle to the Magnesians*, where he declares that "we should be really Christians, not merely have the name."[111] And how do we do so? The burden of this epistle is that we must be subject to the authority of the bishop, who presides "in the place of God."[112]

It cannot, of course, be denied that, for Ignatius, being a Christian involves more than simply moral behavior and obedience to priesthood authority. Still it must not be overlooked that he regards these traits (heavily criticized by anti-Mormons when occuring in The Church of Jesus Christ of Latter-day Saints) as essential to true Christianity. In addition, however, he also gives us a few theological guidelines to follow. Ignatius is the first writer known to have used the term "Christianity," which he explicitly

---

109 Pliny, *Letters X*, 96.

110 Ignatius of Antioch, *Epistle to the Ephesians* 11:2. English translation in Lake (1970): 1:187.

111 Ignatius of Antioch, *Epistle to the Magnesians* 4. English translation in Lake (1970): 1:201.

112 Ignatius of Antioch, *Epistle to the Magnesians* 6:1. English translation in Lake (1970): 1:203; cf. 2:1, 7:1, and esp. 13:2.

contrasts with "Judaism."[113] Much like Paul before Agrippa—and much like the statement of Joseph Smith, quoted above—he bears witness of Christ's birth, death, and resurrection. Against the Docetists, who teach of Jesus that "his suffering was only a semblance," Ignatius affirms that the Savior "was truly born, both ate and drank . . . [and] was truly crucified."[114] "I beseech you therefore," he writes to the Trallians, "live only on Christian fare, and refrain from strange food, which is heresy."[115]

Here, at last, we seem to have a doctrinal criterion for what is and what is not Christian. However, Ignatius's own doctrinal position is not unambiguous. He has, for example, secret teachings which he refuses to reveal in his letters.[116] Furthermore, how enlightening is it, really, to discover that "Christianity" is not identical with "Judaism"? And in answer to the implicit question of how one is to distinguish truth from heresy, Ignatius immediately falls back on lines of priesthood authority.[117] "This will be possi-

---

113 Ignatius of Antioch, *Epistle to the Magnesians* 10:3; *Epistle to the Philadelphians* 6:1; cf. Ignatius, *Epistle to the Romans* 3:3. Also W. Grundmann, "Christos," in Kittel and Friedrich (1974): 9:537, 576, sees the term "Christian" as having arisen with the realization that the followers of Jesus now constituted a group distinct from the Jews.

114 Ignatius of Antioch, *Epistle to the Trallians* 9:1. English translation in Lake (1970): 1:221; cf. *Epistle to the Smyrnaeans* 2, 5-7; cf., in the New Testament itself, 1 John 4:2-3. Docetism was a real threat in Antioch to the form of Christianity advocated by Ignatius. (See J. P. Meier, "Part One: Antioch," in Brown and Meier [1983]: 75.)

115 Ignatius of Antioch, *Epistle to the Trallians* 6:1. English translation in Lake (1970): 1:214.

116 See Ignatius of Antioch, *Epistle to the Trallians* 5.

117 Ignatius of Antioch's view of "priesthood" is not altogether unlike that of the Mormons, who do not accept the notion that priest and prophet are naturally opposed. Writes J. P. Meier, "Part One: Antioch," in Brown and Meier (1983): 76-77: "Ignatius does not view his office as un-charismatic. Rather, in Ignatius we find a peculiar fusion of office and charism, perhaps because Ignatius has come forth from the college of prophets and teachers and still considers himself very much a man of the Spirit. . . . To sum up, then: the presiding teacher-prophet at Antioch became the one bishop, the other teachers and prophets became the college of elders."

ble for you," he declares, "if you are not puffed up, and are inseparable from God, from Jesus Christ and from the bishop and ordinances of the Apostles. He who is within the sanctuary is pure, but he who is without the sanctuary is not pure; that is to say, whoever does anything apart from the bishop and the presbytery and the deacons is not pure in his conscience."[118] And as for the "strange food" of the heretics, which Ignatius contrasts with "Christian fare," is it not reasonable to see in that an allusion by the bishop of Antioch to eucharistic service—which is to say, in Mormon terms, to the administration of the sacrament—conducted by invalid authority? "Let no one," he admonishes the Smyrnaeans, "do any of the things appertaining to the Church without the bishop. Let that be considered a valid Eucharist which is celebrated by the bishop, or by one whom he appoints."[119]

"Let no one be deceived," Ignatius warns the Smyrnaeans. Even the heavenly hosts are subject to judgment. And then the saint applies his ethical standard to the heretics: "Mark those who have strange opinions concerning the grace of Jesus Christ which has come to us, and see how contrary they are to the mind of God. For love they have no care, none for the widow, none for the orphan, none for the distressed, none for the afflicted, none for the prisoner, or for him released from prison, none for the hungry or thirsty."[120] They have, in other words, forgotten what James 1:27 describes as "pure religion and undefiled." But it is not only James who insisted on ethical standards as a means of identifying the real

---

118 Ignatius of Antioch, *Epistle to the Trallians* 7:1-2. English translation in Lake (1970): 1:219.

119 Ignatius of Antioch, *Epistle to the Smyrnaeans* 8:1. English translation in Lake (1970): 1:261. Docetists proper tended to ignore the eucharist, presumably because they denied the incarnation; cf. *Epistle to the Smyrnaeans* 7:1. The word "strange" in Lake's translation of *Trallians* 6:1 renders the Greek *allotrios*. This can also mean "belonging to another," "alien," "hostile," "enemy," or, as a substantive, "other people's property"; cf. Bauer (1957): 40. There may also be a possible reference to idol offerings, as at Acts 15:20, 29; 21:25; 1 Cor. 8:4.

120 Ignatius of Antioch, *Epistle to the Smyrnaeans* 6:1-2. English translation in Lake (1970): 1:259.

followers of Christ, for statements by Jesus himself are recorded in the Gospels which are relevant to the question at issue. The most famous is probably that of John 13:35: "By this shall all men know that ye are my disciples [*mathētai*], if ye have love one to another." Thus, in their emphasis upon behavior as a key to identity as a disciple of Christ, both James and Ignatius faithfully follow their master. For Ignatius, Walter Grundmann notes, "*Christianismos* simply means discipleship." It is "being a Christian as expressed in life-style."[121] This ethical view of Christianity is common to others among the first Christian writers as well. The early second-century *Shepherd of Hermas*, for instance, one of the so-called "Apostolic Fathers," views Christianity as "above all, a series of precepts that must be followed."[122] (The Latter-day Saints, of course, can certainly live with this ethical emphasis found among the earliest Christians. But what of their critics?)

As is implied in the assertion that "the disciples were called Christians first in Antioch," the original word applied to the followers of Jesus was "disciples."[123] It was, states Grundmann, "obviously the term which the original believers used for themselves."[124] K. H. Rengstorf argues that the Greek *mathētēs*, "disciple," is merely a translation of the Hebrew *talmīdh*, and that it derives from the common name which Palestinian Christians used in self-description. It gave way to the term "Christian" only as the Church became more and more Hellenized.[125]

---

121 W. Grundmann, "Christos," in Kittel and Friedrich (1974): 9:576. We have transliterated the Greek of the original.

122 Gonzales (1970): 1:89.

123 This did not forbid the use of other titles; cf. Kittel and Friedrich (1967): 4:457.

124 In W. Grundmann, "Christos," in Kittel and Friedrich (1974): 9:536. P. Parker, "Disciple," in Buttrick (1962): 1:845, surveying the gospels and Acts, calls "disciple" "the most frequent and general term for believers in Christ."

125 K. H. Rengstorf, "Mathētēs," in Kittel and Friedrich (1967): 4:458-59. Irenaeus (d. ca. A.D. 202), notes P. Parker, "Disciple," in Buttrick (1962): 1:845, "used 'disciple' as equivalent to 'Christian.'" A notable fact is that the word

What did the earliest followers of Jesus understand by "disciple-ship"? Rengstorf sees three—largely behavioral—elements in their view: (1) commitment to the person of Jesus; (2) obedience to Jesus; and (3) obligation to suffer with Jesus.[126] "Then said Jesus to those Jews which believed on him, If ye continue in my word, then are ye my disciples indeed" (John 8:31).[127] Commenting on this verse, Bruce Vawter remarks, "Merely to be receptive to the word is not enough; one must also take it in and act on it constantly. Then alone can one be a true disciple of the Lord."[128] "This is my Father's glory, that you may bear fruit in plenty and so be my disciples" (John 15:8, New English Bible).[129]

Being a disciple of Jesus was not an easy thing. "Those who responded," writes Frederick Sontag, "left their family, friends and conventional religious practices to follow an itinerant preaching, healing ministry which was at time subject to danger. To follow Jesus meant to abandon convention and to join a religious cult [!] of the day. . . . Thus, the most obvious definition for 'Christian' would be: 'One called to follow Jesus' no matter what danger or ostracism is involved."[130] Discipleship, thus, demanded behavior, actions—works.

It appears that there are few if any guidelines to be found in the New Testament or in earliest Christianity for ruling on who is, and who is not, Christian. And apart from a condemnation of Docetism,

---

"disciple" [*mathētēs*] occurs about 260 times in the Gospels and in Acts, yet is utterly absent from the rest of the New Testament; cf. P. Parker, "Disciple," in Buttrick (1962): 1:845; K. H. Rengstorf, "Mathētēs," in Kittel and Friedrich (1967): 4:441.

126 K. H. Rengstorf, "Mathētēs," in Kittel and Friedrich (1967): 4:458-59.

127 This is a "classic passage" on the subject. Thus K. H. Rengstorf, "Mathētēs," in Kittel and Friedrich (1967): 4:458.

128 B. Vawter, "The Gospel according to John," in Brown, Fitzmyer, and Murphy (1968): 2:442; likewise R. Russell, "St. John," in Fuller, Johnston, and Kearns (1975): 810h.

129 The New English Bible is slightly clearer here than the KJV.

130 Sontag (1986): 113.

there are no doctrinal criteria given whatsoever. There is, further-more, sufficient ambiguity in the records left behind by the earliest Christians that the question of just which doctrine or practice is authentically "primitive" has historically remained very much open. In late antiquity, each Christian sect claimed apostolicity.[131] And if the situation was confused in ancient times, it has only grown worse with the passage of time. Among nineteenth-century Ameri-can Protestants, Klaus Hansen observes, "each church conceived of itself as conforming more closely to the primitive church than any of its rivals."[132] Despite Walter Martin's complacency about "conform[ing] to the Scriptures," such conformity seems to be both difficult and controversial.

Why should it be so difficult to get a fix on the pure Christianity of the earliest believers? Modern biblical and patristic scholarship would reply that this is because there never was a golden age of unambiguous and unanimously held Christian truth. The important evangelical scholar James D. G. Dunn denies that "orthodoxy" is a meaningful concept within the New Testament period. There is no single preaching or proclamation of the gospel (Greek *kerygma*), but, rather, multiple and conflicting forms of such preaching and proclamation (*kerygmata*). Dunn recognizes "a marked degree of diversity" and "many different expressions of Christianity within the NT."[133] Even fundamentalists are willing to avail themselves of this idea when it proves useful to them: "The fact is," says Loraine Boettner, going after the Catholics, "that [the Church fathers] scarcely agree on any doctrine, and even contradict them-selves as they change their minds and affirm what they had previously denied."[134]

Terms like "orthodoxy" and "heresy" seem increasingly—to modern objective scholarship—to be mere self-congratulatory

---

131 Brox (1983): 149.

132 Hansen (1981): 56.

133 Dunn (1977): 1-32, 372-74.

134 Boettner (1986): 78; cf. 41.

epithets worked up by the victors in the dogmatic skirmishes of Christian history. In earliest Christianity, the two are often impossible to distinguish, at least without the benefit of hindsight. In many areas, the "heretics" were the established church, while the "orthodox" were the damnable minority. And this is not merely the case in later, "apostate" centuries. The New Testament itself contains conflicting perspectives and positions that, many scholars would contend, resist even the most determined harmonizer.

Protestant critics who like to contrast Mormonism with "biblical" Christianity—a uniform Pauline abstraction that never fit the reality of the Christian church, even in its first centuries—argue from a mirage.[135] "The ancient church produced a vast number of theological attempts to interpret Christianity," writes Norbert Brox. "These theologies differ very widely from one another, according to period, environment, points of departure, and intention, and they show the breadth of the options which then existed for understanding the Christian faith."[136]

Clearly, if it is thought to rest upon standards derived from the New Testament or from immediately postapostolic Christianity, the anti-Mormon case for expelling Mormons from Christendom is without substance. Earliest Christians liked to describe their fellowship and their community in ethical terms—terms with which the Latter-day Saints, given their emphasis on good works and "living together in love" (D&C 42:45), can certainly feel comfortable. Their critics, on the other hand, may actually feel less at ease with the early Christians and all their talk of "works" than the Mormons do. Thus, lacking both biblical support and support from the earliest generations of ancient believers, these critics are driven to seek another reason to banish The Church of Jesus Christ of Latter-day Saints from the Christian fold. Is there is another possibility? Is there another weapon?

---

135 Boettner (1986): 78; cf. 41.

136 Brox (1983): 146. Translation ours; cf., for example, Brox (1983): 121-22, on eucharistic debates in the early church.

Can the Councils and Creeds Be Used to Banish Mormonism from Christendom?

The majority of anti-Mormons probably belong to so-called "non-denominational" churches.[137] These predominantly conservative and fundamentalist institutions are typified by the Interlake Christian Church near Seattle, which claims in its advertising to have "No Creed but Christ, No Book but the Bible, No Name but Christian." Of course, the Interlake slogan is itself a creedal statement. And no Christian—least of all a precritical fundamentalist—comes to the Bible or to Christ without presuppositions that reflect his society and upbringing. Further, is it likely that even the most backward Protestant is utterly deaf to the great debates in which Christian theology has been shaped through the centuries? Is it probable that, standing at the end of twenty centuries of doctrinal development, he understands his English Bible in precisely the way that a first-century Palestinian Christian heard and understood the sermons of Peter? Did the great movements of Platonism and Aristotelianism and Neoplatonism and Manichaeanism and Augustinianism and Averroism and Thomism, which surged for centuries about and within Christendom, really have no effect at all? The implied answer given in most anti-Mormon sources is no, none whatsoever. Karl Keating explains this quite well: "Fundamentalists think the intervening centuries have not made the Bible any more confusing for us than it was for people who lived in New Testament times, and they think that way (although they do not realize it) because they begin, not with the Bible, but with an accepted set of beliefs, which they then substantiate by 'searching the Scriptures.' "[138]

---

137 This is implied in the distribution of signers of the Decker petition: The majority were adherents of non-denominational churches. Second best represented were, not surprisingly, the Baptists, with Lutherans coming in a distant third; cf. "Critics Ask LDS Faithful to Stop Calling Themselves Christians," Salt Lake City *Tribune* (26 July 1986).

138 Keating (1988): 322-23.

Mormonism makes no secret of having sources of authority beyond the Bible. Latter-day Saints have never been shy about admitting—nay, proclaiming—that their understanding of the Bible is guided and enriched by revelations through modern prophets. Anti-Mormons, on the other hand, like to think that they represent pure biblical Christianity, arrayed against a Mormonism that is "decadent" and "syncretistic" (precisely because of its extrabiblical sources). Yet this is highly implausible on the face of it. "Fundamentalists use the Bible to protect beliefs that are, in fact, antecedent to the Bible, which is interpreted so it justifies what they already hold, although most fundamentalists think what they believe comes straight out of the sacred text and that they are merely acknowledging its plain meaning."[139] Besides, we have already shown that the Bible offers no real reason to deny that Mormonism is Christian. So anti-Mormons have recourse—overtly in some cases or, as is more common, implicitly—to doctrinal principles that are, at the very best, doubtfully present in primitive Christianity. Quite often, these doctrinal principles derive either directly or indirectly from the classical creeds, which were hammered out in and around the great councils of the ancient postapostolic Christian church.

The so-called "ecumenical councils" of the Church (from the Greek *oikoumenē*, or "world") are normally reckoned as being approximately twenty-one in number. Of these, most Protestants accept only the first seven as binding and doctrinally authoritative. The first was the famous Council of Nicaea (A.D. 325). This was followed by the first Council of Constantinople in A.D. 381, and by the Council of Ephesus, in A.D. 431. The important Council of Chalcedon, in A.D. 451, was succeeded by the second and third Councils of Constantinople, in A.D. 553 and 680, respectively. Finally, the second Council of Nicaea took place in A.D. 787. These councils were essentially legislative sessions, in which bishops and theologians from across the Roman/Byzantine Empire came together to debate each other about doctrinal issues great and small, to identify and condemn heresies and heretics, and to issue declarations or creeds.

---

139 Keating (1988): 26.

These creeds, convenient doctrinal summaries formulated by theologians to express their own beliefs and to rule out the beliefs and formulations of those with whom they disagreed, are usually divided into several categories. First, there are the "ecumenical creeds." These are products—or, at least, claim to be products—of the entire Church, of bishops representing all Christians in the world. There are other categories as well, including Eastern Catholic, Western Catholic, and Provincial creeds. (Later Protestant denominational "confessions" are frequently discussed under a separate category altogether.) We will be concerned here with the "ecumenical creeds." These are the statements which purport to express the universal judgment of Christians. They are generally identified as three—the Apostles' Creed, the Nicene Creed, and the so-called Athanasian Creed. The latter, however, gained its stature only in the thirteenth century, and is most definitely not by Athanasius (d. A.D. 373). It may therefore safely be omitted.

What does the historical record of these assemblies and their resolutions imply about the Christianity of the Latter-day Saints? Distinctly little. The great creeds and the ecumenical councils of mainstream Christendom—while they can clearly be used to demonstrate that Mormonism is out of step with the evolution of "historic Christianity," a proposition no informed Latter-day Saint would care to dispute—furnish very weak grounds upon which to deny that Mormons are Christian. This is so for at least three reasons: (1) the creeds do not include all the groups generally viewed as Christian; (2) they are themselves innovative, and of a nature foreign to the Bible; and (3) the ecumenical councils that generated the creeds have never been viewed as consigning those whom they anathematized to "non-Christianity."[140]

Of course, certain creedlike passages can be located in the Bible itself, although not of the metaphysical type popular in succeeding centuries. Both Protestant and Catholic scholars recognize 1 Corinthians 15:1-11, for example, as a very early Christian creedal

---

140 See Brox (1983): 170, 183-84, on the problematic character of conciliar authority.

statement, not unrelated to Paul's speech before Festus and Agrippa. The Protestant editors of the popular New International Version of the Bible, commenting upon 1 Corinthians 15:3-4, point out that these verses contain "the heart of the gospel," which, following Paul's own language, they summarize as the belief "that Christ died for our sins . . . that he was buried . . . and that he was raised from the dead."[141] The resemblance between this early Christian creed, containing "the heart of the gospel," and Joseph Smith's statement, already cited above, is so striking that the latter is worth quoting here again: "The fundamental principles of our religion," Joseph Smith wrote, "are the testimony of the Apostles and Prophets, concerning Jesus Christ, that He died, was buried, and rose again the third day, and ascended into heaven; and all other things which pertain to our religion are only appendages to it."[142] Mormons accept such propositions fully—and in a much more literal way than do, say, liberal Protestants. In the language of the editors of the New International Version, they thereby accept "the heart of the gospel." Yet this makes no difference in the eyes of their critics, who persist in calling them non-Christians.

Once again, however, the Bible fails to support this expulsion of the Latter-day Saints from Christendom. Thus, a post-biblical instrument is needed to justify such an un-biblical move. J. O. Sanders, for instance, identifies Christianity with the so-called Apostles' Creed,[143] the brief text of which runs as follows: "I believe in God the Father Almighty; Maker of heaven and earth. And in Jesus Christ his only (begotten) Son our Lord; who was conceived by the Holy Ghost, born of the Virgin Mary; suffered under Pontius Pilate, was crucified, dead, and buried; he descended into hell [Hades, spirit world]; the third day he rose from the dead; he ascended into heaven; and sitteth at the right hand of God the

---

141 Barker (1985): 1755.

142 *TPJS*, 121.

143 J. O. Sanders (1962): 15; cf. Boa (1984): 67. The *Forma Recepta* of this creed probably dates back to no earlier than the sixth century.

Father Almighty; from thence he shall come to judge the quick and the dead. I believe in the Holy Ghost; the holy catholic Church; the communion of saints; the forgiveness of sins; the resurrection of the body [flesh]; and life everlasting. Amen."[144] Admittedly, Mormons do not use this creed. But failure to use the text of the creed in liturgy and worship would seem dangerous grounds for thrusting them from Christianity if they accept its principles. "If we take the recognition and use of the Apostles' Creed as our test," writes Einar Molland, "both the Orthodox Church and a number of Protestant Communions will fall outside the limits of Christendom, which would be absurd."[145] But if it is "absurd" to claim that non-use of the Apostles' Creed expels the Orthodox and many Protestants from the Christian fold, it can be no less absurd to claim that such non-use banishes the Latter-day Saints. And indeed, as even some outside observers have noted, the Latter-day Saints do accept the creed's principles.[146] For example, in their first Article of Faith, Latter-day Saints declare a belief in the Father, the Son, and the Holy Ghost. Similarly, Latter-day Saints baptize in the name of the Father, the Son, and the Holy Ghost. Yet consistency sometimes seems too much to ask from anti-Mormons. While declaring acceptance of the Apostles' Creed to be the essence of Christianity, J. O. Sanders denies that the Latter-day Saints are Christians.[147]

If the Bible and the Apostolic Fathers and the simple text of the Apostolic Creed fail to justify denials that Mormons are Christians,

---

144 The English text, with bracketed explanatory glosses, is cited from Schaff (1983): 2:45. "Catholic," of course, is used here in the sense of "universal." The Roman Catholic Church, in the modern denominational sense, did not yet exist.

145 Molland (1959): 355.

146 See Ferm (1945): 432; Broderick (1976): 401. S. E. Robinson (1991): 126, n. 3, agrees. Of course, Mormons would want to watch carefully the phrase *ton sullepthenta ek pneumatos hagious / qui conceptus est de Spiritu Sancto*, the translation of which is sometimes questionable. They are concerned to affirm the divine fatherhood of the Father.

147 J. O. Sanders (1962): 109.

perhaps later and more theologically detailed tools can be located to do the job. Since it is manifestly ridiculous to call the Latter-day Saints non-Christian when they accept a New Testament creed that represents "the heart of the gospel" and when they agree fully with a post-biblical creed which one of their own enemies has effectively described as the least common denominator that links and defines Christians, it will obviously be necessary to purge them from Christianity on the basis of non-essentials—however logically dubious such a course may be. And the later creeds are the obvious place to turn. For inessential speculation and post-biblical innovation, they are mines of unfathomable richness.

Among them, the Nicene Creed is almost certainly the most famous and the most important. Yet its very innovativeness makes it a most questionable basis for banishing the Latter-day Saints from Christendom. "It is impossible for any one," declared Edwin Hatch in his classic 1888 Hibbert Lectures, "whether he be a student of history or no, to fail to notice a difference of both form and content between the Sermon on the Mount and the Nicene Creed. The Sermon on the Mount is the promulgation of a new law of conduct; it assumes beliefs rather than formulates them; the theological conceptions which underlie it belong to the ethical rather than the speculative side of theology; metaphysics are wholly absent. The Nicene Creed is a statement partly of historical facts and partly of dogmatic inferences; the metaphysical terms which it contains would probably have been unintelligible to the first disciples;[148] ethics have no place in it. The one belongs to a world of Jewish peasants, the other to a world of Greek philosophers. The contrast," Hatch continues, "is patent. If any one thinks that it is sufficiently explained by saying that the one is a sermon and the other a creed, it must be pointed out in reply that the question why an ethical sermon stood in the forefront of the teaching of Jesus Christ, and

---

148 This is reminiscent of a currently popular joke, in which Jesus is reported to have asked his disciples, "Whom do you say that I am?" And Peter said unto him, "Thou art very God of very God, the Ultimate Ground of our being." And Jesus said unto him, "What?"

a metaphysical creed in the forefront of the Christianity of the fourth century, is a problem which claims investigation."[149]

Some conservative bishops, even among those who were committed to the doctrinal position taken by the Council of Nicaea, were very much worried by the fact that, in the Nicene Creed, a word utterly foreign to the scriptures—*homoousios*—was proclaimed the dogmatic standard for the church.[150] This consideration ought to, but does not, give pause to those who would make of it—or any of its Hellenistic cousins—the *sine qua non*, the indispensable essence, of Christianity: Who gave the ecclesiastical diplomats of Nicaea the right to set up a definition of Christianity utterly unknown to the prophets, apostles, and evangelists of the Bible, and one which would almost certainly have been incomprehensible to them?

But a yet more fundamental question arises here, for there is no evidence that the statesmen and scholars of the Nicene Council ever *claimed* the authority to define "Christianity." This fact is universally overlooked by those who cite the Nicene Creed as their warrant for determining who is Christian and who is not, but it is of vital importance. While those who framed the Nicene Creed and sought to enforce it were quite willing to expel dissidents from the institutional church, we know of no evidence that they ever claimed they were thereby transforming those excommunicants into "non-Christians." And modern scholarship is unanimous, so far as we have been able to determine, in its implicit denial that condemnation by a creed or expulsion from a council made one a non-Christian. Nevertheless, "Dr." Walter Martin, calling Jehovah's Witnesses "Arians" and attempting thereby to thrust them from the Christian fold, asserts that Arius was excommunicated from the Christian

---

149 Hatch (1970): 1. Mormons, adherents of an essentially creedless Church, access to whose temples depends upon ethical worthiness far more than upon doctrinal purity, would tend to see the change as merely further evidence of the Great Apostasy.

150 Brox (1983): 179.

church at the Council of Nicaea, in A.D. 325.[151] His assertion is technically true but fundamentally misleading, since, as we have just pointed out, excommunication from the institutional church seems not to have been viewed by anyone concerned as making the excommunicant into a non-Christian. (Also excommunicated at Nicaea were the Quartodecimans, for holding a minority viewpoint on the proper date for Easter. Would "Dr." Martin seriously have contended that we should call the Quartodecimans non-Christian because of a quibble over the dating of Easter?) Arianism was given a major blow at Nicaea, it is true, and finally lost at the Council of Constantinople (in A.D. 381), but it is nonetheless routinely referred to as "Christian."[152] And in the half century intervening between Nicaea and Constantinople, Arianism enjoyed much more support than could plausibly have been commanded by a movement officially declared and widely recognized as non-Christian. It was, for example, backed by Constantine's son and successor, Constantius, and indeed was preferred by the majority of the Eastern bishops. Athanasius, on the other hand, who was the guiding force in the formulation of the creedal statement accepted at the Council at Nicaea, was, more often than not, in exile from his bishopric or in disfavor.

Since the Nicene Creed does not seem to have turned any of its dissenting contemporaries into non-Christians, it is frankly difficult to see how it could possibly cause such a metamorphosis in a group of people living a millennium and a half afterwards. And clearly it does not, since it is not accepted even by all those modern churches universally recognized as Christian.[153] Thus, there is no substance to arguments that seek to force The Church of Jesus Christ of

---

151 Martin (1955): 28.

152 Explicitly, in our sampling, by Brandon (1970): 97; Russell (1968): 91; Bruce (1979): 302-4, 321-22, 325; Johnson (1983): 128; implicitly by Kraft (1966): 54-57, and by Cross and Livingstone (1983): 83, where it is opposed not to "Christianity" but to "orthodoxy" and (small "c") "catholicism." The *Oxford English Dictionary* makes no denial.

153 Molland (1959): 356-57.

Latter-day Saints from Christianity on the basis of the Nicene Creed.

After a survey of the various creeds and councils, discussing in greater detail the kinds of problems to which we have alluded here, Einar Molland concludes that the Lord's Prayer is "the one creed of all branches of Christendom."[154] All other creeds exclude one denomination or other that is universally recognized as Christian, which is clearly unacceptable and absurd. Acceptance of the Lord's Prayer, on the other hand, is implied by Molland to be a good demonstration of one's Christianity. What does this imply for the Christianity of Mormonism? The Latter-day Saints would find nothing troubling in Molland's rule, since, while they do not use the Lord's Prayer liturgically—they have very little liturgy to speak of—they certainly do accept it. Indeed, 3 Nephi 13:9-13 has the resurrected Christ teach the same prayer in the New World. Still—strangely, and with striking inconsistency—Einar Molland denies that Mormons are Christian.[155] Once again, Latter-day Saint acceptance of something that makes everyone else Christian, something that their attackers elsewhere recognize as the very definition of "Christian," fails to gain them admission to the club.

Other councils of the ancient church can likewise be shown to furnish no basis for anti-Mormon assaults on the Christianity of the Latter-day Saints. In A.D. 431, for instance, the Council of Ephesus condemned Nestorius and his followers. Yet the Nestorians are invariably described as Christians.[156] Furthermore, the verdict of that council is now generally recognized to have been unjust.[157] The Monophysites, to choose another ancient faction, were condemned at the Council of Chalcedon in A.D. 451. Yet they—

---

154 Molland (1959): 360.

155 Molland (1959): 360.

156 Cross and Livingstone (1983): 962; Peters (1973): 153; Brandon (1970): 468. Several of the specimen sentences given by the *Oxford English Dictionary* call Nestorianism "Christian."

157 As by Brox (1983): 161-62. One of the most passionate of Nestorius's defenders was Friedrich Loofs.

and their numbers include the Coptic, Armenian, Ethiopian, and Jacobite churches—are invariably described as Christian.[158] Is there any authority anywhere who would dispute the claim of, say, the Egyptian Coptic Orthodox church, to the title "Christian"? The idea is preposterous. But is this merely a matter of some bloodless modern "tolerance"? Clearly, no. In 531, that great persecutor of the Monophysites, the Emperor Justinian, sent envoys to the Monophysite Negus of Ethiopia, requesting, "by reason of our common faith," assistance in the war against the Sassanians.[159] If excommunication by a council of the church made one a non-Christian, this fact seems to have escaped Justinian.

The Fifth Ecumenical Council, in A.D. 553, posthumously condemned Theodore of Mopsuestia, who had died in A.D. 428.[160] He appears to have been a victim of the same passionate search for heresies and stumbles that seems to dominate the thinking of some modern fundamentalists. Indeed, Norbert Brox characterizes the period of Theodore's excommunication in terms that could also be used to describe some brands of anti-Mormonism: "A nervous, polemical climate of polarization dominated the era, in which people absolutely waited for their enemies to commit dogmatic or political mistakes."[161] Theodore was caught up in this unpleasant situation even though he had been dead for over a century. But his excommunication did not remove him from Christendom, and modern scholars invariably refer to him as a Christian.[162]

---

158 Farah (1970): 20, speaks of "Christian Abyssinia," while on p. 30 he implicitly so labels the Jacobites. Speaking specifically of the Ethiopians and the Arab Ghassanids, Peters (1973) explicitly calls Monophysites "Christians" at least a score of times. Monophysitism is implicitly identified as Christian by Cross and Livingstone (1983): 932; Brandon (1970): 450. Similar references—these have been found largely at random—could be multiplied indefinitely.

159 Peters (1973): 25.

160 Brox (1983): 186.

161 Brox (1983): 186 (translation ours).

162 Implicitly by Kraft (1966): 485; Brauer (1971): 814-15; explicitly by Moyer (1982): 396-97. These examples have been chosen at random.

A look at other major "heresies" discloses that they are also, in both specialist and common usage, referred to as Christian. The Montanists, for example, were a faction of the second and third centuries A.D. whose chief sin was admitting postbiblical revelation. (In this respect, if no other, they prefigure the Mormons.) Yet they are always called Christians.[163] Their most famous convert, the great Latin father, Tertullian, is indeed described by one historian as "the first Protestant."[164] Similarly, Donatism, condemned as a heresy in A.D. 405, is considered to be Christian by the scholars who deal with it.[165] Even more striking is the fact that authorities are not at all reluctant, in discussing what is perhaps the most radical complex of heresies ever to appear in Christendom, to speak of it as "Christian gnosticism." "Gnostics," writes Yale's Bentley Layton, "in fact made up one of the earliest and most long-lived branches of the ancient Christian movement."[166] James D. G. Dunn is able to speak of "gnostic tendencies within first-century

---

163 On the Montanists, see Johnson (1983): 71. They are implicitly identified as Christians by Johnson (1983): 85-86; Cross and Livingstone (1983): 934. The label is explicitly given to them by Ferm (1945): 505, and by the *Oxford English Dictionary*.

164 Johnson (1983): 50.

165 Ferm (1945): 233; Johnson (1983): 83-85; Manschreck (1985): 59; implicitly, Treadgold (1979): 71.

166 Layton (1987): xi. Examples of similar phrasing include T. W. Leahy, "The Epistle of Jude," in Brown, Fitzmyer, and Murphy (1968): 2:378-79; J. M. Robinson (1978): 4; Jonas (1963): 124; Rudolph (1983): 118; Pagels (1981): xxxvii; Meyer (1986): xvii; Cross and Livingstone (1983): 573-74; P. Perkins, "Gnosticism," in Ferguson (1990): 373; Pétrement (1990): 4-5. Frend (1981): 73, identifies Cerinthus as a "Judeo-Christian Gnostic." The astute reader will recognize that this list reads like a partial "Who's Who" of authorities on gnosticism; cf. Cross and Livingstone (1983): 1423, who clearly imply Valentinian gnosticism to be Christian, and Johnson (1983): 45, who explicitly says that the Valentinians were "quite inside Christianity." Manschreck (1985): 30, identifies both Valentinus and Basilides as Christians, as does the late and much lamented Couliano (1992): 30, 103, who also adds Isidorus as a "Christian gnostic." If Brox (1983): 139, really denies the Christianity of the gnostics—his remarks are ambiguous—he is distinctly in the minority.

Christianity," expressly including the New Testament.[167] Marcion and his followers are also routinely called Christians.[168] Never condemned were the "Christian Platonists of Alexandria"—who surely represent a melding of biblical doctrines with pagan influences, and who count among their number some of the most illustrious thinkers in the history of Christendom.[169] (Even the Docetists, who seem to be the only group that might, on the basis of earliest Christian writings, justifiably be termed non-Christian, are not.)[170]

Some critics of the Latter-day Saints would push the issue yet further, and would claim that Mormons cannot be Christian because they reject the ecumenical councils altogether. This, it is alleged, places them definitively beyond the boundaries of Christendom. However, such reasoning can only be described as arbitrary. As we have seen, Protestants accept but seven of the twenty-one ecumenical councils that have occurred in the course of Christian history. Should they be expelled from Christendom for that fact? Certain Eastern Orthodox Christians—Abyssinian or Ethiopian, Armenian, Coptic, and Syrian—reject all but the first three. Should they be termed pagans? Latter-day Saint scholar Stephen E. Robinson asks very important questions in this context: If the Ethiopians and Armenians and Copts and Syrians "can reject everything in traditional Christianity from the fifth century on and still be Christians, then where is the cutoff that marks how much can be rejected? If it can be as early as the fifth century, then why not as

---

167 Dunn (1977): 275-305.

168 As by Manschreck (1985): 31. Johnson (1983): 46-48, implicitly so recognizes Marcion, as does H. F. Stander, "Marcion," in Ferguson (1990): 568-69. Positive statements of Marcion's Christianity are rather rare because, as in the cases of other "heretics," the question simply does not arise for the vast majority of historians and scholars. As will be seen below, we ourselves are quite willing to grant the title of "Christian" to the Marcionites, despite our deep disagreement with them.

169 See Brox (1983): 160. A classic book on the subject bears the title, *The Christian Platonists of Alexandria*.

170 Johnson (1983): 45, 89, implicitly identifies them as Christians. The *Oxford English Dictionary* nowhere denies this.

early as the second?" Furthermore, Robinson demands, "if the councils and creeds teach doctrines not found in the New Testament, on what authority must they be accepted? And if the councils and creeds merely repeat or summarize the doctrines of the New Testament without adding to them, then why is it necessary to accept them *in addition* to the New Testament itself?" Obviously, the demand that Mormons must accept the creeds and councils or be denounced as heathens rests upon rather shaky grounds. But even "if other churches argue that it is necessary for Latter-day Saints to accept the councils in order to be Christian, then we might well ask, *Which* councils must be accepted? How can these other churches themselves accept only three, or four, or seven, and not all twenty-one?"[171]

The implications of all this should be plain. We have seen that the Bible cannot be used to define The Church of Jesus Christ of Latter-day Saints out of Christendom. Nor can the writings of the Apostolic Fathers. Nor can the ecumenical councils and the classical creeds of postapostolic Christianity be used to achieve such a goal. The essential principles of Christianity as documented in the earliest sources are fully accepted by the Latter-day Saints, who easily qualify as Christians according to the earliest definitions.

The question is now settled, as indeed it was after we had examined the three New Testament occurrences of the word "Christian." Mormons are Christians. Nevertheless, it may be interesting to examine some of the specific standards that anti-Mormons claim to derive from the Bible, and by which they claim to be able to discern "true" Christians from false pretenders. In so doing, we will cite instances from Christian history and biography which illustrate the wide latitude allowed for variation and doctrinal dissent by common usage of the terms "Christian" and "Christianity." Some of the figures we shall cite (e.g., Augustine) are in the mainstream, while some (e.g., Origen and Thomas Münzer) are less representative, chosen precisely because they indicate the range of possibilities allowable under the rubric of "Christian."

---

171 S. E. Robinson (1991): 35, 38.

Specific Reasons Given for Denying
That Latter-day Saints Are Christians

Claim 1. A newspaper advertisement being run by Ed Decker's Saints Alive in Jesus, playing on the Book of Mormon's claim to be "another testament of Jesus Christ," proclaims in bold headlines that "There is a Testament of Another Jesus Christ." "Mormonism claims to be a Christian church, but it does not have the same Jesus. Mormonism worships a false Christ (2 Cor. 11:4)," writes John L. Smith, of the Oklahoma-based Utah Missions, Inc. "Mormon leaders have admitted that they believe in another Jesus. One official of the Mormon church has declared, 'It is true that many of the Christian churches worship a different Jesus Christ than is worshipped by the Mormons.' "[172]

Response. This allegation, if true in the sense claimed for it by Rev. Smith, would be very damning. For if the Mormons were partisans of an individual who simply happened to bear the title "Christ," but was in reality a wholly distinct individual from the Jesus of Nazareth whom mainstream Christians worship the world over, Latter-day Saint claims to be Christian could be dismissed as true but misleading. The situation would be precisely equivalent to a debate between two biologists, both of whom claimed to be Darwinians. Biologist A, an evolutionist and a follower of the nineteenth-century Englishman Charles Darwin, would be absolutely baffled by his opponent's claim to be simultaneously a "scientific creationist," an opponent of evolution, and a disciple of Darwin. "You certainly follow a different Darwin than I do," he would say. But Biologist A would only be puzzled until he realized that the Darwin whom Biologist B followed was the Rev. Jimmy Joe Darwin of the Deadprophets Bible Church in Jenningsbryan,

---

172 J. L. Smith, "Mormonism Has Another Jesus." Cf. Fraser (1977): 61; Decker and Hunt (1984): 11 (vs. Scharffs [1986]: 71-72, 277-78). The official cited is the late Elder Bernard P. Brockbank, in a conference address carried by the *Ensign* (May 1977): 26. 2 Corinthians 11:3-4 is a favorite among anti-Mormons; cf. "What the Mormons Think of Christ REALLY . . .," and Tope, "Can the Mormon Jesus Save You?"

Alabama. Thereupon, Biologist A would probably grow angry, and accuse Biologist B of playing with him—indeed of engaging in deliberate misrepresentation. "You know full well," he would insist, "that 'Darwinian' has a very specific and accepted meaning in common usage, and you were trading on it to cause confusion among your hearers."

It is precisely this accusation, of deliberately misleading outsiders, that is routinely made against The Church of Jesus Christ of Latter-day Saints. It is, however, also a charge that we are strongly tempted to turn against our accusers.

Is the Mormon official's "admission," quoted by John L. Smith, really significant? Almost certainly not, and for a very simple reason. The word "different" can be used in varying ways. Consider the following two sentences: "Paris today is a different city from the one I saw on my first visit many years ago." "Berdyaev was born in Moscow, but died an exile in a different city, Paris." Clearly, the "difference" in the first sentence is merely one of quality, while that in the second is actual or quantifiable or, if you will, numerical. Suppose that Biologist A, having learned that the "Darwin" followed by Biologist B was an entirely distinct individual from the "Darwin" he had thought under discussion, with different nationality, birthdate, location, and fingerprints, now repeated his statement to his opponent. "You *certainly* follow a different Darwin than I do!" It should be clear that this sentence now has a quite distinct meaning, although its wording has not changed in the least. The variation resides entirely in the shift in the word "different" from a qualitative sense to a numerical or quantitative one.

No knowledgeable Mormon would ever "admit" that his church worships a supernatural individual numerically distinct from the God and Christ of the Bible. Clearly the statement cited by Rev. Smith simply acknowledges the undeniable difference between the attributes ascribed to Jesus by Mormons and those ascribed to him by other Christians. Just as clearly, however, the person of whom those attributes are predicated is identical for both Mormons and non-Mormons. Further, it is vital to keep in mind the fact that the difference in attributes between "the Mormon Jesus" and the Jesus of other Christians is only partial: In terms of practical spirituality and prayer, for example, there is little difference between Mormons and other Christians.[173] Mormons share with other Christians, too, the historical data of the New Testament, deviating only very rarely in its interpretation. Indeed, perhaps the greatest irony of the current campaign against Mormonism is that it is almost entirely the work of conservative Protestant Christians. Latter-day Saints have long tended to feel most at home with evangelical Bible commentaries, when they use such scholarly tools at all, because of the belief that we share with them in Christ's literal resurrection, in the historicity of his miracles, in the birth narratives, and in the Savior's divinity.[174] At least until recently, Mormons have thought of conservative Christians as, in many ways, their allies against the threat of theological liberalism and unbelief, as well as against trends toward immorality and family breakdown in the society at large. Hence the shock felt by many Mormons—the present writers among them—at the sometimes venomous attacks now aimed against their Church. Mormons consider Jesus divine, the Only Begotten Son of God, and the only perfect man who ever lived. Their Articles of Faith affirm that men are saved, if they are saved, "through the Atonement of Christ." Most Latter-day Saints can only shake their heads, therefore, at the claim that Mormonism is not Christian.

A comparison of twenty elements of personal identity possessed by "the Mormon Jesus" and "the Jesus of the Bible"—and many, many more elements could be compared if space and the reader's patience did not constrain us—should make it clear to even the most

---

173 One of the authors, for example, considers his participation in an interdenominational choir in Cairo among the highlights of his spiritual life. The choir sang Schubert's "Mass in G," which remains—especially the "Credo"—for him one of the most religiously moving pieces of music he knows. Handel's "Messiah" is beloved among the Latter-day Saints not only for its music, but because they believe every word of it.

174 A survey of the commentators and authorities cited by such Latter-day Saint writers as James E. Talmage and Bruce R. McConkie will easily bear this out.

hardened missing persons detective that the two are the same person.

Category	"The Mormon Jesus"	"The Jesus of the Bible"
1. birthplace	Bethlehem	Bethlehem
2. ethnicity	Jewish	Jewish
3. of David's line?	yes	yes
4. stepfather's name	Joseph	Joseph
5. mother's name	Mary	Mary
6. time period	early first century	early first century
7. occupation	carpenter, preacher	carpenter, preacher
8. taught in temple?	yes	yes
9. sojourn in Egypt?	yes	yes
10. baptized by John the Baptist?	yes	yes
11. walked on water?	yes	yes
12. water to wine?	yes	yes
13. gave parables?	yes	yes
14. public office?	no	no
15. manner of death	crucifixion	crucifixion
16. time of death	under Pontius Pilate	under Pontius Pilate
17. place of death	just outside Jerusalem	just outside Jerusalem
18. sign of death	earthquake	earthquake
19. resurrected?	yes	yes
20. ascent to heaven?	yes	yes

Beyond any question, the Latter-day Saints worship the same Jesus as do other Christians. To make his quotation more damning, therefore, Rev. Smith has chosen to take the word "different" in the quantitative or numerical sense, when it is almost certain that the Mormon leader he cites intended the word in the qualitative sense. In so doing, Smith has, perhaps innocently, perhaps not, committed the logical fallacy of equivocation. This elementary logical error, also known as the Fallacy of the Ambiguous Middle Term, is surprisingly common in anti-Mormon writings, but perhaps its clearest manifestation occurs in connection with this question of Mormonism's allegedly "different Jesus." As one elementary logic textbook defines it, "This fallacy is committed whenever we allow the meaning of a term to shift between the premises of our argument and our conclusion." It is amusingly illustrated in the following short poem:

> I love you,
> Therefore I am a lover;
> All the world loves a lover.
> You are all the world to me—
> Consequently
> You love me.[175]

The poem's error occurs, of course, when the phrase-term "all the world" is allowed to shift meanings between the third and fourth lines. This is precisely analogous to the way in which the word "different" shifts in meaning between the supposed admission of a Latter-day Saint general authority and the triumphant accusation of John L. Smith.

Once this is understood, it becomes apparent that we are talking here merely about differing views of one individual, Jesus, and not about distinct and separate individuals. Rev. Smith's earthshaking

---

175 See Brennan (1961): 210, 208, for the definition and the illustration. (Coincidentally, the very same logical fallacy, involving exactly the same phrase, is also committed by the character Helena, in Shakespeare's *A Midsummer Night's Dream*, Act II, Scene I.)

discovery thereby becomes trivial. After all, the Catholic Jesus is different from the Pentecostal Jesus, and both differ from the Coptic Jesus. Furthermore, given their different human experiences and upbringing and cultural and psychological conditions, it is not surprising that Jane and Joe and Manuel and Yaḥya ᶜAbd al-Masīh and Shusaku Endo and Uri Schwyzer have rather different ideas about Jesus. So what? To have different views of an individual does not magically create different individuals. Citizen C may think Senator Bunkum a paragon of fiscal restraint, as well as a statesman of rare wisdom and moderation, while Citizen D regards him as a heartless skinflint and an indecisive political coward, but we are still, mercifully, left with only one Senator Bunkum. It is with this principle in mind that John Hick and Edmund S. Meltzer can publish a volume about the three Abrahamic traditions of Judaism, Christianity, and Islam, and can quite justly title it *Three Faiths—One God*.[176]

"Christianity begins with Christ," writes C. L. Manschreck, "but who is Christ? The one depicted in the Gospels? Protestantism generally asserts this and uses the Bible as its authority, but examination discloses different views of Christ among the gospel writers, and the apparently older letters of Paul show little interest in the supposed facts about Jesus. Individual Protestants have assumed varied stances for interpreting Scriptures, with the result that widely divergent portraits of Jesus emerge, with no way to determine which is 'true.' "[177] As James D. G. Dunn points out, there was certainly "one Jesus" in history, but there have been "many Christs" in Christian belief—even (or especially) in the period of the New Testament.[178] Jaroslav Pelikan's fine book on *Jesus Through the Centuries* discusses just a few of the various Jesuses that can be documented over the past two millennia. Catholic views of Jesus differ from Protestant views in several

---

176 Vroom (1990): 73-90, argues in much the same direction.

177 Manschreck (1985): 1.

178 Dunn (1977): 203-31.

respects, and anti-Catholics do not lag behind anti-Mormons in exhorting their Roman Catholic readers to "be converted to the true Christ of the Bible," "the Christ of the Bible, not a counterfeit Christ."[179] "Is There Another Christ?" is the title of an anti-Catholic pamphlet published by Chick Publications, of Chino, California.[180] The clear implication is that the Catholics claim to have "another Christ," and that their claims are blasphemously false.

Since it is undeniably the case that many differing ideas are held about Jesus, the question arises just where on the opinion spectrum the line will be placed that separates "Christian" from "non-Christian." And this question, in turn, suggests the more fundamental problem of who has the right to draw such a line, and whence that authority comes. These are precisely the questions that will occupy us in the next few pages.[181]

In the meantime, Rev. Smith offers one seemingly clear distinction between the Mormon view of Jesus and the traditional Christian view: "The Mormon Jesus was the most unforgiving of men. Rather than being a Savior, the Mormon Jesus is a slaughterer." This latter idea he derives from the account of the New World destruction that accompanied Christ's Palestinian crucifixion, as recorded in the early chapters of 3 Nephi in the Book of Mormon. This idea is picked up by the Decker advertisement as well: "The Book of Mormon teaches that Jesus Christ destroyed 16 major cities and killed hundreds of thousands of his 'other sheep' (3 Nephi 8, 9). The Jesus of the Bible gave *new life*, not death!" But is the contrast so patent? The tender portrayal of Jesus blessing the little children in 3 Nephi 17 is only one of many texts that portray the

---

179 Quotations from "Which Will You Believe," and Ciampa, "Catholic or Christian?" respectively.

180 Chick Publications February 1990 Retail Catalog, 8.

181 Drawing on specific issues raised in Rev. J. L. Smith's pamphlet, "Mormonism Has Another Jesus," as well as other anti-Mormon literature.

gentle nature of "the Mormon Jesus."[182] Yet even in the Bible, Jesus is not depicted as sweetness alone. What of the cleansing of the temple? And what of the cleansing of the earth that will accompany his Second Coming?[183] Furthermore, given a trinitarian understanding of the Godhead, is Jesus not rather intimately implicated in such events as the Flood, and the destruction of Sodom and Gomorrah? The Jesus of the Book of Mormon is in fact both judge and Savior, precisely as he appears in the Bible. And our examples need not be restricted to "sacred" history. If Jesus is God, and if God is the Sovereign of all nature—as most Christians would testify, and as Mormons would agree—then it is not immediately apparent that Jesus is unconnected with, say, murderous floods in Bangladesh, or disastrous earthquakes in Turkey, or the burial in Colombia of an entire city by volcanic lava. (These are precisely the kinds of natural destruction reported in the Book of Mormon.) Does Rev. Smith intend here to announce that events in the natural order are (a) of no concern to the Trinity, or (b) beyond the Trinity's ability to control?

Probably the best evidence offered by Rev. Smith for his position is the illustration on the cover of his pamphlet entitled "Mormonism Has Another Jesus." The sightless, staring eyes, the stark features, the long, coal-black hair, the thickly sensuous mouth, the lips parted in devil-may-care lassitude, the lurid red flames that leap around him, all these fairly shout out that this is indeed a different Jesus. But is he "the Mormon Jesus?" No.

Claim 2. Mormons do not really believe in the deity of Jesus because they reject traditional dogma on the Trinity.[184] In Mor-

---

182 And the marvelous seventh chapter of Moses, in the Pearl of Great Price, extends the emotions of sorrow and compassion even to the Father—something that "high" Christian theology, e.g., that of the medieval scholastics, is extremely reluctant if not altogether unwilling to do.

183 Averill (1989): 153-55, argues that the apocalyptic depictions so deliciously savored by many fundamentalists, with their details of the horrible sufferings that will afflict the wicked in the last days, "traduce the character of the God whom we come to know in Jesus as the Christ." He might accurately have said that the fundamentalists have "another Jesus."

184 *The Utah Evangel* 33 (May/June 1986): 4; cf. (July/August 1986): 6; "Is Mormonism Christian?"; Tope, "The Trinity"; Decker and Hunt (1984): 110, 199-

mondom, alleges G. H. Fraser, "Athanasius is scorned and Arius is eulogized."[185] Mormons are "tritheists." And, thus, since they reject the Trinity, "the most basic of all Christian doctrines," they cannot possibly be considered Christian.[186] **Response.** Fraser's accusation is, of course, sheer nonsense. Athanasius and Arius, the Egyptian churchmen who were the principal figures in the theological controversies of the fourth century, are never mentioned in Latter-day Saint sermons and Sunday School classes; not one Mormon in a hundred would even recognize their names. The christological debates of the fourth and fifth centuries are in fact utterly irrelevant to Mormon theology, which does not share the Hellenistic metaphysical presuppositions that alone make them intelligible, and that, indeed, provoked them. (The way in which Latter-day Saint doctrine pierces through the centuries-old debates between Arianism and Nestorianism and Monophysitism and their rivals must surely rank among its greatest if least appreciated achievements.)

Even if the Latter-day Saints could legitimately be classified as "Arians," it would not make them non-Christian since being Arians in the first place did not banish the original followers of Arius from Christendom. Arianism "denied the true Divinity of Jesus Christ.

201, 256 (vs. Scharffs [1986]: 33, 161-62, 257-58); "Questions and Answers"; A. A. Hoekema, "Mormonism," in Douglas (1978): 678; P. B. Smith (1970): 67-68 (p. 67: "this cardinal doctrine of the Christian faith"); Robertson (1983): 16; Spittler (1962): 23: "the Christian conception of the Trinity"; J. O. Sanders (1962): 16; Molland (1959): 357; Tucker (1986): 48: "they do not hold the cardinal doctrines of the Christian faith, such as the trinity of the Godhead and the deity of Christ." Mormons are said by Fraser (1977): 8, 12, to "ridicule" the doctrine of the Trinity; so also Decker and Hunt (1984): 110. Once Mormon nontrinitarianism is twisted to imply disbelief in Christ's deity, Mormons can then be represented as disbelievers in his divinity in an absolute sense. Thus, their christology is reduced to equivalence with that of Unitarians, Jews, and Muslims. This is preposterous, but very common. See, for example, the letter from David E. Richards in the *Wall Street Journal* (24 July 1986).

185 Fraser (1977): 12.

186 *The Evangel* 38 (December 1991): 8; cf. *The Utah Evangel* 34 (July-August 1987): 8.

. . . He was not God by nature, but a changeable creature, His dignity as Son of God having been bestowed on Him by the Father on account of His foreseen abiding righteousness."[187] Yet, as we have seen, Arianism is always termed Christian.[188] (This is altogether appropriate since, as Norbert Brox points out, subordinationism, of which Arianism is a subspecies, represents the original Christian outlook[189]—a point at which, significantly, there probably *is* some affinity with the Mormon view.)

The fact that the Latter-day Saints are neither Athanasians nor genuine Arians, nor indeed any kind of trinitarians at all in the typical meaning of the word, should not mislead observers into thinking that they reject the divine Sonship of Jesus. Unlike such ancient groups as the Ebionites, who are universally referred to as "Jewish Christians," Mormons emphatically affirm the deity of Christ.[190] "We believe in God, the Eternal Father," they declare in their first Article of Faith, "and in His Son, Jesus Christ, and in the Holy Ghost." Thus, while not conventionally trinitarian, they declare forthrightly their belief in a three-person Godhead which is in all crucial respects the functional equivalent of the Greek metaphysical Trinity, and which includes as its second member a fully divine Son. Indeed, so insistent is the Book of Mormon upon the divinity of Christ that Krister Stendahl, former dean of Harvard Divinity School and Lutheran bishop of Sweden, as well as a sympathetic critic of the Latter-day Saints, has suggested that it goes too far![191]

---

187 Cross and Livingstone (1983): 83; cf. the attack on the Arians by J. O. Sanders (1962): 17-18.

188 As, generally, are the Unitarians. The *Oxford English Dictionary* explicitly terms them "Christian," despite their direct denial of the divinity of Christ. At most, the *Oxford English Dictionary* knows one ambiguous hint from 1671 that someone may perhaps have regarded Socinianism as non-Christian.

189 Brox (1983): 171, 175.

190 The title page of the Book of Mormon declares its purpose to be "the convincing of the Jew and Gentile that Jesus is the Christ, the Eternal God."

191 Stendahl (1978): 139-54. The volume in which this essay appears is a fascinating collection of papers by eminent non-Mormon theologians, biblical

We must be clear on the issue here. Despite the frequency with which Christ's divinity and trinitarian metaphysics are identified with each other,[192] the linkage is extremely dubious on both logical and historical grounds. Trinitarianism hardly seems a valid litmus test for determining who is, and who is not, Christian.[193] Indeed, the metaphysical doctrine of the Trinity is a very late development, and hardly to be found with clarity in the Bible.[194] The first Christian author to use the term is Theophilus of Antioch, who flourished in the late second century, and it is very doubtful that he meant by it what contemporary theologians mean, since the term had yet to go through a long philosophical and theological evolution before it reached any kind of stability.[195] Trinitarianism cannot be said to have been fully present among early Christians, in the sense to which the Latter-day Saints are being held. There was, for instance, a tendency in Justin Martyr (d. ca. A.D. 165), as among the apologists of the second century generally, to an idea of two Gods, and not three.[196] The theology of Clement of Alexandria (d. ca. A.D. 215) was also "really Binitarian."[197] W. H. C. Frend believes that the charge of "ditheism" (i.e., having a two-member Godhead) commonly made against Hippolytus (d. A.D.

scholars, and historians—Jewish and Christian—examining Mormon belief and practice in the light of their own specialties. S. E. Robinson (1991): 71-79, provides a useful defense of the Latter-day Saint position on this issue.

192 As by Molland (1959): 357; Tucker (1986): 48; Martin (1955): 12, 52.

193 Roger R. Keller specifically denies that disagreement on the Trinity by itself makes Mormons (or anyone else) non-Christian; cf. Keller (1986a): 5-6.

194 Thus, the trinitarian formula of 1 John 5:7-8—often referred to as the "Comma Johanneum"—is almost certainly a spurious insertion. So Metzger (1971): 716-18; B. Vawter, "The Johannine Epistles," in Brown, Fitzmyer, and Murphy (1968): 2:411; R. Russell, "1, 2, and 3 John," in Fuller, Johnston, and Kearns (1975): 958a; R. W. Orr, "The Letters of John," in Bruce (1986): 1584; Alexander and Alexander (1977): 642; P. B. Smith (1970): 57.

195 Gonzales (1970): 1:117.

196 Gonzales (1970): 1:117; 1:108; Brox (1983): 172.

197 Frend (1981): 358.

235) was probably justified.[198] "The exact theological definition of the doctrine of the Trinity," notes the Protestant Bible commentator J. R. Dummelow, "was the result of a long process of development, which was not complete till the fifth century or even later." Dummelow goes on, it is true, to observe that "the doctrine itself underlies the whole New Testament, which everywhere attributes divinity to the Father, the Son and the Spirit, and assigns to them distinct functions in the economy of human redemption."[199] But we must beware here of shifting meanings. What Dummelow means when he speaks of "the doctrine" that "underlies the whole New Testament" is merely the portrayal of a divine Father, a divine Son, and a divine Holy Ghost, united while nonetheless carrying out their various roles. But this picture of the Godhead is compatible both with the metaphysical Trinity, as that doctrine later evolved, and with the doctrine of the Latter-day Saints. It is far too inclusive to justify expelling the Mormons from Christendom. As Gerhard Kittel's famous *Theological Dictionary of the New Testament* observes, "The NT does not actually speak of triunity. We seek this in vain in the triadic formulae of the NT. . . . Early Christianity itself . . . does not yet have the problem of the Trinity in view."[200] This point cannot be overstressed, for it demonstrates beyond any question that the New Testament does not exclude Latter-day Saints from Christendom over the issue of the Trinity.

Ironically, however, anti-Mormon trinitarianism may well serve to exclude the early Christian Church. We have seen that neither Clement of Alexandria nor Hippolytus nor Justin Martyr held to a full-blown doctrine of the Trinity. Neither, apparently, did the very earliest followers of Jesus. For "the New Testament itself is far

---

198 Frend (1981): 376.

199 Dummelow (1920): cxiii.

200 E. Stauffer, "Theos," in Kittel and Friedrich (1965), 3:108-9.

from any doctrine of the Trinity or of a Triune God who is three co-equal Persons of One Nature."[201] "We cannot," notes one prominent non-Mormon scholar, "read back into the New Testament, much less the Old Testament, the more sophisticated trinitarian theology and doctrine which slowly and often unevenly developed over the course of some fifteen centuries."[202] "To insist that a belief in the Trinity is requisite to being Christian," Bill Forrest aptly remarks, "is to acknowledge that for centuries after the New Testament was completed thousands of Jesus' followers were in fact not really 'Christian.' "[203]

And what of Mormon "tritheism"?[204] A doctrine known as tritheism was taught by a number of prominent theologians in late antiquity, and can be considered "a definite phase in the history of Christian thought."[205] It is never termed "non-Christian."[206] In the sixth century A.D., its leading exponent is John Philoponus, the philosopher and Aristotelian commentator.[207] Not surprisingly, he

---

201 Hill (1982): 27.

202 McBrien (1980): 347; cf. Barth (1936): 1:1:437.

203 See Forrest's effective little pamphlet on the question "Are Mormons Christian?"

204 In view of the definitions given of this word by the *Oxford English Dictionary* and, especially, the *Random House Dictionary*, it is probably not an inappropriate term for Mormon teaching.

205 W. Fulton, "Trinity," in Hastings (1951): 12:463.

206 See, for example, Cross and Livingstone (1983): 1396, where tritheism is implicitly regarded as Christian; also M'Clintock and Strong (1867-91): 10:558; Campenhausen (1960): 6:1043-44. The *Oxford English Dictionary* contains no denial that tritheism is Christian. The opposite extreme from tritheism is perhaps Sabellianism. Yet we located no denials that it was Christian, and Johnson (1983): 90-91, seems implicitly to grant that it was. There seems, thus, to be wide latitude within Christianity—as the term is commonly used by both laymen and experts—for variant views on the Godhead.

207 Cross and Livingstone (1983): 1396.

is always described by scholars as a Christian.[208] But if such figures as Philoponus are too late and too philosophical for our critics, we might point as well to the pseudepigraphic *Ascension of Isaiah*, written sometime between the second and fourth centuries A.D. This early document features a vision of a clearly distinct Father, Son, and Holy Ghost.[209] Yet scholars uniformly refer to it as a Christian text. Obviously, if ancient tritheists were Christians, there is no reason to deny that title to modern tritheists—even if we grant that the term is an adequate one to describe the Mormon understanding of the Godhead, which we do here only for the purposes of argument.

The charge of "tritheism" might surely be leveled at the well-known fundamentalist preacher Jimmy Swaggart. In a brief paper entitled "What is Meant by the Trinity? And When We Get to Heaven Will We See Three Gods?" Swaggart has explained that "the term 'one,' " as applied to the Godhead, "means one in unity." "The three are one in the sense that they are always perfectly agreed; with never any disharmony between them [*sic*]." Yet, he continues, the blessed souls in heaven will actually see three distinct divine beings upon their arrival there.[210] Has Jimmy Swaggart ever been called non-Christian by any evangelical or fundamentalist Protestant? If so, we are unaware of it. How, then, can the Latter-day Saints be barred from Christendom on the basis of a standard that does not serve to expel Jimmy Swaggart as well?

Anti-Mormons who denounce The Church of Jesus Christ of Latter-day Saints as tritheistic need to check the thickness of their glass house's walls before they continue, since their own trinitarian

---

208 For example, by Husik (1970): 247; Peters (1968): 10; Peters (1973): 295; Merlan, "Alexandrian School," in P. Edwards (1967): 1:76; S. Sambursky, "Philoponus, John," in P. Edwards (1967): 5:156; Kraft (1966): 310-11. Further examples would be redundant. The reader will find no contrary opinions. A famous American anti-trinitarian was Ralph Waldo Emerson; cf. Treadgold (1979): 210.

209 *Ascension of Isaiah* 9:27-10:9.

210 Swaggart, "What Is Meant by the Trinity? And When We Get to Heaven Will We See Three Gods?"

understanding of the Godhead looks like tritheism to rigidly monotheistic Jews and Muslims. "Judaism, Islam, and Christianity claim to be monotheistic," noted the late S. G. F. Brandon, "but the title of Christianity is disputed by the other two on the grounds that the doctrine of the Trinity is tritheism."[211] Even dissenters within the Christian tradition have sometimes felt uneasy with trinitarian theology. From the point of view of the Sabellian bishops of early Christianity, the doctrine of the trinity appeared to be tritheistic.[212] But not only by them. Many ordinary Christians of those first centuries were disturbed by such doctrinal innovations. "The beginnings of the church's trinitarian theology were perceived as polytheism and were rejected as heresy in the name of the biblical God."[213]

Claim 3. Mormonism must be considered non-Christian because of its "altogether revolting teaching concerning the Deity."[214] Its anthropomorphism is "anti-Christian," and "pagan."[215] "In fact, the whole matter goes beyond the concept of 'different views of

---

211 Brandon (1970): 450-51; cf. W. Fulton, "Trinity," in Hastings (1951): 12:462, which sees the charge as somewhat justified; Johnson (1983): 89-93.

212 Brox (1983): 174.

213 Brox (1983): 172 (translation ours).

214 Irvine (1921): 133; cf. J. R. van Pelt, "Mormons," in Jackson (1977): 8:18; Tucker (1989): 80; *The Utah Evangel* 31 (March 1984): 8; Decker, "To Moroni with Love," 6-10; cf. the attack on the Christian concept of God, quoted in Minucius Felix, *Octavius* 10, and dating from near the end of the second century A.D.

215 Martin (1985): 200-211, 213; cf. Coe and Coe (1985): 174-77; *The Utah Evangel* 31 (February 1984): 3; *The Evangel* 38 (April 1991): 4; "The Mormon Church and the African"; P. B. Smith (1970): 65-67; "Mormonism: Christian or Cult?"; J. O. Sanders (1962): 109, 113-16; "Questions and Answers"; Decker (1979): 15; Decker, "Petition"; A. A. Hoekema, "Mormonism," in Douglas (1978): 678; Molland (1959): 353. Says Martin (1985): 200: "It will be conceded by most informed students of Christianity that one cannot deny the existence of the one true God of Scripture and at the same time lay claim to being a Christian." Even granting this biblically unprovable proposition, however, Martin's confidence in being able to clearly define that "one true God" is exaggerated.

God'; we are dealing with 'views of different Gods.' "[216] The
Mormon " 'God,' " explain Ed Decker and Dave Hunt, "is an
extraterrestrial from Kolob, definitely not the God of the Bible."[217] In a related vein, one active anti-Mormon ministry laments that Elder Reed Smoot, who served in the United States
Senate for three decades, was "chosen to sit in Congress and make
laws for this Christian country. He would have been more in place
in the Senate of ancient Rome."[218] "Dr." Walter Martin claims
that Mormonism is "a polytheistic nightmare of garbled doctrines
draped with the garment of Christian terminology. This fact, if
nothing else, brands it as a non-Christian cult system."[219]

Response. But polytheism is, to a certain extent, in the eye of
the beholder. There are probably few communicant Mormons who
would agree to being "polytheists," and none who would claim to
worship more than one God.[220] Instead, Mormons are taught to
worship the Father in the name of the Son (D&C 18:40; 20:29).
And the late Elder Bruce R. McConkie's consistent instruction to

---

216 Decker, "To Moroni with Love," 6; cf. Fraser (1977): 32, 36, 45, 75; Decker
and Hunt (1984): 11, 234, 245-46, 259-61 (vs. Scharffs [1986]: 71-72, 337, 352-53,
373-75). On this point, see the discussion of the various senses of "differences,"
under item number one, above.

217 Decker and Hunt (1984): 234. Contrast Scharffs (1986): 337. Such loaded
language is characteristic of Decker and Hunt, as well as of their movie, *The God
Makers*. Mormons never use such terminology, but it is highly valuable if one's
intent is to make Latter-day Saint beliefs appear ridiculous.

218 *Mission Monthly* 13 (February 1992): 7, reprinting with approval a document
from 1904. *Mission Monthly* is published by the California-based Jude 3 Mis-
sions/Utah Gospel Mission.

219 Martin (1985): 226; cf. pp. 200-211, where Mormonism is again, and for the
same reason, branded "pagan." See also Boa (1984): 69-71; A. A. Hoekema,
"Mormonism," in Douglas (1978): 678; P. B. Smith (1970): 64-65, 68; Decker and
Hunt (1984): 121 (vs. Scharffs [1986]: 30, 181); Robertson (1983): 14; Holzapfel
(1925): 84; Molland (1959): 348, 353; *The Utah Evangel* 31 (February 1984): 3;
Mormonism is, says van Baalen (1983): 159, "gross polytheism"; cf. "Is Mormonism Christian?"

220 See, for example, the defense against this charge offered by S. E. Robinson
(1991): 65-69.

worship the Father only and, in a certain sense, not even the Son, must surely be described as monotheistic.[221] Astonishingly, it is also routinely condemned as non-Christian by critics who will then turn around and, with not the slightest inkling of their inconsistency, denounce Mormons as heathen polytheists who worship a pantheon of deities.[222]

As we have noted above, traditional Christianity itself is not straightforwardly monotheistic. Muslims, for example, who are rigidly and purely so, routinely refer to trinitarian Christians as *mushrikīn*, or "polytheists."[223] And they are not alone in their uneasiness with a Godhead that is claimed to be simultaneously one and three. "The metaphysical insanities of Athanasius, of Loyola, and of Calvin," wrote Thomas Jefferson to Jared Sparks in 1820, "are, to my understanding, mere relapses into polytheism, differing from paganism only by being more unintelligible."[224]

Mainstream Christianity's uncertain hold on monotheism probably derives from the fact that Judaism, the religion out of which it grows, was itself perhaps not clearly monotheistic. This may come as a shock, since we usually think of Judaism as a pure monotheism if ever there was one. Our usual thinking, however, may be wrong. Carefully surveying the data, Peter Hayman concludes that "it is hardly ever appropriate to use the term monotheism to describe the Jewish idea of God." "The pattern of Jewish beliefs about God," he says, "remains monarchistic throughout. God is king of a heavenly court consisting of many other powerful beings. . . . For most [pre-modern] Jews, God is the sole object of worship, but he is not the only divine being. . . .

---

221 McConkie (1982): 101.

222 One of Elder McConkie's statements finds its way into John L. Smith's "Mormonism Has Another Jesus." Smith and his Utah Missions, Inc., are in the forefront of those who consider Mormons non-Christian.

223 One definition for the term "Unitarian," given in the *Oxford English Dictionary*, is "any non-Christian monotheist, esp. a Mohammedan."

224 See Hamilton (1926): 244-45.

This pattern is inherited from biblical times."[225] It is a pattern, one might easily argue, that has been inherited by the Latter-day Saints.

Anti-Mormons, as noted above, sometimes charge that Latter-day Saint theology is so radically distinct from traditional notions that we must speak of "views of different Gods," rather than "different views of God." This is an interesting claim. It is closely related to the charge that Latter-day Saints have "a different Jesus." Yet it is very questionable, as an illustration from the history of science should demonstrate. Most ancient observers of the sky imagined it to be a solid structure, with lamps or windows (the stars) that permitted light to reach the earth. They gave various explanations for the moving lights of the planets, the sun, and the moon. Claudius Ptolemy's more scientific view of the cosmos, articulated in the second century A.D. but relying on centuries of Greek astronomy, retained the idea that the earth rested at the center of the solar system. The other planets, along with the sun and the moon, revolved around the earth in a complex combination of cycles and epicycles. Nicolaus Copernicus (d. A.D. 1543) put the sun at the center of the solar system instead of the earth, and had the planets (including the earth) moving in perfect, concentric circles around it. Finally, Johannes Kepler (d. A.D. 1630) kept the sun at the center of his scheme but elaborated a system of elliptical orbits. In doing so, he contradicted 2000 years of scientific tradition. These are decidedly different pictures of astronomical reality. Should we therefore say that we are dealing, not with different views of the same solar system, but with views of different solar systems? That Copernicus represents not a vast improvement upon Ptolemy's theory but a new theory about something utterly unrelated? That the Ptolemaic, Copernican, and Keplerian theories don't even deal with the same subject? (Such a bizarre approach would wreak havoc with the history of astronomy as it is universally understood.) Isn't it more reasonable to say that these theories deal in contradictory ways with exactly the same subject? That the

---

225 Hayman (1991): 2, 15.

ancient Babylonians, Ptolemy, Copernicus, and Kepler were attempting to make sense of and account for the data supplied by astronomical observation, just as, in their own sphere, differing theologies attempt to make sense of and account for the data supplied by revelation?

It is interesting to note that the Church of Rome runs afoul of Protestant fundamentalists on many of the same grounds which are used to expel the Latter-day Saints from Christianity. For instance, according to many of our self-anointed "authorities," Catholicism is "idolatrous."[226] Among its numerous sins is the fact that it recognizes intermediaries, such as the various saints, between God and man.[227] Particularly offensive, in the view of fundamentalist anti-Catholics, is the notion of Mary as mediatrix.[228] Yet reliance on such mediation was widespread in (what has historically been called) Christianity from at least the late second century.[229] Though we do not subscribe to a belief in intermediaries (apart from Christ) and hold no particular brief for that belief, it does seem highly peculiar to claim that millions of believers in Jesus between the second century and the Reformation in the fifteenth—to say nothing of contemporary Catholic and Orthodox believers- —were really non-Christian pagans. However much one may disagree with Catholic theology, any definition of Christianity that excludes the Church of Rome and virtually the entire period of the Middle Ages can only be described as, well, more than a little bit weird. Were the great cathedrals of the Age of Faith erected by pagans? Were Francis of Assisi and Thomas Aquinas heathens?

---

226 Irvine (1921): 140; W. Thompson, "What We Should Know about Roman Catholicism"; Boettner (1986): 279-84; The Conversion Center Newsletter (May/June 1990).

227 Irvine (1921): 142-44; Ironside (1982): 24-31; Zacchello (1984): 145-55.

228 Berry (1979): 96-97; W. Thompson, "What We Should Know about Roman Catholicism"; Zacchello (1984): 113-40; Spittler (1962): 113-14; J. O. Sanders (1962): 25-26, 28; Boettner (1986): 9-10, 46-77, 456.

229 Brox (1983): 133.

But if we admit, as it seems we must, that the acceptance of human intermediaries in prayer does not itself make an individual or a church non-Christian, how can a movement which admits no intermediary but Christ reasonably be dismissed from Christendom? There seems no justification for such a move. Yet this is precisely the case with Mormonism, which admits no human intermediaries in prayer and still is vilified by its fundamentalist enemies as not only non-Christian but "anti-Christian."

And, finally, does anthropomorphism really disqualify those who believe in it from being Christian? It would be odd if it did, for most Christians of the very earliest period were almost certainly anthropomorphists. As a recent article in the *Harvard Theological Review* contends, "ordinary Christians for at least the first three centuries of the current era commonly (and perhaps generally) believed God to be corporeal," or embodied. "The belief was abandoned (and then only gradually) as Neoplatonism became more and more entrenched as the dominant world view of Christian thinkers."[230] And these early Christians had excellent biblical reasons for believing in a corporeal deity, as the contemporary fundamentalist preacher Jimmy Swaggart, an anthropomorphist himself, has noticed.[231] But pursuing this argument would take us too far afield.[232] Roland J. Teske has shown that the great Augustine turned to Manichaeism out of disgust at the anthropomorphism that characterized the Christianity in which he had been raised, and that he had thought was typical of Christianity as a whole. "Prior to Augustine (and, of course, the Neoplatonic group in Milan)," writes Teske, "the Western Church was simply without a concept of God as a spiritual substance."[233] Suffice it to note that the

---

230 Paulsen (1990): 105-16. The quotation is from p. 105.

231 Swaggart, "What is Meant by the Trinity? And When We Get to Heaven Will We See Three Gods?"

232 However, for starters, see the article by Edmond LaB. Cherbonnier (1978): 155-73, where a prominent non-Mormon theologian has much good to say about the Mormon position.

233 Teske (1986): 233-49, especially 242 n. 25, 244 nn. 34 and 35.

Audians, an anthropomorphizing and rigorist group of the fourth and fifth centuries A.D., seem always to be considered Christian by those scholars who discuss them.[234] If anthropomorphism has not disqualified them from being Christians, and if—whatever his other problems—it has also not disqualified Jimmy Swaggart, we find it difficult to understand why anthropomorphism would disqualify the Latter-day Saints. Must one be a Neoplatonist, a disciple of Greek philosophers like Plato and Plotinus, to be a Christian?[235]

Claim 4. Mormonism teaches that human beings can become like God. But this is massively offensive to anti-Mormons of all stripes and persuasions. "Any church who [sic] preaches a gospel such as this is definitely not Christian."[236] The doctrine is, according to many critics, pagan, occultic, and Satanic.[237] It is so troubling to many mainstream Christians that the producers of one slickly dishonest anti-Mormon film chose it as their central attention-getting theme, and entitled their pseudo-documentary *The God Makers.* (Their efforts have since spawned a book of the same name, and an even more inflammatory sequel titled *Temples of the God Makers.*)

---

234 In our survey, we found no explicit assertions of their Christianity, probably because nobody had ever thought to deny it. But they are distinctly implied to be Christians by Brauer (1971): 70; Cross and Livingstone (1983): 106; G. Krüger, "Audians," in Jackson (1977): 1:360; M'Clintock and Strong (1867-91): 1:537; Campenhausen (1960): 1:688.

235 See S. E. Robinson (1991): 79-89, for another Latter-day Saint perspective on this favorite anti-Mormon claim.

236 Breese et al. (1985): 49; also *The Utah Evangel* 31 (January 1984): 12, and (December 1984): 1, and (July/August 1986): 1, 4; Decker, "To Moroni with Love," 18-19; A. A. Hoekema, "Mormonism," in Douglas (1978): 678; Fraser (1977): 31, 45, 74; "Questions and Answers"; P. B. Smith (1970): 64, 68; Robertson (1983): 15, 18; Holzapfel (1925): 85; Decker (1979): 15, 27; "Mormonism: Christian or Cult?"; Decker and Hunt (1984): 24-25, 261 (vs. Scharffs [1986]: 77-79, 375-76); J. R. van Pelt, "Mormons," in Jackson (1977): 8:18; "The Mormon Church and the African"; Decker, "Petition"; cf. Boa (1984): 69-71, who, for this reason, declares that "Mormon theology is definitely not a form of Christianity." Indeed, he lists Mormonism among "Major Pseudo-Christian Religions of the West"—along with Christian Science and Seventh-Day Adventism.

237 Sackett, "A Mormon Temple Worker," 7.

Response. Even a cursory glance at early Christian thought reveals that the idea of human deification—known in Greek as *theōsis* or *theopoiēsis*—is to be found throughout ancient Christianity.[238] We are, of course, under no illusions that such figures as Athanasius and the Byzantine fathers—given their very different metaphysical and theological presuppositions—understood *theōsis* in precisely the same way as do the Latter-day Saints. It is certain that the ancient doctrine had undergone massive dislocations by the time it reached the sixteenth century. Clearly, it had already been "spiritualized" by the time of Pseudo-Dionysius, around A.D. 500, and, given the evolution of Christian teaching on God, probably well before.[239] Latter-day Saints, though, are in an enviable position here. Given our belief in an apostasy, we fully expect there to be differences, even vast differences, between the beliefs of the Fathers and Mormon doctrine. Any similarities that exist, however, are potentially understandable as survivals from before that apostasy. When any similarities, even partial ones, exist between Latter-day Saint beliefs and the teachings of the Fathers *but are absent between contemporary mainstream Christendom and the Fathers*, they can be viewed as deeply important. And the simple fact is that, on the specific question at issue here, Latter-day Saints teach a doctrine of deification, and many of the Fathers teach a doctrine of deification, but the Protestant brand of Christianity espoused by most anti-Mormons does not. We suspect, in fact, that even relatively late statements on *theōsis* represent the Hellenization of an earlier doctrine—one that was perhaps much closer to

---

238 See, for example, the index entries in Pelikan (1971) and Pelikan (1974) under "Salvation—defined as deification," as well as the appropriate index entry in A. Nygren. Probably the most complete treatment of the issue—with references and data far beyond what we are able to include here—is found in Norman (1980); cf. Beggiani (1983): 73-78, on the Syriac tradition. G. I. Mantzarides (1984) deals particularly with St. Gregory Palamas, an important fourteenth-century Greek theologian, but is useful for the Orthodox tradition generally. S. E. Robinson (1991): 60-65, is a handy Latter-day Saint discussion of this issue, with references, in the light of anti-Mormon claims.

239 On Pseudo-Dionysius, see Nygren (1982): 584-88.

Mormon belief. According to a very early formula, "God became man that man might become God."[240] According to Clement of Alexandria (d. A.D. 215), "By thus receiving the Lord's power, the soul studies to be God."[241] And in a chapter on "Why Man Is Not Made Perfect from the Beginning," Irenaeus (d. A.D. 180) wrote, "For we cast blame upon Him, because we have not been made gods from the beginning, but at first merely men, then at length gods."[242]

The doctrine of human deification existed early because it is deeply rooted in the Bible. "Be ye therefore perfect," says the Savior at Matthew 5:48, "even as your Father which is in heaven is perfect." Indeed, according to the apostle Paul, the Church itself was established to bring us to this perfection (Ephesians 4:11-13). How far will the process of perfection extend? Quite far indeed. "The Spirit itself beareth witness with our spirit, that we are the children of God: And if children, then heirs; heirs of God, and joint-heirs with Christ; if so be that we suffer with him, that we may be also glorified together" (Romans 8:16-17). We are the sons of God, Paul repeats in Galatians 4:6-7—"And if a son, then an heir of God through Christ." First John 3:2 agrees completely. "Now are we the sons of God," says that letter, declaring that "we know that, when he shall appear, we shall be like him." Again, Paul, speaking of "the glory of the Lord," says that we "are changed into the same image from glory to glory" (2 Corinthians 3:18). The promise, says 2 Peter 1:4, is that we will be made "partakers of the divine nature." When, at John 10:30, Jesus says, "I and my Father are one," the Jews immediately "took up stones . . . to stone him" (John 10:31). Why? Because, with entire justification, they understood the claim to be one with God as a clear claim of deity. "For a good work we stone thee not; but for blasphemy; and

---

240 See Norman (1975); Barlow (1983): 13-18.

241 Clement of Alexandria, *Stromata* VI, 14. English translation in Roberts and Donaldson (1979): 2:506.

242 Irenaeus, *Against the Heretics* IV, 38, 4. English translation in Roberts and Donaldson (1981): 1:522; cf. Barlow (1983): 16.

because that thou, being a man, makest thyself God" (John 10:33). It would seem, then, with this episode in mind, that a promise of deification for his faithful followers is implied in the Savior's great intercessory prayer, when he asks on behalf of the disciples "that they all may be one; as thou, Father, art in me, and I in thee, that they also may be one in us" (John 17:21). "To him that overcometh," says the Savior in Revelation 3:21, "will I grant to sit with me in my throne, even as I also overcame, and am set down with my Father in his throne." How much more clearly can it be said?

Theōsis or *theopoiēsis* can easily be traced in both biblical and post-biblical Judaism as well. "The theme of 'becoming like one of us' reveals itself as the lurking subtext of Judaism from Adam to Nachman of Bratslav," writes Peter Hayman in an important study. "But how does this material square with the supposed transcendental monotheism of Judaism from the post-exilic period on? Not at all, as far as I can see!" Nevertheless, Hayman points out, "many [Jewish mystical texts] presuppose that humans can become divine and dispose of the powers of God."[243] Indeed, Jewish tradition can name at least one specific historical individual who has attained divine status, for the so-called Hekhalot literature claims "that a man, Enoch, ascended to heaven and was metamorphosed into Metatron, the 'little Yahweh.' "[244]

The notion of deification is characteristic of Clement of Alexandria.[245] It is fundamental to Athanasius.[246] Indeed, so pervasive was it in the fourth century that it was also held by Athanasius's archenemies, the Arians, and played a vital role in the dispute between

---

243 Hayman (1991): 4-5.

244 Hayman (1991): 5; cf. 11-12. On notions of ascension as deification, with reference both to Enoch and to earliest Christianity, see the extensive treatment of Segal (1990): 34-71; cf. 22.

245 Butterworth (1916): 157-69; Nygren (1982): 356.

246 Norman (1980): 77-106; cf. Manschreck (1985): 62; Treadgold (1979): 57. Boettner (1986): 82, acknowledges Athanasius as "the champion of orthodoxy at the Council of Nicaea."

the two factions.[247] Athanasius opposed the Arians because he feared that, in their belief, Christ's deity was not sufficiently robust to sustain redemption as deification.[248] Even in subsequent centuries, the doctrine of *theōsis* continued to play a central role in Christian thinking. John Chrysostom (d. A.D. 407) taught that "man can, by his own efforts, attain the likeness of God by mastering his passions."[249] "The chief idea of St. Maximus," who died in A.D. 662, "as of all of Eastern theology, [was] the idea of deification."[250] Are we to toss out the entire Greek and Syriac patristic traditions as "non-Christian"? Perhaps some Protestant fundamentalists would be willing to do so. But most reasonable people would find it a very strange definition of Christianity that excluded almost all Christians. And, besides, the western Christian tradition is not at all free from the doctrine of human deification, which often appears in the most unexpected places.[251] C. S. Lewis, for instance, is an author dear to many evangelical Christians. Yet Lewis's writings are full of the language of human deification.[252] Would anyone claim that he was not a Christian?[253]

---

247 Nygren (1982): 428, n. 3. And the Arians, as we have seen above, are routinely described as being Christians.

248 J. H. Crehan, "Original Sin," in Davis, Williams, Thomas, and Crehan (1971): 3:382; cf. Brox (1983): 189.

249 Kelly (1978): 348.

250 Pelikan (1974): 10, citing S. L. Epifanovic; cf. Nygren (1982): 428, n. 3. Nellas (1987) offers a good discussion of deification in the modern Orthodox understanding.

251 Bouzignac (1986): 8-9, offers an example of the doctrine in the Latin text of a French Christmas carol: "Cur Deus factus homo? Ut homo Deus fieret" ("Why did God become man? That man might become God").

252 See, for example, C. S. Lewis (1963): 84-85; (1960b): 9; (1965): 14-15; (1960a): 38-40, 174, 187; (1973): 45. Note that the bulk of the references above are to a book entitled *Mere Christianity*; this demonstrates the centrality of the concept in Lewis's thought. We are indebted to Todd Compton and Karen Lewis for having tracked down these passages in Lewis. Barlow (1983) offers evidence that other post-Reformation authors have held similar beliefs. Apparently even Martin Luther was capable of speaking of "the deification of human nature," although in what sense or context we are unable to say; cf. Pressau (1977): 57; Nygren (1982): 734.

"One can think what one wants of this doctrine of progressive deification," comments the important German Protestant church historian Ernst Benz, "but one thing is certain: with this anthropology Joseph Smith is closer to the view of man held by the Ancient Church than the precursors of the Augustinian doctrine of original sin were, who considered the thought of such a substantial connection between God and man as *the* heresy, par excellence." Discussing the doctrine of human deification as held by the Latter-day Saints, Benz expressly terms it Christian.[254]

One response to Latter-day Saint teaching on deification, a brief item entitled "One God: A Response to Mormon Apologists," tries to argue that "the early Church" did not teach the doctrine at all.[255] However, it gives examples that extend down to John of Damascus (d. A.D. 750), who can hardly be considered a representative of "the early Church." But even its use of the early Apologists like Aristides of Athens (d. A.D. 140) and Justin Martyr (d. A.D. 155) is somewhat problematic from a Latter-day Saint viewpoint, since precisely these "Apologists" were Hellenized, and were attempting to show that Christians worshiped the same God as their sophisticated pagan neighbors. This was also the position of Origen.[256] The eminent historian Robert Wilken is helpful here, in the context of a discussion of the great third-century pagan critic of Christianity, Porphyry. "For over a century," he says, "since the time when the Apologists first began to offer a reasoned and philosophical presentation of Christianity to pagan intellectuals, Christian thinkers had claimed that they worshiped the same God

---

253 In another context, P. B. Smith (1970): 43, obviously unaware of the hideousness of the demon he is hugging to his breast, ridicules "the incredible concept that men like . . . C. S. Lewis did not understand nor preach the Gospel."

254 Benz (1978): 215-16 (emphasis in the original).

255 "One God."

256 Prestige (1940): 63. On p. 65, Prestige endorses Origen's own self-description: "Origen, and not the third-rate professors of a dying sophistry and nerveless superstition, stood in the true succession from Plato and Aristotle in the history of pure thought."

honored by the Greeks and Romans, in other words, the deity adored by other reasonable men and women. Indeed, Christians adopted precisely the same language to describe God as did pagan intellectuals. The Christian apologist Theophilus of Antioch described God as 'ineffable . . . inexpressible . . . uncontainable . . . incomprehensible . . . inconceivable . . . incomparable . . . unteachable . . . immutable . . . inexpressible . . . without beginning because he was uncreated, immutable because he is immortal' (*Ad Autolycum* 1.3-4). This view, that God was an immaterial, timeless, and impassible divine being, who is known through the mind alone, became a keystone of Christian apologetics, for it served to establish a decisive link to the Greek spiritual and intellectual tradition."[257]

Such efforts to demonstrate that the Christian God was identical to the God of sophisticated paganism continued as long as there were pagans to impress—i.e., well into the fifth century.[258] Yet it appears that the majority of early rank-and-file Christians deeply distrusted the attempts of these intellectuals to clothe Christianity in the garments of pagan Greek philosophy.[259] Thus, it seems that Latter-day Saints have very good reason to be skeptical of Aristides and Justin and their fellow Apologists as spokesmen for earliest Christian beliefs. Their pagan audiences were rather skeptical as well, and for an intriguingly relevant reason: "The gods are hostile to you," the pagans replied, "because you maintain that a man, born of a human being . . . was God . . . and you worship him in daily prayers."[260] This sounds rather like certain criticisms of the Latter-day Saints—except that we are seldom accused of *worshiping* deified humans.

The citation by "One God" of G. L. Prestige to express the Fathers' position does little to silence our suspicion that it has

---

257 Wilken (1984): 151.

258 Wilken (1984): 151-52, 154.

259 Wilken (1984): 78-79.

260 Wilken (1984): 154, citing Arnobius, *Adversus Nationes* I, 36.

overlooked their Hellenistic taint. God, says Prestige, has "all those positive qualities which man does not possess, the attribution of which is made by adding the negative prefix to the common attributes of humanity."[261] Prestige is talking about the well-known Greek alpha-privative, the use of which was so notoriously characteristic of such Alexandrian thinkers as Clement, and so typical of the milieu that produced Neoplatonism. Yet such "negative theology," as it is termed, is not to be found in the Bible.

The response entitled "One God" also cites Prestige as asserting that the early Fathers did not "obliterate the distinction" between God and man. "The gulf is never bridged between Creator and creature. . . . Man remains a created being: God alone is *agenē-tos*."[262] The point of this, of course, from the standpoint of anti-Mormon polemic, is to say that, since humans are entirely distinct and different in quality from God, they cannot possibly ever partake of real divinity. Therefore, whatever the early Christians may have meant by "deification," it cannot, so the argument goes, have been anything like what the Mormons claim.

But "One God" is not giving the entire story. As late as the time of the Emperor Julian (d. A.D. 363), Professor Robert Wilken notes, "the term ungenerate (*agenētos*) was a point of contention among Christians. For several decades Christian thinkers had been debating whether the son was 'ungenerated' or 'generated.' If the son was generated—that is, came into existence—then he could not be divine [according to current philosophical assumptions]. Only God is ungenerated, for he exists eternally without change. At the

---

261 Unless otherwise noted, quotations from G. L. Prestige are taken from "One God."

262 Latter-day Saints, of course, would disagree with this formulation. "All learned men and doctors of divinity say that God created [the essential human intelligence or personality] in the beginning; but it is not so: the very idea lessens man in my estimation. I do not believe the doctrine; I know better. Hear it, all ye ends of the world; for God has told me so. . . . I am going to tell of things more noble. We say that God himself is a self-existent being. Who told you so? It is correct enough; but how did it get into your heads? Who told you that man did not exist in like manner upon the same principles? Man does exist upon the same principles" (*TPJS*, 352).

time Julian was writing his *Contra Galilaeos* the Christians were engaged in a debate as to whether the Holy Spirit was generated or ungenerated—in other words, whether the Spirit was truly divine."[263]

However, it would seem that God the Father alone remained *"agenētos"* in patristic belief. The Son is distinguished from the Father precisely by the fact of his Sonship, which, as in earthly sonship, relates him to the Father as effect to cause. G. L. Prestige makes this quite evident in one of his other books. "God the Father, who alone enjoys a being that is both absolute and underived (*agenētos* and *agennētos*), is the sole source of whatsoever deity belongs to His Word and His Spirit. The second and third Persons of the Trinity, inasmuch as their being is derivative, are subordinate to Him in respect of existence. These propositions represent substantially the position of Tertullian, and so far there is nothing heretical in affirming them. Tertullian in fact laid the permanent foundation of the Latin doctrine of the Trinity."[264]

One of the great Christological contributions of the illustrious third-century theologian Origen was his doctrine of the Eternal Generation of the Son. Alan Richardson, the late Dean of York, provides a clear explanation of this doctrine: "God's nature is eternally to be a Father, and therefore the Son could not have been born at a specific moment in time, but must be eternally Son. He is eternally being begotten by the Father, for the latter is the ultimate ground of all that is, begetting the Logos and creating the world and finite spirits. It is in this sense that the Son is subordinate to the Father, for whereas the Father is the Supreme Being and ground of all other existents, the reality of the Son is derived from that of the Father."[265]

Of course, Latter-day Saints do not agree with Origen's position. But they can afford to disagree with it. The anti-Mormon response

---

263   Wilken (1984): 183.

264   Prestige (1940): 83.

265   Richardson (1990): 42; cf. 43-44, 52.

"One God," alas, cannot. If it wants to argue that being "*genetos*" means one cannot be truly divine, it will have to reject Origen's position, which is also that of most if not all of the classical creeds of Christendom, since they assert both the "begottenness" of the Son and his full and complete deity.

The so-called Athanasian Creed, of the fifth century, makes things especially clear. It affirms that "the Godhead of the Father, of the Son, and of the Holy Ghost, is all one: the Glory equal, the Majesty coeternal. Such as the Father is: such is the Son: and such is the Holy Ghost. . . . So the Father is God: the Son is God: and the Holy Ghost is God." However, Father, Son, and Holy Ghost are distinguished precisely by their origination, or lack thereof. "The Father is made of none: neither created, nor begotten [*nec genitus*]." The situation is rather different, however, with the Son. "The Son is of the Father alone: not made, nor created: but begotten [*sed genitus*]." The Holy Ghost's origination is different from the Son's, but this third member of the Trinity is no less dependent upon another—or, more properly, upon others—for its being. "The Holy Ghost is of the Father and of the Son: neither made, nor created, nor begotten: but proceeding."[266]

This is virtually the universal teaching of mainstream Christianity. Ignatius of Antioch (A.D. 107), for example, in his *Epistle to the Trallians*, preached of a Jesus Christ "who truly was born [both to God and of the Virgin]."[267] Tertullian (A.D. 200) taught that Christ is the Son of the Father, "his Word [Logos] who proceeded from him."[268] Origen (A.D. 230) said that he "was born of the Father before all creation."[269] Gregory Thaumaturgus (A.D. 300) held that God the Father is "the perfect origin (begetter) of the perfect (begotten): the Father of the only-begotten Son. . . . And there is one Holy Ghost, having his existence from God." Yet,

---

266 Schaff (1983): 2:66-68.

267 Schaff (1983): 2:11.

268 Schaff (1983): 2:18.

269 Schaff (1983): 2:23.

together, Father, Son, and Holy Ghost constitute "a perfect Trinity, not divided nor differing in glory and eternity and sovereignty."[270] Lucian of Antioch (A.D. 300) said that Christians believe in Jesus Christ as "the only-begotten God . . . who was begotten of the Father before all ages, God of God, Whole of Whole, One of One, Perfect of Perfect, King of King, Lord of Lord, . . . the first-born of all creation."[271] Arius of Alexandria (A.D. 328) maintained that the Son was begotten of the Father before all ages.[272] Eusebius of Caesarea (A.D. 325), as reported in the *Ecclesiastical History* of Socrates, affirmed Christian belief in Jesus Christ, "God of God, Light of Light, Life of Life, the only-begotten Son, the first-born of every creature, begotten of God the Father before all ages."[273] Cyril of Jerusalem (A.D. 350), in his *Catechetical Lectures*, said that Christians believe in Jesus Christ, "the only-begotten Son of God, begotten of the Father before all ages, very God."[274] Epiphanius (A.D. 374), in the *Ancoratus*, declared Christian belief in Jesus Christ, "the only-begotten Son of God, begotten of the Father before all worlds, that is, of the substance of the Father, Light of Light, very God of very God, begotten, not made, being of one substance with the Father."[275] Epiphanius also affirmed Christian belief in the Holy Ghost, "who proceedeth from the Father," yet who "with the Father and the Son together is worshiped and glorified."[276] In a somewhat different formula, he declared

---

270 Schaff (1983): 2:24-25. (Gregory specifies that the origin of Son and Holy Ghost did not take place in time, but is timeless.)

271 Schaff (1983): 2:26. Lucian declares, of course, that the begetting of the Son was preceded by no time. He also denounces any who will say that the Son "is a creature as one of the creatures, or generated as one of the things generated, or made as one of the things made" (Schaff [1983]: 2:27-28).

272 Schaff (1983): 2:28.

273 Schaff (1983): 2:30.

274 Schaff (1983): 2:31.

275 Schaff (1983): 2:33.

276 Schaff (1983): 2:34.

Christian faith in Jesus Christ as the Son of God, "the only-begotten Son of God the Father, that is, of the substance of the Father, God of God, Light of Light, very God of very God, begot-ten, not made, being of one substance with the Father."[277] The Holy Spirit is declared to be "uncreated, proceeding from the Father."[278]

References could be multiplied yet further. In the Nicene Creed (A.D. 325)[279] and in the Nicæno-Constantinopolitan Creeds (A.D. 381),[280] as in most of the other materials we have cited in this connection, words related to *genētos* and *genitus* are used to describe the Son. And even when etymologically distinct terms are used, the meaning is much the same. The Son is both "generated" and fully divine. The Symbol of Chalcedon, dating to 22 October, A.D. 451, teaches that the Son is "perfect in Godhead," while at the same time affirming him to have been "begotten before all ages of the Father according to the Godhead."[281] The Apostles' Creed, which originated in the sixth century or later, speaks of the Father and then expresses belief "in Jesus Christ his only (begotten) Son our Lord."[282]

The argument that humans cannot be deified because, unlike God the Father, they are not "unoriginated" would, if accepted, deny the deity of the Son, Jesus Christ. If his deity is accepted, despite his having been "generated" or "originated," then the doctrine of human deification cannot plausibly be rejected on that score.

---

277 Schaff (1983): 2:35-36.

278 Schaff (1983): 2:34, 38. In both formulae, the origination of Son and Holy Spirit is said to be timeless, and it is denied that either was created *ex nihilo*.

279 Schaff (1983): 2:60.

280 Schaff (1983): 2:57-58.

281 Schaff (1983): 2:62.

282 Schaff (1983): 2:45. Compare the various versions of the old Roman and African form of the Apostles' Creed, dating to before A.D. 341 (Schaff [1983]: 2:47).

Some critics of Latter-day Saint doctrine make much of the allegedly unbridgeable chasm, the abyss, that separates humanity from deity. And it is true that, as the years went by, that gulf widened in the teachings of the Church Fathers. But it is not at all clear that the gulf was always there, or that it is present in biblical doctrine. And even to the extent that a gulf was seen to exist, the Incarnation of Christ was viewed, to a great degree, as bridging it. (G. L. Prestige says of the ancient theologians of Antioch that "they shrank in horror from the idea that [the incarnate Son] was not in all respects as truly kin to us as He was kin to God.")[283]

Alan Richardson notes of the theologians who produced the famous Definition of Faith of the Council of Chalcedon in A.D. 451 that "they were inclined to set too great a gulf between God and man. They tended to conceive of God and man as two substances differing from each other in kind and having no properties in common. Of course we can now see that this tendency of their thought was principally due to the accommodation of their thinking to the current philosophy of their day." Richardson credits the Chalcedonian Fathers for rejecting much of "the old Greek or pagan idea of a transcendent, perfect and far-away Deity, which underlay such heresies as Docetism and Arianism." But he suggests that they did not, perhaps, go far enough. "If a real incarnation has taken place at all, this means that God and man cannot be absolutely dissimilar in essence, since they have been brought together in the one Person of Jesus Christ. Wholly dissimilar substances can never be brought together in such a way that a real, organic union is effected. . . . If God was incarnate in Jesus Christ, there must be that in man which is fundamentally capable of being united with Deity." Richardson affirms, for his part, that "God and man are fundamentally akin, as is surely implied by the belief that man was made in the image of God." And he concludes from this that "it is possible for one person to be both divine and human because God incarnate is human nature perfected."[284] G. L. Prestige, discuss-

---

283 Prestige (1940): 133.

284 Richardson (1990): 85-87; cf. 88.

ing one important fourth-century Christian thinker, remarks that "What Apollinaris says about the Heavenly Man is quite normal and orthodox. God and manhood had been united. Therefore inasmuch as God had become incarnate the two elements together are properly called man; and inasmuch as the manhood had been deified the two elements together are also properly called God (*frag.* 147 puts this point with the utmost clarity)."[285]

Now, Anglican divines like Alan Richardson and G. L. Prestige would presumably have been shocked by the Mormon doctrine of human deification. We do not mean to suggest that they were crypto-Mormons. Nevertheless, in teaching—contrary to many of their opponents—that human beings are of the same race as God, Latter-day Saints merely teach what the Bible says. "Ye are gods," says the Psalmist (82:6), "and all of you are children of the most High." In the New Testament, Jesus expressly quotes this passage with approval, and declares of it that "the scripture cannot be broken" (John 10:34-35). In ancient Judaism, there was a continuum of divine beings, which included not only God but also the angels and archangels. "Yahweh belongs to this class of beings," says Peter Hayman, "but is distinguished from them by his kingship over the heavenly host. However, he is not different from them in kind."[286] The apostle Paul tells his Athenian audience that they and he are the "offspring" of God (Acts 17:28-29). That, at least, is how the King James translation of the Bible renders the Greek *genos*—which, of course, is related to the Latin/English word *genus*. (It means "race" or "descent.") What Paul is saying, clearly, is that human beings are of the same race or genus as God—precisely the teaching for which their critics often condemn the Latter-day Saints. This is also the doctrine that undergirds Hebrews 2:11, where that epistle says of Christ, the divine Son, and of those whom he saves that "both he that sanctifieth and they who are sanctified are all of one [*ex henos*]: for which cause he is not ashamed to call them brethren." The doctrine of human deifica-

---

285 Prestige (1940): 108.

286 Hayman (1991): 5.

tion follows logically from the fact that human beings and God are of the same *genos*.

It is quite true that, as certain critics of the Mormon doctrine of deification have alleged, no ancient Christian text seems to teach that God the Father was once a man, or that he advanced from that condition to his current status. But we probably should not expect to find such a doctrine widely taught among early Christians, much less among later apostates. Recalling the revelation to him of the famous principle "As man is, God once was; as God is, man may become," sometime around the year 1840, Lorenzo Snow testified that "I felt that I had learnt something that I ought not to communicate to others."[287] And, indeed, Joseph Smith himself only disclosed the doctrine to his people at the very end of his ministry—less than three months before his martyrdom in 1844, to be exact. And he seems to have regarded himself as revealing a wonderful mystery: "God himself was once as we are now," the Prophet taught, "and is an exalted man, and sits enthroned in yonder heavens! That is the great secret. . . . We have imagined and supposed that God was God from all eternity. I will refute that idea, and take away the veil, so that you may see."[288]

The Lord's words to Moses may help us to understand why this would have remained a secret for thousands of years. "Worlds without number have I created. . . . But only an account of this earth, and the inhabitants thereof, give I unto you" (Moses 1:33, 35). And, relative to this earth, God was already in existence, in his exalted state, when things began. Even on a Latter-day Saint understanding, he was, for all practical purposes, *agenētos* or "ungenerated." Analogously, when we consider the father of an ordinary earthly family, we do not consider him in his capacity as effect, but as cause, not as begotten, but as begetter. He may be—certainly he is—the son of another father, but that is not relevant to our consideration of the nuclear family as such.

---

287 Williams (1984): 1.

288 *TPJS*, 345.

Besides, it is not the *agenētos* Father to whom we are to look as our model for deification—not, at least, as the doctrine of *theōsis* was taught among the early Christians. Rather, it is the Son who is, in this as in so many other respects, our forerunner and ideal. "Let this mind be in you," wrote Paul to the saints at Philippi (2:5-6), "which was also in Christ Jesus: Who, being in the form of God, thought it not robbery to be equal with God." In that sense, it is irrelevant whether or not early Christians had a view of the Father as having come to be. For the full deity of the begotten Son was quite enough to sustain a doctrine of human deification.

Related to the issue of *theōsis* is the charge that Mormons are not Christian because their God is "mutable," while the God of Christianity is "immutable."[289] The God worshiped by the Latter-day Saints seems to be in process, while many mainstream Christian theologians would insist that God is beyond change. But isn't this rather tenuous ground upon which to declare people non-Christian? Recent academic articles with titles like "The Pagan Dogma of the Absolute Unchangeableness of God" would suggest that it is.[290] After all, the venerable notion of the "Unmoved Mover" comes not from the Bible but from Aristotle, however deeply it may have rooted itself in scholastic theology. And it is not at all clear that a theory of unchanging divinity can be reconciled with the God disclosed in biblical revelation. "Of all the current debates about the divine attributes," writes the evangelical philosopher of religion Ronald Nash, "the disagreement over the property of immutability is the most heated."[291]

The Anglican church historian Alan Richardson labels the notion that the Supreme Being is "utterly impassible and transcendent" a "pagan idea of God," and links it with the rise of the Arian heresy in fourth-century Alexandria. "The Arians, holding the pagan view of God as unknowable, impassible, unchangeable and unreachable, could

---

289 *The Utah Evangel* 31 (February 1984): 3; cf. A. A. Hoekema, "Mormonism," in Douglas (1978): 678; J. L. Smith; "Is Mormonism Christian?"

290 See R. B. Edwards (1978): 305-13. "It is not self-evident," wrote Lovejoy (1964): 12, "that remaining forever unchanged should be regarded as an excellence."

291 Nash (1983): 99.

not conceive of the Incarnation of such a being. God could have no direct relationship with the world. Moreover, there could only be one Supreme Being of such a kind, and therefore Christ must be a subordinate, created Deity, a mediator between the unknowable Godhead and the world. The Arian Christ was thus neither properly God nor properly man, but a mean between the two; he was not an Incarnation of God but a creature of God's. Certain consequences follow from the Arian conception of God. [Among these consequences is the fact that] no incarnation of God is possible, if God be the God of Greek philosophy, since no man can be the vehicle of that which transcends all human experience."[292]

A further corollary claimed for the doctrine of human deification by anti-Mormons is that the Latter-day Saints do not view Jesus as uniquely divine.[293] Such an assertion is fundamentally misleading. The phrase, "only begotten Son," for example, occurs with its variants at least ten times in the Book of Mormon, fourteen times in the Doctrine and Covenants, and nineteen times in the tiny Pearl of Great Price. Surely this by itself should suffice to demonstrate the uniqueness of Jesus in Latter-day Saint scripture and theology. However, Mormons will confess to taking seriously such passages as Psalm 82:6, John 10:33-36, and Philippians 2:5-6. Were the authors of these passages (including Jesus himself) truly Christians? It does not seem that a hope for human deification can disqualify believers in Jesus from being Christians. After all, the Origenist monks at Jerusalem divided over this very question, "whether all men would finally become like Christ or whether Christ was really a different creature."[294] And both Origenists and Origen himself are always described as Christian.

---

292   Richardson (1990): 50-51.

293   Fraser (1977): 58-59, 62, 94; van Baalen (1983): 159.

294   Manschreck (1985): 52. So widely held was the Origenist position in (particularly Eastern) Christendom that it took hold as a minority *Islamic* viewpoint, following the Arab conquest of the old Christian lands. Ibn al-Rawandī makes the same charge against Abū Hudhayl that Jerome had earlier made against Origen, claiming that Abū Hudhayl taught that the final state of the believer would be the same as that of his Lord (the Arabic, in transliteration: *fī hālatin wāhidatin*); cf. Seale (1964): 71-72.

Indeed, if the Latter-day Saints were inclined to do so, they could point out that they alone, among contemporary followers of Jesus, seem to possess the ancient Christian doctrine of *theōsis*. And they might be entitled to wonder if those who lack it can truly be considered Christian. However, this would be to engage in the same illegitimate semantic game as do the anti-Mormons.

Claim 5. "It is an established doctrine of the LDS Church that the Holy Ghost is a spirit in the form of a man, who has size and dimensions, who does not fill the immensity of space, and cannot be everywhere present in person at the same time, and is different from the Holy Spirit. . . . But the Bible teaches, and Christians through the ages have affirmed, that the Holy Ghost and the Holy Spirit are one and the same, and, being part of the nature of the one true God, does [*sic*] indeed fill the immensity of space and is [*sic*] indeed everywhere present."[295]

Response. Even if we accept this statement, which forms a part of Ed Decker's petition against the LDS church, as an adequate summary of Mormon doctrine on the subject—among the false impressions given is that, in Mormonism, the Holy Ghost is not divine, and that the influence of the Spirit is not everywhere present—one is immediately struck by the problematic character of its assertions about "Christianity." According to an eminent Jesuit theologian, the late Karl Rahner, "The teaching on the Holy Spirit developed very slowly in the faith of the Church. . . . Pneumatology always lagged behind Christology."[296] We have already noted above that many of the earliest Christian writers could actually be described as "binitarians," as believers in a Godhead of only two members, the Father and the Son, rather than of three. This is not surprising, since, as E. F. Scott notes, "in the New Testament there is no direct suggestion of a doctrine of the Trinity. The Spirit is conceived as an impersonal power by which God

---

295 See Mr. Decker's "Petition." We have attempted to bring the petition's punctuation into line with accepted canons of English grammar; cf. also J. L. Smith's pamphlet "Is Mormonism Christian?"

296 Rahner (1968-70): 3:53.

effects His will through Christ."[297] Even if Scott's reading of the New Testament is not wholly accurate, it at least shows a way in which the documents could be read, and suggests why early Christian views of the third person of the Godhead were slow to develop. At least as late as the latter part of the third century, formal doctrine on the Holy Spirit—including its relationship to God and Christ—was basically unarticulated.[298]

"In general," writes Karl Rahner, "Scripture speaks more of the Spirit's function in our salvation than of his nature."[299] This is, of course, just what one would expect from an as yet largely un-Hellenized religious movement such as primitive Christianity—or from Mormonism, for that matter. In earliest Christianity before its Hellenizing, and in Semitic Judaism and Islam even to the present day, heavy emphasis is placed rather on law and on history than on theology, on practice rather than on theory. It was only later that, as Edwin Hatch pointed out, the metaphysical and speculative Nicene Creed replaced the ethically and behaviorally oriented Sermon on the Mount as the central Christian text.[300] And the supplanting of an ethical emphasis by a speculative one was, on the whole, the source of great problems in Christendom, in the matter of the nature of the Holy Spirit as elsewhere. "The precise relationship of the Spirit to the Father and the Son is nowhere stated in Scripture, and it has caused discussion and even division in the church."[301]

But it is vitally important to recall that this development was late, and that it is a very questionable procedure to expel the Latter-day Saints from Christendom on the basis of questions that did not even arise until centuries after the death of Christ and the apostles.

---

297 In Ferm (1945): 344; cf. also G. W. H. Lampe, "Holy Spirit," in Buttrick (1962): 2:626-39.

298 Brox (1983): 171.

299 Rahner (1968-70): 3:53.

300 Hatch (1970): 1.

301 L. Morris, "Holy Spirit," in Douglas (1978): 478.

Only after about A.D. 360 did the doctrine of the Spirit become a matter of acute controversy. A group of theologians known as Macedonians or Pneumatomachi ("Spirit Fighters"), while maintaining the full divinity of the Son, denied that of the Spirit. That they did so with at least some biblical plausibility is demonstrated by the comment of one standard reference work, which says that they "were characterized by an overliteral interpretation of the New Testament."[302] Finally, in 381 at the Council of Constantinople, their position was repudiated. Shortly thereafter, they fell victim to massive imperial persecution, and the standard trinitarian view of the Holy Spirit received general acceptance.[303]

Even within that standard view, however, there are crucial disagreements. The main reason for the schism between Eastern and Western Christendom, for example, was a dispute over the relationship of the Spirit to the Father and the Son—evidently caused by a copyist's mistake. Which view of the "Filioque" clause is the "Christian" one? What is the "Christian" stance on "the Double Procession of the Holy Spirit?"[304] Of course there is no single "Christian" position on the metaphysics of the Spirit. There is no single "Christian" position on any metaphysical issue. The earliest Christians knew nothing of metaphysics. Only with the progressive Hellenization of the church did such issues come to be seen as vital. But even in today's Hellenized Christendom, nobody thinks to deny the Christianity of the Pneumatomachi nor that of their leader, Eustathius of Sebaste.[305]

---

302 J. P. Kenny, "Holy Ghost," in Davis, Williams, Thomas, and Crehan (1971): 3:30: "They certainly failed to produce any theologian or metaphysician of distinction." Hardly grounds, it would seem, to bounce anybody out of Christendom. St. Peter was no metaphysician, either.

303 See Cross and Livingstone (1983): 660-61.

304 See, on these issues, Cross and Livingstone (1983): 423-24, 512-13; Elwell (1983): 524; Rahner (1968-70): 3:56-58.

305 Eustathius is plainly implied to be Christian by Williams, "Eustathius," in Douglas (1978): 357, and Davis, "Pneumatomachi," in Douglas (1978): 790; Cross and Livingstone (1983): 483; Kraft (1966): 214; Moyer (1982): 136; Brauer (1971): 313. The

Thus, although the Pneumatomachi denied the deity of the Holy Ghost they are recognized as Christian. Yet Mormons, who affirm the deity of the Holy Ghost, are said to be non-Christian simply because they vary somewhat from standard trinitarianism in their pneumatology. Latter-day Saints are held to a theological standard never stipulated by any reputable scholar as a requirement for Christian legitimacy, a standard that was wholly unknown to the first four centuries of Christianity, and which has, frankly, no demonstrable relevance to the term "Christian."

Claim 6. Christianity teaches creation *ex nihilo*. Mormonism does not. Therefore, Mormonism is not Christian.[306] "As in all nature (witchcraft) religions," say Ed Decker and Dave Hunt, "so in Mormonism there is neither creator nor creation."[307]

Response. "Yet medieval Jewish thinkers . . . held that the account of creation in Genesis could be interpreted to mean that God created from pre-existing formless matter, and ancient Jewish texts state that he did so."[308] This doctrine of the ancient and medieval Hebrews is precisely the same doctrine as that taught by Mormon texts such as Abraham 3:24-4:1. It is highly doubtful that the doctrine of *ex nihilo* creation is to be found in Genesis or anywhere else in the Old Testament.[309] There is good reason to believe that the doctrine was "far from being commonly accepted" by the classical rabbis.[310] "We have to wait until the second half

---

Macedonians or Pneumatomachi are implied to be Christians at Cross and Livingstone (1983): 1104-5; Brauer (1971): 518. Under the relevant articles, the *Encyclopaedia Britannica* "Micropaedia," 1986 ed., identifies the Macedonians as "a 4th century Christian heresy," and the Pneumatomachi as "Christian heretics."

306 Decker and Hunt (1984): 258. But see also Scharffs (1986): 370.

307 Decker and Hunt (1984): 259 (vs. Scharffs [1986]: 372). So now Mormonism is a "nature (witchcraft) religion." And all along we thought it was Hindu! Or Buddhist? (Of course, it doesn't matter, since they're all alike!)

308 Goldstein (1984): 127. For further references on the subject, see Peterson (1990): 1:584-610.

309 B. W. Anderson, "Creation," in Buttrick (1962): 1:728.

310 Winston (1986): 91.

of the second century to find unambiguous Christian statements of creation *ex nihilo.*[311] The fact is that among rabbinic Jews of the ancient and medieval periods, and among Christian Fathers of the second century, there were those who affirmed a creation from preexistent matter.[312] It is a very strange definition of Christianity which would redefine the Church Fathers of the second century as pagan adherents of a "nature" religion and accuse them of "witchcraft." Should Mormons be driven from Christianity over a doctrine so ambiguously attested in the earliest church? Clearly, no. (Incidentally, some militant anti-Catholics argue that Roman Catholicism is witchcraft.)[313]

Claim 7. The Mormon doctrine of the premortal existence of souls is not Christian, reports G. H. Fraser.[314]

Response. This charge is hardly plausible, however, since even Fraser himself mentions that "Origen and others" taught it.[315] Origen of Alexandria is always described as a Christian. He is always ranked as a "Christian scholar, teacher, and thinker," and indeed as "one of the greatest of all time."[316] Nevertheless, sounding the newly fashionable theme of Mormon Hinduism—a

---

311 Goldstein (1984): 132. Goldstein (1984): 133, thinks that he has found an "unequivocal" Jewish insistence on *ex nihilo* creation in Rabban Gamaliel II, "at the latest early in the second century C.E." But see the reply by Winston (1986): 88-91. See also Hayman (1991): 2-4; F. Young (1991): 139-51. On pages 3-4 of his important article, Hayman asks the question, "Is a doctrine of monotheism conceivable without a doctrine of *creatio ex nihilo?*" He thinks not, and this is one of the reasons for his denial that early Judaism was truly monotheistic.

312 Goldstein (1984): 135.

313 See the description of Rebecca Brown's *Prepare for War*, as given in the Chick Publications February 1990 Retail Catalog.

314 Fraser (1977): 85.

315 Fraser (1977): 79.

316 So Ferm (1945): 551; cf. Treadgold (1979): 9-50; Manschreck (1985): 49; Brox (1983): 157; Bruce (1979): 259; Johnson (1983): 58-59; Kraft (1966): 393-401. It is to be doubted that any contrary opinions will be found among reputable scholars. This, significantly, despite the fact that Origen was condemned by the Fifth Ecumenical Council, in Constantinople in 553.

marvelously effective method of guilt by theological association—
Fraser terms this unusual Mormon teaching "reincarnation." Gerald
B. Stanton pulls essentially the same trick, falsely equating the
Mormon doctrine of the premortal existence of spirits with Hindu
reincarnation, and then condemning the doctrine for implying
something about God's judgment that it does not imply and that
Latter-day Saints deny—only because Hindu *karma*, associated with
the doctrine of reincarnation but totally foreign to Mormon belief,
would imply such an idea.[317]

Such antics raise an important question, one that may already
have been in readers' minds long before now. We have seen that
the arguments advanced by anti-Mormons are often unreliable, but
can their audience even rely on their "facts"? Sadly, the answer is
often "No." G. H. Fraser's book is, for instance, not only rather
heavy-handed, but often wildly inaccurate. In this regard, as in
others, anti-Catholicism and anti-Mormonism are intimately
related.[318] Catholic writer Karl Keating speaks of "the way fundamentalist opponents of the Church bend facts to the snapping point.
Little printed by professional anti-Catholics—those who make their
living by attacking 'Romanism'—can be taken at face value. The
reader cannot assume blithely all is on the up and up."[319]

So it is in this case. Mormonism teaches nothing remotely like
the doctrine of Hinduism. Indeed, Joseph Smith denounced the
theory of reincarnation as being "of the devil."[320] Fraser may

---

317 G. B. Stanton, "Pre-Existence of Souls," in Harrison, Bromiley, and Henry
(1960): 418.

318 The virulently anti-Catholic Chick Publications February 1990 Retail Catalog
carries not only its own pamphlets against the Latter-day Saints, but also John L.
Smith's *Witnessing Effectively to Mormons* (1975) and *Hope or Despair?* (1976) as
well as Floyd C. McElveen's *The Mormon Illusion*. Additionally, it advertises books
explaining how Jesuit priests assassinated Abraham Lincoln.

319 Keating (1988): 73.

320 *TPJS*, 105.

even be aware of this, for, perhaps realizing that even the most superficial acquaintance with real Hinduism would reveal his analogy between it and Mormonism to be ludicrously inappropriate, he redefines "reincarnation" in such a way that his accusation loses all of its force.[321]

Claim 8. "Mormonism is a 'cult' and not a Christian church or denomination, because it is built entirely on Joseph Smith."[322] "I chose Jesus over Joseph," says one Ex-Mormon for Jesus.[323]

Response. Surely this accusation is somewhat odd. Even if we grant for purposes of discussion that Mormonism is built upon the account of the appearance of God and Christ given by Joseph Smith, how does that make it inferior to traditional Christianity, which claims to be built upon the accounts of God and Christ given by Matthew, Mark, Luke, John, Simon bar Jonah, and Saul of Tarsus?[324] Both Mormon Christianity and traditional Christianity appeal to the authority of certain men who are believed to have possessed supernatural insight. The difference is that Latter-day Saints are open to insights from recent and even still living prophets, while their critics accept only prophets who have long been dead. In fact, ordinary Latter-day Saints believe that even they have direct access to God and the Spirit, and that they are not entirely dependent merely upon the records of ancient people who claimed such access. Thus, while Mormonism encourages personal revelation and the seeking of testimony through prayer, it appears

---

321 Fraser (1977): 76.

322 Morey (1983): 13; cf. Geer, "Who Is This Man . . .?"; *The Utah Evangel* 31 (March 1984): 8; (May 1984): 3; (December 1984): 12; *The Evangel* 38 (September 1991): 2; *The Evangel* 38 (October 1991): 3.

323 Decker and Hunt (1984): 245. Contrast Scharffs (1986): 350. We might note here that Dr. Scharffs's book is, on the whole, devastating to Decker and Hunt. Not only are they inaccurate, but their inaccuracies appear to have been perpetrated in bad faith.

324 "Be ye followers of me," writes Paul, "even as I also am of Christ" (1 Corinthians 11:1).

that its fundamentalist opponents restrict the pursuit of religious truth to biblical exegesis.[325]

But this appearance may be deceiving. It can be argued that fundamentalists, too, take their guidance from living human sources as well as from dead prophets. Protestant theologian Lloyd Averill makes this point well: "Given fundamentalism's authoritarian character, it succumbs regularly and readily to the cult of personality. For Protestant fundamentalists, the Bible is the professed source of authority for faith and life. The difficulty is that the Bible does not interpret itself authoritatively. Given the symbolic and poetic nature of much that it contains and its consequent opaqueness for even the most devout general reader, an authoritative Bible requires an authoritative interpreter, presumably gifted and authorized by the Holy Spirit, who can read its signs and penetrate its mysteries for the saving edification of ordinary believers not gifted with that kind of putative insight. So the leader is the essence of the move-ment—shapes its persona, gives it legitimation, infuses it with his own rhetorical power. This is the significance of the following that gathers around such television personalities as Oral Roberts, Jimmy Swaggart, Jerry Falwell, Kenneth Copeland, Pat Robertson. For such audiences, coherence comes not from a common creedal confession, as in the Reformed churches, nor from a prayer book, as in the Anglican Communion, nor from a history of witness, as among Friends—not even from the Bible itself, given the unin-terpreted confusion of its voices. What provides coherence is the spirit-filled interpreter, who can tell the faithful authoritatively just how things are in the mind of God."[326]

The difference between the Mormons and their fundamentalist critics on this point is not merely that the Latter-day Saints look to modern men for help in understanding the Bible and their religion, while conservative Protestants listen to the pure teachings of the

---

325 See, for example, Decker and Hunt (1984): 115, 170 (vs. Scharffs [1986]: 177-228); Tope, "Why Should I Pray"; Tope, "But I Have a Testimony." Decker (1979): 25, mocks the idea of praying for a testimony.

326 Averill (1989): 112-13.

Bible itself. The difference is not merely that the Mormons admit their reliance upon authoritative living teachers, while their "Bible-believing" critics do not realize—or pretend not to realize—that they are doing exactly the same thing. The real difference is that Latter-day Saints look to prophets who claim modern-day divine revelation of the same nature and authority as that received by the biblical writers themselves, while fundamentalist anti-Mormons rely upon men who do not even *pretend* to revelation.

But Latter-day Saints vigorously reject the accusation that their religion is "based entirely on Joseph Smith." They fully accept the writings of ancient prophets and apostles in both the Old and New Worlds. They see rich biblical evidence for their beliefs, and see themselves as members of the ancient Church restored, as citizens of modern-day Israel. Where their adversaries accept dead prophets but reject living ones, Mormons are free to learn from both.

The April 1991 *Evangel*, published by Oklahoma-based Utah Missions Incorporated, offers an amusing argument on this issue. "Who was Joseph Smith?" the paper asks rhetorically. "He was to Mormonism what Christ is to Christianity! If it had not been for Christ there would have been no Christianity, if it had not been for Joseph Smith there would have been no Mormonism. . . . If Joseph Smith is to Mormonism as Christ is to Christianity—and Joseph Smith and Christ are not one and the same—then Mormonism must not be Christian!"[327] But Joseph Smith's relationship to Mormonism is not identical to the relationship between Christ and Christianity, except in the bare sense that Jesus founded the early Church and Joseph Smith was the earthly founder of the latter-day Church. The differences between their roles are numerous and essential, as the editors of *The Evangel* know full well. Joseph Smith does not atone for Mormon sins. He is not a redeemer; he is not divine. A paraphrase of *The Evangel*'s argument will be sufficient to show its weakness. "Who was Martin Luther? He was to Lutheranism what Christ is to Christianity! If it had not been for Christ there would have been no Christianity, if it had not been for Martin Luther there

---

would have been no Lutheranism. . . . If Martin Luther is to Lutheranism as Christ is to Christianity—and Martin Luther and Christ are not one and the same—then Lutheranism must not be Christian!" Given such arguments, could Calvinism survive as "Christian"? Would the Mennonites or the Wesleyan Methodists or the Swiss Evangelical Reformed Church (founded by Zwingli) or the Campbellites pass such a test? Had it not been for Henry VIII, would there be a Church of England?

Claim 9. Mormonism is a non-Christian cult because it believes that salvation is in some sense mediated through a church.[328] Real Christians know that salvation is not achieved through any denominational affiliation.[329] Real Christians know that it is the "invisible church," the fellowship of the truly born-again, which is crucial: "One who has not been the object of the regenerating power of the Holy Spirit [is] therefore . . . not a Christian."[330] Real Christians are not obsessed with priesthood and ordinances and hierarchy and ecclesiastical structure; they are opposed to sacerdotalism.[331]

---

328 Fraser (1977): 87, 96, 174; "The Mormon Church and the African"; Decker, "To Moroni with Love," 45-46, 48; "Mormonism: Christian or Cult?"; *The Utah Evangel* 31 (March 1984): 8; (May 1984): 3; (December 1984): 12; 33 (July/August 1986): 5; Geer, "Who Is This Man . . .?"; Decker and Hunt (1984): 246-47 (vs. Scharffs [1986]: 36, 354-55).

329 So O. J. Smith, "Which Church Saves?"; Bishop Ryle, "The Only True Church"; W. Thompson, "What We Should Know about Roman Catholicism"; Boa (1984): 67; P. B. Smith (1970): 24, 54-55; J. O. Sanders (1962): 16, 113; Decker (1979): 31; "Mormonism: Christian or Cult?" Berry (1979): 91, contra Roman Catholicism, writes: "The word 'church' in the New Testament refers to all who have personally trusted Jesus Christ as Saviour, regardless of their religious affiliations on earth." Yet anti-Mormons consistently deny the possibility that one might be "saved" within the Mormon Church. Similarly, after much prodding and with great reluctance, a woman volunteer at the Ex-Mormons for Jesus visitor's center, in Santa Fe Springs, California, admitted to one of the authors in the summer of 1984 that it was "impossible" for someone to become a Christian "and remain a Catholic" (and W. Thompson, "What We Should Know about Roman Catholicism," agrees).

330 Boettner (1986): 90.

331 Martin (1985): 199-200; Coe and Coe (1985): 180-82; Ridenour (1979): 27-51.

Response. But who is being most true to the biblical evidence? "The term *ekklēsia*," notes J. P. Meier, "certainly means for Matthew the church as a visible structure and society, having authoritative officials and authoritative functions."[332] Was the evangelist Matthew a Christian? It would be an odd definition of the term that excluded him. And the New Testament nowhere defines "Christians" as only those who have been "born again." It knows nothing of such a vintage Protestant equation since, in fact, as we have already demonstrated above, it does not define the term "Christian" at all.[333]

By the anti-ecclesiastical standards of our "experts," Ignatius of Antioch—perhaps the most influential of the "Apostolic Fathers"[334]— was most definitely not a Christian. For him, alas, Church, sacraments, and bishop were vital to Christianity.[335] "Let us then," he writes to the Ephesians, "be careful not to oppose the bishop, that we may be subject to God."[336] "We must regard the bishop as the Lord himself."[337] To the Magnesians, he writes that the bishop presides "in the place of God."[338] "Let all respect the

---

332 J. P. Meier, "Part One: Antioch," in Brown and Meier (1983): 66.

333 Being "born again" is, of course, a desirable state; Alma 5, one of the most famous chapters in the Book of Mormon, deals extensively with the theme. Mormons tend not, however, to view the subject in quite the same revivalistic way as do very conservative Protestants. Nevertheless, the similarities are considerable—after all, both views have their roots in the Bible—and should not be overlooked.

334 Gonzales (1970) 1:97, has him sharing the honor with Clement of Rome.

335 See Ignatius of Antioch, *Epistle to the Ephesians* 3:2; *Epistle to the Magnesians* 3:1-2, 7:1; *Epistle to the Trallians* 2:1-3; 3:1-3, 7:1-2; *Epistle to the Philadelphians* 2:1; *Epistle to the Smyrnaeans* 8:1; Gonzales (1970): 1:76-77.

336 Ignatius of Antioch, *Epistle to the Ephesians* 5:3. English translation in Lake (1970): 1:179.

337 Ignatius of Antioch, *Epistle to the Ephesians* 6:1. English translation in Lake (1970): 1:179; cf. *Epistle to the Magnesians* 2:1.

338 Ignatius of Antioch, *Epistle to the Magnesians* 6:1. English translation in Lake (1970): 1:203; cf. 13:2.

deacons as Jesus Christ, even as the bishop is also a type of the Father, and the presbyters as the council of God and the college of Apostles. Without these, the name of 'Church' is not given."[339] For the *Shepherd of Hermas*, too—a second-century document that is counted among the writings of the "Apostolic Fathers"—the Church is of essential importance.[340] And similar citations could be given to literally scores of early Christian documents. Many of the most bitter debates in earliest Christendom, in fact, presumed the necessity of affiliation with the proper ecclesiastical body.[341] We are therefore led to ask the obvious question: Were early Christians "non-Christian"? If concern with membership in a visible, institutional church disqualifies the Mormons from being Christian, then it must, for consistency's sake, exclude the early Christian Fathers as well.

However, it is not merely *ancient* Christians who would be purged from Christendom by this particular anti-Mormon rule. Hundreds of millions of contemporary believers in Jesus would meet a similar fate, for, as the ex-Catholic Stella Ciampa points out, churches do not save[342]—by which she, along with many other fundamentalist Protestants, means to say that ordinances and rituals and priesthood and institutions are not necessary for salvation. Let us first of all consider the various branches of Orthodox Christianity, which include Russian, Greek, Armenian, Coptic, and other varieties. Reporting on a dialogue between Lutherans and the Eastern Orthodox churches, W. G. Rusch has noted that, for the latter, a specific hierarchical organization is "essential for the

---

339 Ignatius of Antioch, *Epistle to the Trallians* 3:1. English translation in Lake (1970): 1:215.

340 Gonzales (1970): 1:90.

341 See, for example, Brox (1983): 124-32.

342 Ciampa, "Catholic or Christian?"

church."[343] There are 200 million Eastern Orthodox believers.[344] Surely any definition of Christianity which would make non-Christians of them must be dismissed as unrealistic and bizarre. But what of Roman Catholicism? It represents an even larger proportion of living believers in Jesus, and its views on the question under consideration here are, in some ways, analogous to those of the Latter-day Saints. For instance, "Mormons agree with Catholics that apostolic authority and succession are of crucial importance."[345] Indeed, the historical position of the Roman Church has been that affiliation with the church is essential to pleasing God. One need only think of the famous phrase, *Extra ecclesiam nulla salus*, "Outside the Church there is no salvation."[346] "A study of the New Testament," declared Archbishop John F. Whealon in a pastoral letter, "shows the importance of belonging to the Church

---

343 Rusch (1986): 12. Molland (1959): 358, notes that the Anglicans, too, share a certain sacerdotalism with the Orthodox tradition.

344 Rusch (1986): 11.

345 Hansen (1981): 36.

346 John Adams, writing in his diary for 16 February 1756, complained that "The church of Rome has made it an article of faith that no man can be saved out of their church"; cf. Zacchello (1984): 6-7, 186; P. B. Smith (1970): 22. Official Catholic teaching leaves no doubt about how "church" is to be understood: "The Church is the congregation of all baptized persons, united in the same true faith, the same sacrifice, and the same sacraments, under the authority of the Sovereign Pontiff and the bishops in communion with him." (See *This We Believe* [1962]: 102; cf. Zacchello [1984]: 193; Molland [1959]: 358). We realize that Catholic teachings are not quite as exclusive as they sound at first hearing (cf. *This We Believe* [1962]: 130-31; P. B. Smith [1970]: 29). But neither are Mormon teachings (despite such misunderstandings as that of Holzapfel [1925]: 84; Decker and Hunt [1984]: 9. Contrast Scharffs [1986]: 67). For a good summation of Catholic thinking on the role of the Church, see G. H. Joyce, "Church," in Herbermann (1908): 3:744-61; cf. Holzapfel (1925): 16-34. Horace Greeley remarked on this similarity between Mormon and Roman Catholic ecclesiology already in 1859. And Brigham Young agreed with him (see Greeley [1968]: 9:132). S. E. Robinson (1991): 41, correctly points out that "in the areas of priesthood, ordination, and apostolic succession, the Latter-day Saints are actually more 'orthodox' than Protestants, sharing the older, more traditional view with Roman Catholics."

started by Jesus Christ. . . . It is all-important to be in union with Peter's successor and in the Catholic Church."[347] Father John A. Hardon's *Question and Answer Catholic Catechism* puts the matter clearly: " 'Is the Church necessary for salvation?' 'Yes, the Church is necessary for salvation.' "[348] "All are obliged to belong to the Catholic Church in order to be saved," according to the Baltimore Cathechism.[349] The Syllabus of Pope Pius IX asserts that "the eternal salvation of any out of the true Church of Christ is not even to be hoped for!"[350] The Roman Church is "in its inmost essence nothing but the everliving Christ."[351] "The Pope is Christ in office, Christ in jurisdiction and power," declared the First Vatican Council in 1870. "We bow down before thy voice, O Pius, as before the voice of Christ, the God of truth; in clinging to thee, we cling to Christ."[352] "Priests and bishops are the representatives of God on earth," according to the sixteenth-century Council of Trent. "Justly, therefore, they are called not only angels, but gods."[353]

---

347 Cited in Whealon (1986): 17. Rev. Whealon is the current archbishop of Hartford, CT; cf. the "Oath of Faith for Converts" to Catholicism, cited by Zacchello (1984): 170. Keating (1988): 23, dismisses fundamentalist Protestant anti-institutional feelings (discussed also on p. 89) as "unalloyed Christian individualism."

348 Hardon (1981): 98.

349 *This We Believe* (1962): 129; but cf. 130-31. Spittler (1962): 110-11, 115-16, with eye firmly fixed on Rome, denies the need for organized religion.

350 Cited by Zacchello (1984): 185.

351 Holzapfel (1925): 8-19: "Sie ist in ihrem innersten Wesen nichts anderes als der fortlebende Christus."

352 Cited by Zacchello (1984): 34. The reader may judge for himself whether this, or Zacchello's *sola scriptura* denunciation of it, resembles most closely the testimony of St. Ignatius from early Christianity. Zacchello (1984): 35, further notes that on June 20, 1894, Pope Leo XIII proclaimed: "We hold upon this earth the place of God Almighty."

353 Cited by Boettner (1986): xi.

Such statements as this draw forth thunderous denunciations from our experts,[354] even though they have their parallels in the statements of Ignatius of Antioch (d. A.D. 117), quoted immediately above. Rome "makes blasphemous claims for her priests," and her followers have a "slave-mentality."[355] "The Romish Mass," proclaims H. A. Ironside, is a "mysterious mixture of Judaism and Paganism, and a perversion of apostolic teaching."[356] Rev. Donald F. Maconaghie refers to the "blasphemy" of "the unbiblical, unscientific black magic of the Roman mass."[357] "And so, my dear Roman Catholic friend," admonishes Wes Thompson, "the next time you go to Mass . . . don't you just assume everything is just fine. Because you are attending an idolatrous ceremony and anyone who is a practicing idolator cannot enter the kingdom of heaven." In Thompson's view, it is clear, Catholics are bound for

---

354 E.g., Zacchello (1984): 11-16; W. Thompson, "What We Should Know about Roman Catholicism"; Boettner (1986): 19-74, 261, 270-97, 456-57.

355 Irvine (1921): 141, 147; cf. Green (1984d); J. O. Sanders (1962): 24; Green (1984b); Zacchello (1984): 76, 102. Irvine (1921): 141-42, denounces claims that the Pope stands in for God—claims that sound very much like Ignatius speaking of the bishop, or like D&C 21:5 speaking of the Mormon prophet. Passages like the latter convince its critics that Mormonism is a "non-Christian cult."

356 Ironside (1982): 23. Green (1984a) sees the ritual as idolatrous paganism. In terms very reminiscent of the Ed Decker school of anti-Mormonism, Green (1984b) describes the chief Roman sacrament as "a system which is not only unbiblical, but is actually steeped in mysticism, bordering dangerously on the occult!" The process by which "mysticism" became a term of reproach is not altogether clear to us. Such connotations are nevertheless common among fundamentalist muckrakers, who have, perhaps, not heard of the rich Christian mystical tradition, of St. John of the Cross, of St. Teresa of Avila, of Meister Eckhart, or of Dionysius the Areopagite. For a representative specimen of the genre, see Pat Means's exposé, *The Mystical Maze* (cf. "Dr." Walter Martin's presumed exposé of the Latter-day Saints, *The Maze of Mormonism*; we should, it seems, be grateful to them for guiding us through the labyrinth). A few of our "experts" are more mild: Spittler (1962): 111, refers gently to how, in the Church of Rome, "meaningless liturgical acts were substituted for personal worship." It is presumably better to be ineffectual than idolatrous; concomitantly, to be idolatrous is presumably to be effectual; cf. P. B. Smith (1970): 25-26, 35; J. O. Sanders (1962): 22-25.

357 Newsletter, The Conversion Center (May/June 1990).

hell.[358] "True Christians must never have unity with those who bow to idols, such as Catholics," warns one active Protestant ministry. "Rather, we must win them to Christ. . . . A Catholic, once born again, can never return to the idolatrous sacrifice of the Mass."[359]

Not all critics of Latin Christianity are so forthright. Some conservative Protestants, intimidated by the sheer size of the Church of Rome, allude shyly to "basic differences between Romanism and biblical Christianity."[360] R. P. Spittler is willing to admit that Catholics may perhaps be "nominally Christian."[361] Many others, however, are not at all reserved. Writes J. O. Sanders: "We place Roman Catholicism at the head of the list of heresies, since it is the largest and most influential of them all. . . . No Bible-believing Christian can intelligently be or become a Roman Catholic."[362] "Is the Roman Catholic Church Christian?" asks Wes Thompson. "I say that until it repents and stops practicing these heresies, it should be thought of in the same way as Mormons . . . or any other non-Christian cult. However, the Roman Catholic Church makes those other cults look like pikers—and I am astounded that the real Christian community tolerates it."[363]

---

358 See W. Thompson, "What We Should Know about Roman Catholicism." This is a charge repeatedly brought against Mormon ritual, as well—notably by Ed Decker and followers. But aren't we saved by grace? Nonetheless, for anti-Catholic Donald Spitz, as cited by Keating (1988): 104, Catholics are damned if they remain Catholic.

359 Chick Publications February 1990 Retail Catalog, 28, 31. On p. 8, the catalog advertises a pamphlet on the Roman Catholic mass, referring specifically to the consecrated wafer, entitled "The Death Cookie."

360 Whealon (1986): 16.

361 Spittler (1962): 109; cf. 117.

362 J. O. Sanders (1962): 20.

363 W. Thompson, "What We Should Know about Roman Catholicism." Thompson's inventory of adjectives for Catholicism is rich. It includes "demonic," "idiotic," "disgusting," "sick," "demented," etc. It should not be mistakenly assumed that we are drawing on the lunatic fringe of fundamentalist anti-Catholicism

Claim 10. Mormons practice baptism for the dead. But "the whole idea of a vicarious work for our ancestors is totally foreign to the Christian faith."[364] Clearly, then, Mormons cannot be Christians. But it is not only the Latter-day Saint practice of vicarious baptism that enrages their critics. Mormon temple ritual in general is a point of contention. Secrecy itself, say Ed Decker and Dave Hunt, is un-Christian.[365] "No genuine Christian church has any secret rituals; nor are there any secret rituals in the New Testament. Such things are much more appropriate to the pagan mystery religions of antiquity."[366]

Response. The argument that baptizing for the dead is un-Christian presumes that the problem of 1 Corinthians 15:29 has already been solved, and that it has been solved in a way that contradicts the faith and practice of The Church of Jesus Christ of Latter-day Saints. However, this is far from the case. Try as they might, commentators have been unable to talk their way out of the clear meaning of the text, which is that living Corinthians were

---

in order to discredit anti-Mormons by association. We cite nothing from the likes of Tony Alamo. Every pamphlet and book referred to herein was obtained either at mainstream "Christian" bookstores or from mainstream "Christian" periodicals.

364 *The Utah Evangel* 31 (January 1984): 7; cf. Fraser (1977): 107-12. *The Evangel* and others simply don't like ordinances; cf. Fraser's attack on baptism: Fraser (1977): 97-106. For the quite different attitude of Christianity in late antiquity, see Brox (1983): 112-18.

365 Thus Decker and Hunt (1984): 141-42 (vs. Scharffs [1986]: 200-202). Mr. Decker's "Petition," along with the materials which generated controversy a few years ago over the dedication of the Denver temple, may be taken as representative of yet another point of controversy connected with Mormon temple worship: Alleged Latter-day Saint mockery of traditional Christianity. We choose not to discuss this accusation, refusing to acquiesce in the thrusting of temple ritual into the public domain—a cherished goal of Mr. Decker and his associates. On the other hand, we emphatically deny that the effect of temple worship on any of those we know has ever been to inculcate contempt for Christian clergy. And since no Latter-day Saint known to us interprets the temple ritual as cutting Mormonism off from Christianity *per se*, we find extremely dubious the attempt by non- and anti-Mormons to portray it as doing so.

366 *Saints Alive in Jesus Newsletter* (July 1990): 5.

allowing themselves to be baptized on behalf of those who had died. "None of the attempts to escape the theory of a vicarious baptism in primitive Christianity seems to be wholly successful," observes Harald Riesenfeld.[367] Thus, reluctant though they might be, the majority of scholars has now come around to a position very much like that of the Latter-day Saints. As the eminent Lutheran New Testament scholar Krister Stendahl has recently noted, "the text seems to speak plainly enough about a practice within the Church of vicarious baptism for the dead. This is the view of most contemporary critical exegetes."[368] The anti-Mormon claim that those who baptize for the dead cannot be Christian also ignores the fact that such groups as the Montanists—whom we have already seen to be universally recognized as Christians—practiced a similar rite.[369] It would further seem to question—yet again—the Christianity of Roman Catholics: "The faithful on earth," Rome teaches, "through the communion of saints, can relieve the suffering of the souls in purgatory by prayer, fasting, and other good works, by indulgences, and by having Masses offered for them."[370] It ques-

---

367 H. Riesenfeld, "Hyper," in Kittel and Friedrich (1972): 8:512-13.

368 Stendahl, "Baptism for the Dead: Ancient Sources," in Ludlow (1992): 1:97. Among the commentators, including Catholics as well as both liberal and conservative Protestants, who agree that 1 Corinthians 15:29 most likely refers to a practice among Corinthian Christians of receiving vicarious baptism on behalf of the dead, see Fee (1987): 763-67; R. Kugelman, "The First Letter to the Corinthians," in Brown, Fitzmyer, and Murphy (1968), 2:273; Orr and Walther (1976): 335, 337; Marsh, "1 Corinthians," in Bruce (1986): 1384; Mays (1988): 1187; J. J. O'Rourke, "1 Corinthians," in Fuller, Johnston, and Kearns (1975): 883h-m; W. F. Flemington, "Baptism," in Buttrick (1962), 1:350; Conzelmann (1975): 275-77. Nibley (1987): 100-167.

369 Ferm (1945): 54; Fraser (1977): 110. The Marcionites, also invariably referred to as Christians, observed the practice as well. The practice was condemned in A.D. 393, by the Council of Hippo, which certainly implies that it was still a live issue in the late fourth century of the Christian era.

370 *This We Believe* (1962): 134; cf. 134-35, 144; cf. Boettner's attack, in Boettner (1986): 7, 295-96. Prayers for the dead are a central motif in Dante's *Purgatorio*. Was Dante Christian? Says Jeffrey B. Russell's *Medieval Civilization*: "Thomas Aquinas and Dante were the crowns of their age" (376). "The *Divine*

tions, too, the Christianity of one of the largest and oldest Protestant churches, the Church of England, and its related communions, who also teach prayer for the dead.[371] Can any definition of Christianity which excludes both the Roman Catholic Church and the Church of England possibly be taken seriously?

And what of the claim that secrecy is itself un-Christian?[372] It is significant to note that both of the major categories of the sacred—"sacred word" and "sacred act/ritual"[373]—were, under certain circumstances and for varying periods of time, maintained in secrecy in early Christianity. The eminent New Testament scholars Joachim Jeremias and Morton Smith have demonstrated that such esotericism—secrecy—was present throughout early Christianity and the religious milieu from which it grew.[374] What has been referred to as the "Messianic secret," the constraint placed (at least temporarily) by Jesus on his disciples, and others as well, against revealing his Messiahship is found throughout the Gospel accounts, but particularly in the gospel of Mark.[375] Jeremias and Smith also specifically include the apostle Paul in their judgment about secrecy in early Christianity. Paul describes himself and his

Comedy of Dante Alighieri (1265-1321) was the masterpiece of medieval literature. . . . [I]t is a *summa* of medieval thought. In [it], Christian theology is summarized" (552; cf. 138). But, imply our "experts," do the mediaevalists know what they are talking about? Was the "Age of Faith" in Western Europe really Christian? Perhaps Dante was a Hindu?

371 Boettner (1986): 295.

372 For another Latter-day Saint response to this charge, with useful references, see S. E. Robinson (1991): 96-98, 99-103.

373 Heiler (1961): 176, 266.

374 See Jeremias (1966): 125-37, with his copious notes; M. Smith (1973): 38, 44, 91-92, 94, 197-202; G. Bornkamm, "Mysterion," in Kittel and Friedrich (1967): 4:802-28. For Latter-day Saint perspectives on this question, see Compton (1990): 611-42; Hamblin (1990): 202-21; Nibley (1987a): 10-99 (esp. 14-15, 30-33); Nibley (1988): 84-110; and Welch (1990): 70-72.

375 There is considerable literature on this topic and its implications for the New Testament; cf. Wrede (1971); Boobyer (1959): 225-35; Schweizer (1965): 1-8; Powell (1969): 308-10; Aune (1969): 1-31; Blevins (1981); Tuckett (1983).

coworkers as "stewards of the mystery of God" in 1 Corinthians 4:1. As Smith demonstrates at length, the word "mystery" was regularly used by the early Christians to refer to secret rites or ordinances.[376] He also states that "this [the rite of baptism] was the mystery of the kingdom—the mystery rite by which the kingdom was entered."[377] Secrecy is a feature found not only in the early Christian community but also in ancient Judaism, among the Essenes, and very widely in the ancient world generally.[378] According to the historian of religions Kees Bolle, "Not only is there no religion without secrecy, but there is no human existence without it."[379]

Critics of the early Church were not slow in noticing this penchant for secrecy. And, like today's anti-Mormons, they were quick to exploit it in their attacks. "The cult [!] of Christ," declared a second-century anti-Christian named Celsus, "is a secret society whose members huddle together in corners for fear of being brought to trial and punishment."[380] "Why," demanded Caecilius Natalis in the early third century, "do they endeavor with such pains to conceal and to cloak whatever they worship, since honourable things always rejoice in publicity, while crimes are kept secret? . . . Why do they never speak openly, never congregate freely, unless for the reason that what they adore and conceal is either worthy of punishment, or something to be ashamed of?" "Assuredly this confederacy ought to be rooted out and execrated," Caecilius

---

376 M. Smith (1973): 179-84.

377 M. Smith (1972): 96; cf. M. Smith (1973): 178-81. K. W. Bolle, "Secrecy in Religion," in Bolle (1987): 10-11, notes that "the Greek word *mysterion* was translated into Latin as *sacramentum*. . . . Even when referring to specific church acts, it was more than the sacraments of baptism and holy communion. . . . All these church acts are mysteria, i.e., acts in which God is at work and therefore distinct from ordinary, profane, natural occurrences."

378 Jeremias (1966): 136; M. Smith (1973): 197-99; Wewers (1975).

379 Bolle (1987): 1.

380 Celsus (1987): 53. Much like his latter-day co-workers, Celsus even wrote a handbook of advice for ex-Christians.

declared. "They know one another by secret marks and insignia. . . . Certainly suspicion is applicable to secret and nocturnal rites."[381] The Christians defended themselves against such charges much the way today's Latter-day Saints do: They affirmed the high morality of their faith and the behavior it asked of them, but they did not deny that secrecy was a part of their religious belief. And, furthermore, they did not fall into the trap of revealing the secrets that had been entrusted to their care—even when revealing those secrets might have strengthened their defense. "God orders us in quietness and silence to hide His secret," wrote Lactantius in the fourth century, "and to keep it within our own conscience. . . . For a mystery ought to be most faithfully concealed and covered, especially by us, who bear the name of faith. But they accuse this silence of ours, as though it were the result of an evil conscience; whence also they invent some detestable things respecting those who are holy and blameless."[382]

For such secret doctrines and practices lay at the very heart of the doctrine that the early Christians had received, and that they were trying against great odds to preserve. We have seen already that Ignatius of Antioch held secret doctrines early in the second century. He himself explained one of the reasons for this. "For," he wrote to the Trallian saints, "might not I write unto you of things more full of mystery? But I fear to do so, lest I should inflict injury on you who are but babes [in Christ]. Pardon me in this respect, lest as not being able to receive their weighty import, ye should be strangled by them."[383] At the end of the second century, Clement of Alexandria advised keeping certain teachings from "the multitude" because, while "those of noble nature" find them "admirable" and "inspiring," the masses, unable to understand such

---

381 Cited in Minucius Felix, *Octavius X*, 9. English translation in Roberts and Donaldson (1979): 4:178, 177.

382 Lactantius, *Divine Institutes* VII, 26. English translation in Roberts and Donaldson (1979), 7:221.

383 Ignatius of Antioch, *Epistle to the Trallians*, 5.

doctrine, would regard them as "ludicrous."[384] Early in the third century, the Latin church father Tertullian could write that the apostles "did not reveal all to all men, for . . . they proclaimed some openly and to all the world, whilst they disclosed others [only] in secret and to a few."[385] At the same time, Hippolytus was writing about secrets to be conveyed by the bishop to the faithful alone—secrets that Hippolytus linked with the white stone of John's Revelation.[386] Secret Christian teachings are also a major theme of the *Clementine Recognitions* and the *Clementine Homilies*, which seem likewise to have originated at some point in the third century.[387]

The central doctrines of Christianity were doubtlessly well known in antiquity among Christian and non-Christian alike. Thus Origen, in responding to the ancient Christian-baiter Celsus (who has himself written a manual for ex-Christians), states: "Moreover, since he frequently calls the Christian doctrine a secret system (of belief), we must confute him on this point also, since almost the entire world is better acquainted with what Christians preach than with the favorite opinions of philosophers. For who is ignorant of the statement that Jesus was born of a virgin, and that He was crucified, and that His resurrection is an article of faith among many, and that a general judgment is announced to come, in which the wicked are to be punished according to their deserts, and the righteous to be duly rewarded? And yet the mystery of the resurrection, not being understood, is made a subject of ridicule among unbelievers. In these circumstances, to speak of the Christian doctrine as a *secret* system, is altogether absurd."

---

384 Clement of Alexandria, *Stromata* I, 12. English translation in Roberts and Donaldson (1979): 2:312-13.

385 Tertullian, *On the Prescription against Heretics* 25. English translation in Roberts and Donaldson (1980): 3:254-55.

386 Hippolytus, *Apostolic Tradition* 23:13-14, cited in Hanson (1962): 32. Compare Revelation 2:17; D&C 130:10-11.

387 See, for instance, *Clementine Recognitions* 2:4, 3:1, 3:34; *Clementine Homilies* 19:20.

But, to forfend the charge that he is disingenuously claiming that the Christians had no doctrines not made generally known, Origen continues: "But that there should be certain doctrines, not made known to the multitude, which are (revealed) after the exoteric ones have been taught, is not a peculiarity of Christianity alone, but also of philosophic systems, in which certain truths are exoteric and others esoteric. Some of the hearers of Pythagoras were content with his *ipse dixit*; while others were taught in secret those doctrines which were not deemed fit to be communicated to profane and insufficiently prepared ears. Moreover, all the mysteries that are celebrated everywhere throughout Greece and barbarous countries, although held in secret, have no discredit thrown upon them, so that it is in vain that he endeavors to calumniate the secret doctrines of Christianity, seeing he does not correctly understand its nature."[388]

This latter quotation is also interesting since its argument is essentially *tu quoque*: we may do it, but so do you. It cites, apparently without embarrassment, the Greco-Roman mysteries whose secrecy provides parallels to the secrecy with which some Christian doctrines were maintained.

As we have noted above, rites were also maintained in secrecy in the early Church. The ancient Christian *arcani disciplina* (secret discipline) was the "practice of . . . keeping certain religious rites secret from non-Christians and catechumens."[389] The very word from which "mass" may be derived, *missa* (in the phrase *missa*

---

388 Origen, *Contra Celsum* I, 7. English translation in Roberts and Donaldson (1979): 4:399.

389 H. Mulder, "Arcani Disciplina," in Palmer (1964): 1:390. In the numerous studies on the subject—P. Batiffol, "Arcane," in Vacant and Mangenot (1894): 1:1738-54; Bonwetsch (1873): 203-99; Casel (1927): 329-40; Gravel (1902); Hanson (1962), 22-35; Jacob (1990; this is the most recent study on the topic and contains a rich bibliography); Mensching (1926): 126-32; O. Perler, "Arkandisziplin," in Klauser (1950): 1:667-76; Douglas Powell, "Arkandisziplin," in Krause and Müller (1979), 4:1-8; Schindler (1911)—there seems to be little argument about the existence of the *disciplina arcani*. Even the most exacting—thus Hanson (1962): 22—expresses no doubt on that score, but restricts its practice to the fourth and fifth centuries. Others are more generous in this regard.

est), appears to have been the point in the Christian worship service when those who were not yet members in full standing were "invited . . . to leave the church building. Then the doors were closed, and the ushers assumed their places in order to inquire of anyone who still desired to enter if he was baptized."[390] The practice of the *arcani disciplina*—including exclusion from participating in the Eucharist, from the baptismal service, and from other rites as well—persisted through several centuries, probably from the end of the second century until the end of the fourth or the beginning of the fifth century. According to Mulder, the early Church may have had certain secret practices that were not to be made known under any circumstances, whose secrecy were sometimes maintained by an oath.[391]

As late as the fourth century, efforts were being made within the church to return to the earlier, lost, Christian tradition of esotericism.[392] The motivation was "a concern to keep the most sacred things from profanation"—a concern shared by the Latterday Saints, and shown by such anti-Mormon efforts as the film *The God Makers* to be wholly justified.[393] Athanasius, for example, angrily notes that the people he views as apostates "are not ashamed to parade the sacred mysteries . . . even before the heathens: whereas, they ought to attend to what is written, 'It is good to keep close the secret of the king;' and as the Lord has charged us, 'Give not that which is holy unto the dogs, neither cast ye your pearls

---

390 H. Mulder, "Arcani Disciplina," in Palmer (1964): 390.

391 H. Mulder, "Arcani Disciplina," in Palmer (1964): 390. Mulder believes that, in the taking of these oaths, "the church may have imitated" the practices of certain Eastern religions that "contained a number of secret ceremonies . . . related especially to the initiation, [which] had to be kept quiet under all circumstances by the adherents. Sometimes an oath was required at the initiation; at other times the death penalty was pronounced in the eventuality of a breach"; cf. G. Anrich, "Arkandisziplin," in Gunkel and Zscharnack (1927): 1:523-33; Bolle (1987): 10, on the other hand, sees the origins of such practices arising from within the Christian communion itself; cf. Nock (1924): 58-59; Benko (1986): 12-13.

392 Brox (1983): 134.

393 Jeremias (1966): 130.

before swine.' We ought not then to parade the holy mysteries before the uninitiated, lest the heathen in their ignorance deride them, and the catechumens [i.e., investigators] being over-curious be offended."[394] Likewise, Basil of Caesarea reminds his readers of the "unpublished and secret teaching which our fathers guarded in silence out of the reach of curious meddling and inquisitive investigation." The apostles and fathers of the church, Basil continues, "laid down laws for the Church from the beginning [and] thus guarded the awful dignity of the mysteries in secrecy and silence, for what is bruited abroad at random among the common folk is no mystery at all. This is the reason for our tradition of unwritten precepts and practices."[395] Jeremias argues that this concern with preserving sacred things from mockery was the very motive that led the writer of the Gospel of John consciously to omit an account of the Lord's Supper, "because he did not want to reveal the sacred formula to the general public."[396]

We have seen that esoteric or secret teachings were an important component of Christianity in its early centuries. The fact that such teachings are clearly absent from mainstream Christianity today may explain, to a large degree, why some anti-Mormons are so irritated by Latter-day Saint claims to possess them. If we don't have those secret teachings, the reasoning seems to run, then they must not be important. Certainly they aren't essential; perhaps they are even evil. (One is reminded of Aesop's fable about the fox and the "sour grapes.") This is manifestly not the way in which early Christians thought of their own esoteric doctrines, however. They treasured them.

But fundamentalist anti-Mormons have announced that claims of secret doctrine bar us from being Christians. Do such claims also excommunicate the early saints? Was John a Christian? Was Paul?

---

394 Athanasius, *Defence against the Arians*, 1:11. English translation in Schaff and Wace (1979): 3:254-55.

395 Basil, *On the Spirit*, XXVII, 66. English translation in Schaff and Wace (1978): 8:42; cf. Cyril of Jerusalem, *Procatechesis* 12.

396 Jeremias (1966): 125, 136-37.

Was Jesus? If a definition of Christianity that excludes Roman Catholicism seems rather absurd, what of a definition that excludes Jesus himself?

Claim 11. Mormons are not Christians because they do not accept the Bible as their sole authority in faith and doctrine, but claim other sources.[397] "To the Mormons," says J. O. Sanders, speaking for them, "the Bible is not the sole and infallible Word of God but only a convenient tool to forward their subtle and misleading teaching."[398] "Dr." Walter Martin helpfully points out that "the Bible is only a convenient tool by which they attract attention to their subtle and ever-misleading dogmas of deception."[399] Orthodox Christianity teaches that "the Bible is the inspired, authoritative, inerrant Word of God."[400] But Mormons believe the Bible contains errors. Therefore, they are not Christians.[401] "Mormons rely on the 'revelations' of the authorities," complains Robert McKay. "Christians rely on the revelation of God in His written Word."[402]

Response. But what is the Bible, if it is not the writings and revelations of "authorities" from an earlier day? Is being ancient

---

397 Decker and Hunt (1984): 44, 110, 114 (vs. Scharffs [1986]: 32, 89, 159, 176); *The Utah Evangel* 34 (July-August 1987): 8; *The Evangel* 38 (April 1991): 4; "What Is a Cult?"; A. A. Hoekema, "Mormonism," in Douglas (1978): 678; "Mormonism: Christian or Cult?"; van Baalen (1983): 145, 168; "The Mormon Church and the African"; P. B. Smith (1970): 18, 57-61; Decker, "To Moroni with Love," 17-19; Spittler (1962): 14, 22-23, 27; J. O. Sanders (1962): 110-11, 119-21; Decker (1979): 15; Johnson (1983): 434. This is the issue that, rather inconsequently, irks Barrett (1982): 57-58.

398 J. O. Sanders (1962): 119.

399 Martin (1955): 54. Note the similarity between this quotation and the one preceding it. Hugh Nibley has drawn attention to the almost incestuous polemical inbreeding among anti-Mormons; cf. Nibley's classic essay on "How to Write an Anti-Mormon Book (A Handbook for Beginners)," in Nibley (1991): 474-580.

400 Ridenour (1979): 8; "Mormonism: Christian or Cult?"; J. O. Sanders (1962): 16, 28; cf. Ironside (1982): 47, against the Catholics.

401 See the discussion of this point by Forrest, "Are Mormons Christian?"

402 *The Evangel* 36 (December 1989): 3.

and dead really the chief requirement for true prophethood or apostleship? "Woe unto you," declared Jesus to the critics of his day, "scribes and Pharisees, hypocrites! because ye build the tombs of the prophets, and garnish the sepulchres of the righteous, and say, If we had been in the days of our fathers, we would not have been partakers with them in the blood of the prophets" (Matthew 23:29-30). "Woe unto you! for ye build the sepulchres of the prophets, and your fathers killed them" (Luke 11:47).

Apart from Robert McKay's rather frivolous complaint, there seem to be two fundamental points at issue here. First, the Latter-day Saints accept a scriptural canon that is larger than the canon accepted by Protestant Christians. Second, Latter-day Saints are uncommitted to the notion of biblical infallibility. We shall examine these two issues in turn.

It is true that Mormons irritate their critics by accepting other books of scripture not included in the traditional canon. But is this enough to exclude them from Christendom? It seems odd to take such drastic action on so flimsy and uncertain a basis. The Hebrew canon had not yet been fixed in the time of Jesus. Josephus (d. ca. A.D. 100) was among the first to identify an authoritative collection of Hebrew scriptural texts. But the collection of which Josephus spoke consisted merely of the Pentateuch, thirteen prophetic books, and four books of "writings"—for a grand total of twenty-two, seventeen short of the canon insisted upon by fundamentalist anti-Mormons. Even today, there are some uncertainties as to the extent of the Old Testament canon. Do those who accept Psalm 151, found in the Greek Septuagint but not in most other versions of the Bible, commit self-excommunication? Roman Catholics and the Orthodox churches tend to accept the Apocrypha as canonical. Indeed, the conciliar decree *De canonicis scripturis*, issued on 8 April 1546 by Session IV of the Catholic Council of Trent, declares all who do not accept the Apocrypha as Christian scripture—in other words, the Protestants—to be anathema or accursed.[403] The Greek Ortho-dox churches add 2 *Esdras* and 3 *Maccabees* to the Apocryphal or

---

403 See S. E. Robinson (1991): 54.

Deuterocanonical books, placing *4 Maccabees* in an appendix. The Russian Orthodox add *3 Esdras* and omit *4 Maccabees*. The Ethiopian biblical canon, which claims links back to the fourth century, contains eighty-one books—as opposed to the traditional Protestant Bible, which contains only sixty-six. Indeed, as Loraine Boettner notes, Eastern Orthodoxy has never really settled the question of the canon—which is, of course, rather odd if that question is all-important.[404] Have the Catholics and the Orthodox excluded themselves from Christendom? Are they heathens? The illustrious Athanasius of Alexandria omitted Esther from his Old Testament canon, but accepted both Baruch and the Epistle of Jeremiah. Was he a pagan cultist?

The question of the New Testament canon is very nearly as difficult as that pertaining to the Old. It is quite difficult, in fact, to see a distinction being made between canonical and non-canonical writings in earliest Christianity. Ancient evidence shows, however, that many Christian communities may not have accepted 2 Peter. More dramatic still is the case of the Revelation of John, which was rejected by such eastern writers as Cyril of Jerusalem (d. A.D. 386), John Chrysostom (d. A.D. 407), Theodore of Mopsuestia (d. A.D. 428), and Theodoret (d. ca. A.D. 466), as well as by the mid-fourth century Council of Laodicea, and which the Armenian version of the New Testament originally failed to include. The extremely important Syriac version of the New Testament known as the Peshitta not only excluded 2 Peter and the Revelation of John, but 2 and 3 John and Jude as well.[405] More interesting for our purposes, though, are the many Christians, ancient and modern, who have regarded as sacred or authoritative books that are not included in the Western Protestant version of the New Testament.

---

404 See the attack by Boettner (1986): 80-87, on Rome's acceptance of the Apocrypha.

405 Cross and Livingstone (1983): 1183; R. J. Owens, "Peshitta," in Ferguson (1990): 719; Turro and Brown, "Canonicity," in Brown, Fitzmyer, and Murphy (1968): 2:515-34; and Brown, "Apocrypha; Dead Sea Scrolls; Other Jewish Literature," in Brown Fitzmyer, and Murphy (1968): 2:535-60.

The Latter-day Saints are hardly unique among Christians in accepting an expanded canon. The so-called Muratorian Fragment, for instance, which dates from somewhere between the late second century and the middle of the fourth century A.D., shows that at least some Christians of the period accepted the *Apocalypse of Peter* and the *Wisdom of Solomon*. Clement of Alexandria, writing around A.D. 200, seems to have admitted a New Testament canon of some thirty books, including the *Epistle of Barnabas* and *1 Clement*—both of which he called "scripture"—and the *Preaching of Peter*. Origen called *1 Clement* a "catholic epistle," and recognized *Barnabas* and the *Shepherd of Hermas* as authoritative. The fifth or sixth century Codex Claramontanus includes the *Epistle of Barnabas*, the *Shepherd of Hermas*, the *Acts of Paul*, and the *Apocalypse of Peter*. On the other hand, it omits Hebrews. Codex Alexandrinus, dating from the fifth century, includes both *1* and *2 Clement*. So does the eleventh century Codex Constantinopolitanus, which also contains the *Epistle of Barnabas*, the *Didache*, and certain texts of Ignatius. The vastly important fourth century manuscript of the New Testament known as the Codex Sinaiticus includes *Barnabas*.

Are we to conclude that the devoted monks who copied the codices Alexandrinus and Constantinopolitanus and Claramontanus and Sinaiticus were pagans? Certainly not. Such a conclusion would be absurd. Yet, like today's Latter-day Saints, they do seem to have accepted a larger canon than that tolerated by today's anti-Mormons. And what of Ephraem of Edessa (d. A.D. 373)? He accepted as scripture an apocryphal exchange of letters between Paul and the Corinthians, taken from the *Acts of Paul*, which is now generally regarded as spurious. Was he merely mistaken, or was he non-Christian? (Anti-Mormons should think long and hard before they start dismissing canonized Christian saints as "non-Christian." It will make neutral observers suspicious. No clearer illustration could possibly be furnished of the fact that the denial of Mormon Christianity involves a massive, if surreptitious, redefinition of the word "Christian.") It was not until A.D. 367 that Bishop Athanasius —he of the enlarged Old Testament—identified the present twenty-seven-book New Testament as comprising the exclusive Christian canon.[406] And even then, as the various codices cited above clearly demonstrate, not everybody seems to have accepted the limits set by Athanasius.

Given anti-Mormon standards, it is not even clear that the New Testament itself will survive as a "Christian" document. The Epistle of Jude, for instance, draws heavily on non-canonical books such as *1 Enoch* and the *Assumption of Moses*. Indeed, as an eminent contemporary scholar says of *1 Enoch*, "it influenced Matthew, Luke, John, Acts, Romans, 1 and 2 Corinthians, Ephesians, Colossians, 1 and 2 Thessalonians, 1 Timothy, Hebrews, 1 John, Jude (which quotes it directly), and Revelation (with numerous points of contact). There is little doubt that 1 Enoch was influential in molding New Testament doctrines concerning the nature of the Messiah, the Son of Man, the messianic kingdom, demonology, the future, resurrection, the final judgment, the whole eschatological theater, and symbolism."[407] When Matthew the evangelist says (at 2:23) that Jesus "came and dwelt in a city called Nazareth: that it might be fulfilled which was spoken by the prophets, He shall be called a Nazarene," he is citing a prophetic text unknown to the Bible as we have it. When, at Acts 20:35, the apostle Paul exhorts the elders of the Ephesian branch "to remember the words of the Lord Jesus, how he said, It is more blessed to give than to receive," he is pointing their minds toward a famous statement that does not occur in the New Testament books that we possess today. To put it bluntly, both Matthew and Paul seem to accept a canon of scriptural materials broader than that accepted today by the critics of the Latter-day Saints. This hardly bothers the Mormons, but it should give real pause to our detractors. How can they denounce us for receiving scriptures beyond their limited canon without simulta-

---

406 For discussions of the variability of the canon through Christian history, see Manschreck (1985): 33; Averill (1989): 67-68; Bauer (1957): 10-11; L. M. McDonald, "Canon," in Ferguson (1990): 169-73. On the ambiguity of early Christian notions of canon, and on Orthodox and Roman views, see, generally, M. S. Enslin, "Apocrypha," in Buttrick (1962): 1:161-69. S. E. Robinson (1991): 45-56, also offers a Latter-day Saint response to this issue.

407 E. Isaac, "1 Enoch," in Charlesworth (1983): 1:10.

neously condemning Jude, Matthew, and Paul? Did devious non-Christian cultists manage to creep into the New Testament?[408] Was primitive Christianity Christian?

To summarize our argument thus far: If acceptance of extra-biblical scriptures bars the Latter-day Saints from consideration as Christians, it must also bar the Catholics, the Orthodox, and a great many of the early believers in Jesus, including the authors of more than half the books of the New Testament.

Further, Roman Catholics even today accept "Tradition" as an authority along with the Bible, especially on matters arising after the close of the biblical canon. "Catholicism asserts tradition and Scripture as equal authorities, both being products of the Holy Spirit, who dwells supremely in the Pope, the infallible interpreter of the Christ of Scripture and tradition."[409] Rome often dismisses the idea of "the Bible alone" as mere Protestantism. (Catholic anti-Mormon W. J. Whalen, in fact, remarks that Latter-day Saints reject "the sole sufficiency of the Bible, another *Reformation* principle.")[410] Rome does not hesitate to declare that the Church has priority, both logically and historically, over the Bible.[411] "It was the Church that formed the Bible," writes the Catholic apologist Karl Keating, "not the Bible that formed the Church. . . . In the beginning, teaching was oral and was under the authority of the Church, which eventually decided what books belonged to the Bible and what did not." "How," Keating demands, "is one to know what interpretations are right? The same Church that authenticates the Bible, that establishes its inspiration, is the

---

408 On Jude, see D. F. Payne, "Jude," in Bruce (1986): 1590-92.

409 Manschreck (1985): 2.

410 Whalen (1963): 167 (emphasis ours); cf. also Holzapfel (1925): 15-34.

411 See the statements of Archbishop Whealon (1986):17; cf. Zacchello (1984): 4, 18; Holzapfel (1925): 20, 23-37. Johnson (1983): 22, supports the view that the canonical gospels are "products of the early Church."

authority set up by Christ to interpret his word."[412] Such a critic
of Mormonism as G. H. Fraser, who would thrust the Mormons
from Christendom because of their belief in the authority of a
Mormon prophet, compares that prophet's authority to that of a
"Romanist" pope.[413] Will he follow his insight through to its
logical implication?

The Eastern Orthodox, too, reject the Reformers' view of
Scripture and Tradition as competitive. Instead, they choose to see
them as complementary.[414] Are Roman Catholics and Eastern
Orthodox non-Christians? Loraine Boettner, for one, certainly
seems willing to show Rome the door.[415] And Bill Jackson makes
the point with horrifying bluntness: "The addition of blasphemous
Tradition and changeable Papal teaching," he cries, "is as bad as
looking for inspiration in . . . *The Book of Mormon.*"[416] But if
Rome and the Orthodox tradition were to be expelled, most people
would perceive this as an extraordinarily strange use of the word
"Christian." Still, fundamentalist strictures on this issue are
severe.[417] Christianity accepts the Bible alone.[418] But Catholi-

---

412 Keating (1988): 312, 34. On pp. 312-13, Keating argues eloquently and
plausibly against the notion of the Bible as the sole and exhaustive rule of faith.

413 Fraser (1977): 40. Coming from the opposite direction, Boettner (1986): 102,
too, has noticed the resemblance.

414 Rusch (1986): 12. A similar view, held by a modern German church historian,
is expressed by Brox (1983): 149. Further, Draper (1984), a former president of the
Southern Baptist Convention, acknowledges in his book that *sola scriptura* is a
Reformation doctrine—and, in so doing, reflects a sense of history and historical
process that is rather rare in the conservative Protestant camp.

415 Boettner (1986): 3, 14, 24, 49, 71, 90, 98, 260, 272, 276-77, 450, 460. Of
course, the real question is Does the Christian "house" really belong to the likes of
Boettner? Or, indeed, to any man?

416 Cited in Keating (1988): 83.

417 Thus, Berry (1979): 89, 91-92; Irvine (1921): 140; Boettner (1986): 24, 75-
103, 455-56; W. Thompson, "What We Should Know about Roman Catholicism";
Green (1984d); Green (1984a); Ironside (1982): 41-48; Zacchello (1984): 12-16, 24-
28; P. B. Smith (1970): 13-15, 17, 18 (where Catholics are linked with Mormons),
23; Spittler (1962): 14, 112-16; J. O. Sanders (1962): 21-22. They have been

cism departs strikingly from Christianity, says Jimmy Swaggart. "Obviously, church (human) tradition has taken precedence over the Word of God within the Catholic church, with awesome and eternal suffering the end product of adherence to such policies." Furthermore, he says, "the Roman Catholic church has added books to the generally accepted Bible and has officially declared these books to be God-breathed and God-inspired—when it is obvious that they are not."[419] "The Roman Catholic Church," writes Keith Green, "has constructed one of the most unbiblical doctrinal systems that has ever been considered 'Christian.' "[420] According to Wes Thompson, head of Concerned Christians for Catholics, "this Church's doctrine comes from Satan himself."[421] So, given their assumptions, it is not surprising that many fundamentalists summon Roman Catholics, in the words of Joseph Zacchello, "to discover the errors of their church and become Christians."[422]

---

known to pronounce excommunications from Christendom for far lesser offenses. Irvine (1921): 136-39, has an entire chapter on "Pseudo-Christianity, or Modern Religious Education."

418 P. B. Smith (1970): 17-20.

419 Swaggart (1985b): 38.

420 Green (1984c); Swaggart (1985a): 38, 41, attacks the Catholic practice of auricular confession as unscriptural; Swaggart (1985b): 37-38, attacks the immaculate conception of Mary, her bodily assumption into heaven, the mass, and papal infallibility. The anonymous pamphlet entitled "Which Will You Believe? The Holy Scriptures, God's Unchangeable Word or The Human Traditions of Men" [sic], lists, among unscriptural beliefs and practices, purgatory, confession or penance, the mass, idolatry, priesthood, prayers to Mary and the saints, and alleged Catholic claims that the Church of Rome does not change.

421 W. Thompson, "What We Should Know about Roman Catholicism." He is echoing a charge made scores of times in the propaganda of such people as J. Edward Decker and Utah Missions, Inc., against the Mormons. It should not come as a surprise that the group's title resembles that of "Concerned Christians," once one of the leading anti-Mormon groups. Both emerge from the same spiritual demimonde.

422 Zacchello (1984): vii.

Ephraem and readers of the Septuagint may seem dispensable to the average fundamentalist anti-Mormon, who has never met the former and may never have heard of the important ancient Greek translation of the Hebrew Bible. Even the Catholics and the Orthodox may lightly be jettisoned. But if critics of the Mormons persist in claiming that acceptance of the modern Protestant canon of the Bible, nothing more, nothing less, is essential to being a Christian, they will soon find their sword cutting closer to home. Martin Luther is a case in point. "That Luther was critical of the scriptures," writes Otto Scheel, "is too well known for me to have to emphasize it."[423] Luther's critical attitude, Scheel contends, continued throughout his career as a reformer. His famous negative judgment of the Epistle of James, for instance, was repeated over a period of many years. In the "Vorrede" (preface) to his translation of that letter, he denied its apostolic authorship, and declared that it fell short of the gospel as defined by Paul.[424] Luther characterized James as "an epistle of straw," having "no gospel quality to it"[425]—largely, we must point out, because it seemed to disagree with his teaching of justification by faith alone.[426] "We should throw the Epistle of James out of this school [i.e., out of the University of Wittenberg]," he declared, "because it's worthless [*denn sie soll nichts*]. . . . I hold that some Jew wrote it who probably had heard about Christians but had never run into any. Since he had heard that Christians put so much emphasis on faith

---

423 Except where specifically noted, the argument of this paragraph is based upon Scheel (1902): 47-55; also Bainton (1950): 332; Averill (1989): 72-73; and Stephens (1986): 56. For a general survey of Luther's views on scripture, see Althaus (1966): 72-102.

424 Luther (1972): 2:2454-55.

425 Luther (1929): Ser.3:6:10: "eyn rechte stroern Epistel . . . denn sie doch keyn Evangelisch art in ihr hat." See also Holzapfel (1925): 27; Bainton (1950): 177, 331-32; T. Carson, "James," in Bruce (1986): 1536. Some have wished to dismiss such remarks as merely "tongue-in-cheek," not representing Luther's real view on the matter. This, however, will not wash. Luther was too consistent in expressing the opinion, in contexts which simply cannot be written off as humorous.

426 See Lackmann (1949) for a discussion of this issue.

in Christ, he thought [to himself]: 'Wait a minute! I'll oppose them and emphasize *works* [*opera*].' And that's what he did."[427] Martin Luther may never have acted on his own advice, but later reformers like Karlstadt and Oecolampadius actually wished to exclude the Epistle of James from the canon, and to give it "deuterocanonical" status instead.[428]

Luther also felt that there were "hay," "wood," and "straw" among the biblical prophets. Both Luther and the great Swiss reformer Zwingli mistrusted the Revelation of John (which, as we have seen, had never been accepted by the Syriac church in the first place). Jude and Hebrews were of dubious value. 2 Peter, Luther said, fell off from apostolic standards. Esther, the great reformer felt, deserved no more place in the canon than did 2 Maccabbees, but 1 Maccabbees should have been canonized. He preferred Romans among the epistles of Paul, for reasons that should be obvious enough, and said that John stood out among the four gospels. He did not much like the synoptic gospels (Matthew, Mark, and Luke), since, again, they do not emphasize his pet doctrine of salvation by grace alone. Astoundingly, Luther was willing to call the Sermon on the Mount "the devil's masterpiece" since its emphasis on works seemed incompatible with his understanding of grace.[429] (He enjoyed the Acts of the Apostles, however, since he imagined that book to teach his theology.) Most of Luther's judgments, as should be clear, were based on personal theological criteria—i.e., on how well the particular book or passage suited his own beliefs—rather than on historical ones, but he was very far from being a believer in scriptural infallibility. The

---

427 Luther (1919), 5:157. Our translation. The text from which this passage comes is a mixture of German and Latin. The switch from German to Latin in the word *opera* is reflected by our emphasizing "*works.*"

428 Reicke (1964): 9.

429 Luther (1906): Ser.1:32:299: "Das heist ein meister stuck des Teuffels." Luther's preface to his commentary on the Sermon on the Mount is a wandering and occasionally ill-tempered text. Luther seems to be blaming the devil for misinterpretations of the Sermon on the Mount, but it often seems that he blames the Sermon itself.

books of Kings, he argued, were more trustworthy (*glaubwürdiger*) than the Chronicles. On the whole, however, both Luther and Zwingli were notably indifferent to the question of biblical inerrancy in historical and other details.

The Protestant writer Lloyd Averill summarizes this point well, meanwhile bringing in yet another figure beloved among evangelical and fundamentalist anti-Mormons: "It is clear," he writes, "that Calvin cannot be identified with the scriptural literalism affirmed by present-day fundamentalists. Nor, indeed, can any other major figure in the history of Christian thought prior to 1800. Contrary to fundamentalist claims, the doctrine of biblical inerrancy as they have formulated it is not a return to primitive Christianity or to Christian orthodoxy. Rather, it was an innovation fashioned scarcely more than a hundred years ago as a weapon to be used against the modernist movement."[430]

Can Luther and Zwingli and John Calvin and the Syrian fathers still be considered Christian? If they can, so, on this point, can the Latter-day Saints. In fact, the claim that "orthodox Christianity" insists always and everywhere upon the inerrancy of scripture is a flagrant oversimplification. Such books as Harold Lindsell's famous polemic, *The Battle for the Bible*, make it abundantly clear that even contemporary conservative Protestants are not at one on this issue. Their division is not surprising, since "the Bible cannot properly be said to make a claim of inerrancy for itself."[431] And it is not true that even all fundamentalists believe the Bible to be the sole source of redeeming truth. There are notable divisions within their own camp.[432] Furthermore, the Catholic Karl Keating quite properly notes that the boast of fundamentalists that they (alone) approach the Bible without preconceived notions or extrabiblical intellectual baggage is, simply, false. The difference between the Catholics and the fundamentalists on this point rests largely on the

---

430 Averill (1989): 73-74.

431 Averill (1989): 66.

432 Averill (1989): 43-45.

fact that Rome is aware of what it is doing, and explicit about it, while conservative Protestants tend to smuggle foreign ideas into their interpretations silently, and probably without even being aware of it themselves. Fundamentalists, Keating observes, "do not really 'find' their doctrines through a literal reading of the Bible. They approach the Bible with already-held views, their own tradition, one might say, and they use the Bible to substantiate those views."[433]

But the anti-Mormon case does not end here. Paul B. Smith speaks for most conservative critics of Mormonism when he says of the Latter-day Saints and other intended fundamentalist targets, "If they contradict the written word of God, they are not Christian."[434] However, the Bible itself lays down no such rule. It cannot be repeated too often that the Bible offers no definition of Christianity at all. Besides, it is doubtful that anybody who claims to be Christian would ever willingly admit to contradicting scripture—although he might want to argue about how one is to interpret it correctly. And, as we have already noted, "conformity to scripture" is largely in the eye of the beholder. As we have outlined here in only the sketchiest and most inadequate fashion, agreement on just what is and is not contained in "the written word of God" is by no means unanimous.

Latter-day Saint writer Stephen E. Robinson makes another point that deserves mention here, one in which he takes a position very much like that attributed above to Roman Catholics. He agrees that the Church as an institution has logical and historical priority over the New Testament canon. "Since it is clear that there were Christians before the New Testament was written," he notes, "it cannot be maintained that the Bible is what makes one a Christian."[435]

To repeat and stress the point: There seems, on the matter of scripture and canon, to be no reason whatever to deny that The Church of Jesus Christ of Latter-day Saints is Christian.

---

433 Keating (1988): 188.

434 P. B. Smith (1970): 20.

435 S. E. Robinson (1991): 56.

Claim 12. "The Christian position," asserts "Dr." Walter Martin, "has always been based upon a literal acceptance" of the virgin birth.[436] Certain early Mormon leaders speculated about the mode of Jesus' conception along quite nontraditional lines. Therefore, Mormonism is not Christian.[437]

Response. We will ignore the fact that these scattered nineteenth-century speculations were never canonized by the Mormon Church, and that no comparable statements occur in Latter-day Saint scripture. We will pass over the unfairness of holding Mormons to statements that they and their own leaders have never deemed authoritative or binding (and we will deprive ourselves of the great entertainment that would ensue were we to call our Protestant critics to account for every speculation advanced by their pastors and reformers of the past five centuries).[438] We will ignore the fact that the New Testament is not specific about the mechanism of Jesus' conception. We will decline to notice the fact that some denunciations of Mormonism seem to betray a Neoplatonic and gnosticizing disdain for the material cosmos, a discomfort with the body and with sexuality that is utterly foreign to the Bible.[439]

---

436 Martin (1985): 214; cf. *The Utah Evangel* 31 (March 1984): 8.

437 So, for example, *The Utah Evangel* 31 (January 1984): 12; 31 (February 1984): 3; 33 (July/August 1986): 4; *The Evangel* 37 (November 1990): 1; Decker, "Petition"; P. B. Smith (1970): 68; Robertson (1983): 7; J. O. Sanders (1962): 109, 115-16; Decker and Hunt (1984): 199-201 (vs. Scharffs [1986]: 258). Martin (1955): 53, finds these rare and isolated speculations "shocking and vile," and makes the obligatory allusions to Greek mythology. He alleges that such ideas spring from the immoral and sensual character of Mormonism and its leaders; cf. pp. 50, 53-54.

438 S. E. Robinson (1991): 9-21, is worth consulting on this sort of thinking, which he labels "exclusion by misrepresentation."

439 Orson Hyde speculated that Jesus was married. Robertson (1983): 17, finds the suggestion "horrifying." Gnosticism would respond so, as would a Christianized Neoplatonism. But where in Judeo-Christian scripture is such a horror of sex and materiality to be found? If Mr. Robertson takes the Incarnation seriously, he must allow for some pretty gritty physiological attributes—at least as much so as sexuality—to be predicated of Jesus. If he does not, he is a Docetist. And Docetism,

Is it not relevant that Mormonism resolutely proclaims the divine Sonship of Jesus? The speculations that most incense the critics are simply literalistic interpretations of the divine paternity alluded to in the title, "Son of God." While certain early Mormon leaders may occasionally have reinterpreted the concept of "virgin birth," they never for a moment suggested that Jesus was begotten by a mortal man, nor that his father was any other personage than God.

On the other hand, history is replete with such groups as the ancient Ebionites and the modern Unitarians, to whom both scholarly and common usage refer as Christian, who nonetheless reject the Virgin Birth and deny the divinity of Christ.[440] How can those groups be described as Christian, and the Mormons not? The professional anti-Mormon Robert McKay stumbles into this dilemma himself when he claims, first, that "belief in [the] literal virgin birth of Jesus Christ" is an "essential part of Christianity," and then immediately declares that "historically the vast majority of Christians have believed this doctrine."[441] While he clearly intends to isolate the Latter-day Saints from the Christian main-stream—no great achievement, of course, since most Latter-day Saints would enthusiastically agree that we are outside the main-stream—the clear implication of his statement that "the vast

---

as we have seen, is the one heresy that our ancient sources might justify us in expelling from Christianity. Hayman (1991): 6, 14, points out that, in popular Jewish belief (as held by "many, perhaps the majority, of ancient Israelites"), God himself had a female consort.

440 On "Jewish Christianity," which includes the Ebionites, see, for example, Bruce (1979): 255; Ferm (1945): 241; Frend (1981): 353; Bauer (1957): 201, 243. References could be multiplied indefinitely. The standard work on the subject is H.-J. Schoeps, *Theologie und Geschichte des Judenchristentums*; cf. also J. Danielou, *Théologie du judéo-christianisme*. Cf. also J. O. Sanders (1962): 17, who attacks the Judeo-Christians. The *Oxford English Dictionary*, perhaps the ultimate arbiter of English usage, explicitly terms the Unitarians "Christian." We have in mind, as the *Oxford English Dictionary* necessarily did as well, more the Unitarians of several decades ago. Some contemporary Unitarians probably cannot be described as Christians in any meaningful sense. But—and this is crucial—many of these people no longer claim to be Christians.

441 *The Utah Evangel* 34 (July-August 1987): 8.

majority of Christians" have been believers in the virgin birth is that some Christians, at least, have *not* believed in it. And once this is admitted, there seems no justifiable reason to exclude Latter-day Saints from Christianity for a denial that has not excluded others. And for a denial, it cannot be repeated too often, that the Latter-day Saints have never accepted as official doctrine.

On the other hand, those who would deny the Christianity of Mormons for taking the divine Sonship of Christ too literally commit a monstrous irony, one which allows that unbelievers in the divinity of Christ can be Christians while certain believers in his divinity are not. This seems absurd. If they wish to avoid this absurdity, however, anti-Mormons must redefine the word. They must reject the consensus of historians of the Christian church and contradict normal English usage of the word "Christian." This seems to be the path they have chosen. But it is important that neutral observers, Latter-day Saints, and the anti-Mormons themselves, be fully aware of the redefinition that is occurring.

Claim 13. The conspicuous absence of the cross from Mormon iconography constitutes an admission that Mormonism is not Christian. Indeed, it proves Mormonism to be a mere "superstition and cult."[442] Critics cite such Mormon statements as that of Elder Robert E. Wells: "To us, the cross is a symbol of His passion, His agony. Our preference is to remember his resurrection. We seek to honor the living Christ who was brought forth in glory from the tomb on the third day. . . . We remember Him resurrected and glorified, having overcome death. We see Him as a strong, masculine, healthy Saviour of mankind, not an emaciated and

---

442 *The Evangel* 37 (November 1990): 1; cf. *The Utah Evangel* 33 (May 1986): 8; cf. Decker and Hunt (1984): 136 (and the rebuttal by Scharffs [1986]: 193-94); "Introducing Ex-Mormons for Jesus." With equal hostility, but for quite another purpose, Fraser (1977): 144, tries the following argument: "We would hasten to remind Mormons that the cross on which the Saviour died was a palus, or pole, without a transom member. The classical cruciform developed later in Christian art." In other words, one set of anti-Mormons assaults the Latter-day Saints for the failure to use a symbol that another prominent anti-Mormon rejects as inauthentically biblical. The left anti-Mormon hand knoweth not what the right one doeth.

suffering one."[443] "One Mormon," recalls *The Utah Evangel*'s Robert McKay, "said to me at the 1984 Utah State Fair that putting a cross on a church building is the same as giving a place of respect to a butcher knife that was used to murder one's brother."[444]

Response. It is possible to disagree with these Mormon statements. But is it reasonable to call those who make them "anti-Christian"? Is it reasonable to call people "anti-Christian" because, out of respect and love for Jesus, they are uncomfortable with the cross? If so, what are we to make of the most ancient Church? According to Colles and Child, "In the first three centuries A.D. the cross was not openly used as a Christian symbol, for the early believers looked beyond the Crucifixion to the Resurrection, and the emphasis was not on the cross of suffering and humiliation but on the Promise of Life with Christ here in the world and hereafter in the life beyond the grave."[445]

Protestant theologian Lloyd Averill makes essentially the same point: "The power of salvation, Paul says, is not in the cross, as fundamentalist evangelists have claimed, but in the resurrection."[446] "Christians preferred to glorify the founder of their faith rather than emphasize his shameful end."[447] The similarity of

---

443 Wells (1985): 24. This is partially cited by *The Utah Evangel* 33 (May 1986): 8. It is likely that, in the last sentence, Elder Wells has in mind the Catholic crucifix, so common in Latin America where he has spent much of his life.

444 In *The Utah Evangel* 33 (May 1986): 8.

445 Child and Colles (1971): 10; cf. Kirschbaum (1970): 2:571; *Newsletter*, The Conversion Center (March/April 1989). Miller (1956): 26, finds possible evidence of the use of the cross in Syria by the beginning of the third century; cf. also Boettner (1986): 286-87, assaulting the Catholics. No Mormon is more hostile to the cross than Rev. Boettner. We know next to nothing of Christian art before A.D. 200, and precious little of it during the third century; cf. Janson (1969): 158. The very close relationship between pagan art, on the one hand, and early Christian art and iconography, on the other, is well portrayed in de la Croix and Tansy (1980): 212-26, and Janson (1969): 157-69. It is impossible, in the earliest centuries, to speak of one single "Christian" artistic tradition.

446 Averill (1989): 88.

447 Miller (1956): 25.

early Christian attitudes, as sketched by these scholars, to contemporary Latter-day Saint opinions is almost uncanny. Were the Christians of the first three centuries really Christian? If they were, so are the Mormons.

Claim 14. Mormons are not Christian because they deny the doctrine of original sin.[448]

Response. This charge rests on an exaggeration. Latter-day Saint scriptures uniformly declare that the human condition has been one of sin and suffering since the fall of Adam.[449] The Mormon view resembles that held by the classical rabbis—who, after all, spent a great deal of time in meditation upon the text of Genesis. As S. G. F. Brandon summarizes their position, "Jewish Rabbinic thought traced man's tendency to actual sin to Adam's Fall, and explained death thereby."[450] While the rabbis knew "actual" or "individual sin," they seem to have known little or nothing of the notion of "essential sin"—something which anti-Mormon "experts" tell us is essential to Christianity. So too with the restored gospel. What Latter-day Saints reject is the full-blown doctrine of original sin as developed by such a relatively late Christian thinker as Augustine—a doctrine that so eminent a historian as W. H. C. Frend has characterized as "inhuman," "obsessive," and rooted in "persistent mistranslation."[451]

But why single out the Mormons for condemnation on this issue? "In the history of the church, fierce controversy has raged about the

---

448 Lanczkowski (1972): 210. Eggenberger (1969): 58, hints only vaguely at the same position, but he made the charge explicitly during a conversation with one of the authors in Zürich, Switzerland, in early 1974. This accusation may be a purely European fashion, although the pamphlet "Is Mormonism Christian?" published in Grand Rapids, Michigan, in 1989, makes an implicitly related point.

449 As at 1 Nephi 10:6; Mosiah 3:11, 16, 19; 4:5, 7; 16:3-4; Alma 12:22; 22:12-14; 34:9; 42:2-26; Helaman 14:16; Mormon 9:12; Ether 3:2; D&C 20:18-20; Moses 6:48-49, 53-55.

450 Brandon (1970): 481.

451 Frend (1981): 206-7.

doctrine of original sin."[452] The Pelagians of the fifth and sixth centuries denied that doctrine, too, as did Theodore of Mopsuestia (d. A.D. 428).[453] Yet, as we have already seen, Theodore's Christianity is never denied. And neither is that of Pelagius.[454] No real doctrine of original sin is detectible in either Justin Martyr (d. ca. A.D. 165) or Tatian (d. ca. A.D. 160), although nobody would dream of denying their Christianity.[455] In fact, the notion of original sin as it is usually understood today is distinctly late, evolving out of the controversies of the fourth and fifth centuries.

J. N. D. Kelly, while he sees in certain Greek fathers "the outline of a real theory of original sin," acknowledges that "it is easy to collect passages from their works which . . . appear to rule out any doctrine of original sin."[456] Athanasius, for instance, "never hints that we participate in Adam's actual guilt, i.e. his moral culpability, nor does he exclude the possibility of men living entirely without sin." Indeed, he claims at one point that Jeremiah and John the Baptist actually did lead sinless lives. And Gregory of Nyssa (d. ca. A.D. 395), Gregory Nazianzen (d. A.D. 389), and John Chrysostom "teach that newly born children are exempt from sin."[457] Paul M. Blowers, writing in a recently-published reference work that bears official endorsements from both the American Society of Church History and the North American Patristic Society, offers a useful summary of the earliest situation: "There is

---

452 C. G. Kromminga, "Sin," in Harrison, Bromiley, and Henry (1960): 488; Kelly (1978): 168.

453 Rahner (1968-70): 4:329; Cross and Livingstone (1983): 1011.

454 Frend (1981): 205. On the Pelagians, see Bruce (1979): 371 (although Bruce comes perilously close to excommunicating Pelagius at p. 336); Kraft (1966): 415-16; Manschreck (1985): 73; D. F. Wright, "Pelagianism," in Douglas (1978): 760-61; O'Brien (1970): 385-87. Rahner (1968-70): 4:384, claims that "Pelagius appears as a Christian still under the spell of the Old Testament." The *Oxford English Dictionary* does not deny that Pelagians were Christian.

455 Kelly (1978): 167-68.

456 Kelly (1978): 351, 349.

457 See, for Athanasius, the two Gregorys, and Chrysostom, Kelly (1978): 347-49.

little evidence among the Greek fathers for a notion of inherited guilt or physically transmitted sinfulness. With the apologists, culpability was principally a matter of the individual's exercise of free will, of personal sins for which Adam's disobedience was only a prototype. Greek writers consistently espoused the sinlessness of infants, thereby precluding original guilt as a basis for infant baptism. . . . Origen . . . stressed that individual souls were punished precisely according to their respective sins. This characteristic emphasis on personal responsibility, coupled with the belief that moral evil had no 'natural' status in creation but resulted only from human volition, continued to militate against a doctrine of genetically transmitted sin in the Christian east." In the Latin West, Blowers admits, there evolved a somewhat "graver picture" of the question. But even in the West, the leading authors prior to the time of Augustine had "concluded that individuals were ultimately accountable only for their own sins."[458] Tertullian (d. ca. A.D. 220), for instance, who was very concerned with the idea of individual sin, appears to know nothing of any doctrine of collective guilt deriving from Adam.[459] The early Christian position seems to have been, essentially, that "men will be punished for their own sins, and not for Adam's transgression." We are, of course, quoting from the second Article of Faith of The Church of Jesus Christ of Latter-day Saints. It is difficult to see why the early Saints could hold such a view and remain Christians, while the Latter-day Saints are to be driven from Christendom for holding it today.[460]

---

458 Blowers, "Original Sin," in Ferguson (1990): 669; cf. also Cross and Livingstone (1983): 1010-11; Placher (1983): 96-97; Kelly (1978): 354-55. We have omitted the extensive listing of patristic references supplied by Blowers; cf. also E. Ferguson, "Baptism," in Ferguson (1990): 133, with references.

459 Although Kelly (1978): 175, thinks he was "close."

460 The comments by Roman Catholic theologian Herbert Haag, in Haag (1969): 107, are strongly reminiscent of the second Article of Faith: "No man enters the world a sinner. As the creature and image of God he is from his first hour surrounded by God's fatherly love. Consequently, he is not at birth, as is often maintained, an enemy of God and a child of God's wrath. A man becomes a sinner only through his own independent and responsible action."

Original sin, then, was an innovation. Early Christians did not know of it, and the Jews, who have known the story of Adam and Eve since long before the time of Christ, reject it still today.[461] The doctrine was not clearly enunciated until the time of Augustine. He elaborated it in his battle with the Pelagians, who found it abhorrent, and it can be securely associated with the Council of Carthage in A.D. 418. "Properly considered, Pelagian theology was the traditional one, especially in Rome. But the Africans, under the theological leadership of Augustine, managed to make their charge of heresy stick within the church, thereby establishing the Augustinian theology of grace as the basis of the Western tradition."[462]

By Augustine's time, the idea that some single great sin lay behind the visible decay of Roman society was common to both pagans and Christians, and the relatively late Christian doctrine of original sin appears clearly to have grown out of this overwhelming sense of malaise.[463] Augustine, indeed, may have been even more inclined toward it than most of his contemporaries because of his Manichaean past, which he never entirely outgrew. He was often accused, even after his conversion, of still being a Manichaean, rather than a Christian.[464] (Manichaeism, founded by the Persian prophet Mani [A.D. 215-277], held a dualistic view of creation,

---

461 The doctrine's absence from the Dead Sea Scrolls was noted by Gaster (1964): 19-20.

462 Brox (1983): 141 (translation ours). Note Prof. Dr. Brox's specification that, even triumphant, Augustine's innovation became only the "Basis der *westlichen* Tradition" (emphasis ours). For brief accounts of Augustine's development of the doctrine, and of some of the opposition it aroused, see Placher (1983): 115-18; Kelly (1978): 361-66; Frend (1981): 205.

463 P. Brown (1969): 388.

464 See P. Brown (1969): 203-4, 370-71, 386, 393-94; Frend (1981): 207. Teske (1986): 233-49, discusses the vastly important role played by Manichaeism in the intellectual development of Augustine—and, thus, in the development of Christianity. On p. 240, n. 20, Teske quotes Prosper Alfaric on Augustine, to the effect that "moralement comme intellectuellement c'est au Néoplatonisme qu'il s'est converti, plutôt qu'à l'Evangile" (morally and intellectually he was a convert more to Neoplatonism than to the gospel). Alfaric had special reference to the question of anthropomorphism.

which it divided between light and darkness, and saw the physical cosmos as essentially evil.) Some modern scholars now argue that it was Augustine, "the paradigm of Western theology," who introduced foreign notions into Christianity, and that it was he, and not Pelagius, who was the archheretic.[465] Augustine triumphed over his opponents. But it may well be that, on the question of original sin, it is the heirs of an ancient pagan Iranian heresy who denounce the Latter-day Saints for remaining true to original Christian belief. And, if the distinguished Protestant scholar Ernst Benz is to be believed, it is very likely that Mormon views on this subject are closer to those of primitive Christianity than are those of Augustine and his disciples.[466]

J. N. D. Kelly offers a suggestion for understanding the early Greek fathers of the church that bears quotation here. He laments what he terms "the customary verdict" of scholars (that the Greek fathers lacked a notion of original sin), and remarks that it "seems unjust to the Greek fathers, perhaps because it depends on the assumption that no theory of original sin holds water except the full-blown Latin one [like that advanced by Augustine]. It is imperative to get rid of this prejudice. Admittedly there is hardly a hint in the Greek fathers that mankind as a whole shares in Adam's guilt, i.e. in his culpability. This partly explains their reluctance to speak of his legacy to us as sin, and of course makes their indulgent attitude to children dying unbaptized understandable."[467] So, too, is it unjust to condemn the Latter-day Saints for rejecting a theory that originated centuries after the death and resurrection of the Savior. It is imperative that such prejudice be rooted out or, at least, exposed for what it is.

---

465 See Phipps (1980): 124-33, with accompanying references. The quotation is from Manschreck (1985): 67.

466 Benz (1978): 216.

467 Kelly (1978): 350.

Claim 15. "The only way to obtain salvation is by personally receiving Jesus Christ as Saviour."[468] Mormonism is non-Christian because it rejects the biblical doctrine of salvation by grace alone, solafidianism, which is the core of Christianity.[469] Jan Karel van Baalen and G. H. Fraser even allege that Latter-day Saints deny the atonement of Christ.[470]

Response. As the most cursory glance at Mormon writings would indicate, this is a slanderous misrepresentation. (Latter-day Saints, for instance, believe that Christ's grace is essential for

---

468 Berry (1973): 18. So too Gruss (1976): 56-62; Martin (1985): 216-26; Berry (1973): 14-18; Breese et al. (1985): 49. *The Utah Evangel* is fond of referring to the Mormon practice of baptism for the dead as "dead works for dead people"; cf. the tract, "Baptism for the Dead."

469 Thus Rowe (1985): 26-31; "The Mormon Church and the African"; Fraser (1977): 112-23, 171, 188; P. B. Smith (1970): 70; Spittler (1962): 24, 27; J. O. Sanders (1962): 16, 109, 117-18, 121; *The Utah Evangel* 31 (January 1984): 12, and (February 1984): 4; *The Utah Evangel* 34 (July-August 1987): 8; *The Evangel* 37 (October 1990): 4; *The Evangel* 38 (April 1991): 4, 8; *The Evangel* 38 (October 1991): 10; Tope, "Faith without Works"; Tope, "Would You Risk"; J. L. Smith, "Mormonism Has Another Jesus"; Decker, "To Moroni with Love," 10-19; B. McKeever; "What Is a Cult?"; J. K. van Baalen (1983): 151; "Those Plain & Precious Things"; Decker (1979): 13-14, 15, 21-23; "Jesus Is Sufficient!"; A. A. Hoekema, "Mormonism," in Douglas (1978): 678; "What the Mormon Church Teaches about Jesus Christ"; Tope, "Are You REALLY Good Enough"; Decker, "Petition"; Witte, "And It Came to Pass"; Decker and Hunt (1984): 54, 135-36, 138, 178-79, 210. (Decker [1979]: 23: "That basically is the difference between Mormonism and Christianity.") Once again, Forrest, "Are Mormons Christian?" contains a brief summary of the charge, and a concise but effective reply; cf. also Scharffs (1986): 18-19, 21-22, 39, 96, 191-95, 198-200, 241-42, 275. Pressau (1977): 1, is apt here: "It is a scandal that the widest credibility gap among Christians is caused by the many meanings of this central doctrine of 'the faith which was once for all delivered to the saints.' It's ironic that the salvation understanding gap generates so much condescension and pride from some Christians and so much suspicion and ill will from others when *both* were exhorted to 'love one another.' "

470 Van Baalen (1983): 159; Fraser (1977): 59. Sometimes this charge is associated with a claim that Mormons place unbiblical limits on the efficacy of Christ's atonement—a rather self-contradictory association, by the way. Without debating that particular issue, we might note the controversies in the early church on the limits of forgiveness; cf. Brox (1983): 124-32.

salvation and is sufficient to atone for personal sins as well as Adam's transgression.) We shall therefore not take this claim up in detail. Mormons simply do not view the atonement in precisely the terms to which Fraser and van Baalen are accustomed; the Latter-day Saint position probably diverges far less from normative Christianity than their portrayal implies. V. M. Bonniwell says Mormons "teach the heresy called Galatianism. 'Galatianism' is the false doctrine condemned in Galatians. It is mixing grace and works in salvation, the mixing of Jesus's blood with our own merits in order to save us from our sins."[471] This idea is sometime termed synergism, from the Greek words *syn* ("together with") and *ergon* ("work"). It is opposed to "monergism," (*monos*, "alone"). "Implicit in solafidianism is the doctrine of divine monergism, which declares that man's salvation is totally dependent upon God's activity and is in no way conditioned by the action of man."[472] Mormonism is often linked as well, even by sympathetic observers, to the doctrines of the fifth-century British monk, Pelagius, who was fiercely combatted by Augustine and, finally, condemned by Pope Zosimus in A.D. 418.[473] Konrad Algermissen, a Catholic, sees in Mormon teaching "a Pelagianism . . . which devalues the significance of grace in justification and sanctification."[474]

---

471 In *The Utah Evangel* 31 (May 1984): 5. It is highly ironic that Martin (1955): 103-05, 113-14, seems to make one single exception to his rule that salvation is by grace without works: Agitation against "cults" is a positive requirement of true Christianity. Martin denounces a publisher who would not assist him in his crusade: "Here was a man who ignored the commands of Scripture without blinking, and yet expressed as his motto complete trust in the promises of God." (See p. 105. This could, incidentally, serve as a Mormon's description of a fundamentalist!) "The Christian today who . . . refuses to engage in apologetics when he realizes its import, is in direct disobedience to the revealed will of God and cannot forever escape judgment of a severe nature" (p. 114).

472 Elwell (1983): 1032.

473 So, for example, McMurrin (1965), foreword: "Mormon theology is a modern Pelagianism in a Puritan religion."

474 Council of Trent, Session VI, Canon 12, in Algermissen (1962): 7. It should be noted, however, that Algermissen does *not* deny Mormon Christianity.

But are Mormons uniquely guilty here? "If anyone," proclaimed the Catholic Counter-Reformation's Council of Trent (1545-1563), "saith that justifying faith is nothing else but confidence in the divine mercy which remits sin for Christ's sake alone; or, that this confidence alone is that whereby we are justified, let him be anathema."[475] Father Heribert Holzapfel noted years ago that the "Sekten" and the Catholics frequently share a common attitude on the question of justification, an attitude quite different from that of the churches of the Reformation.[476] The Catholic anti-Mormon, W. J. Whalen, revealingly remarks that the Latter-day Saints reject "the distinctive Protestant doctrine of justification by faith alone."[477] The *Oxford English Dictionary* quotes a certain Bishop Montagu, from 1625: "In the point of Freewill the Church of Rome absolutely and wholly Pelagianizeth."[478] To put it bluntly, if the Mormons are Pelagians, are not the Catholics, too?

Some Protestant fundamentalists are not at all shy about saying just that. "Catholicism teaches a salvation based on works in addition to faith," notes a volume entitled *Exposing the Deceivers: Nine Cults and What They Teach*. This causes some to "question whether or not they are a New Testament church."[479] Catholic doctrine on salvation "is an impostor. It is a counterfeit, a fraud, a hoax." It is "of Satan."[480] Our fundamentalist heresiographers

---

475 Cited by Boettner (1986): 261.

476 Holzapfel (1925): 10-11.

477 Whalen (1963): 167.

478 The *Oxford English Dictionary* also quotes one H. Burton, who wrote, in his 1629 *Truth's Triumph*, of "those Pelagianizing enemies of the grace of God."

479 Breese et al. (1985): 56; cf. Green (1984b); Green (1984c). Cattau (1986): 8-10, describes what a thorny issue this has been in Lutheran-Catholic dialogue. Yet he does not label Catholicism a "non-Christian cult." Our "experts," on the other hand, are not always so circumspect. For quotations from the Council of Trent containing Roman Catholic denunciations of Protestant teachings on salvation by grace alone, see Zacchello (1984): 99-100.

480 Dunlap, "Alex Dunlap Answers Roman Catholic Priest," 9.

routinely attack Rome for "legalism."[481] H. A. Ironside accuses Rome of "the Galatian heresy"—just like the Latter-day Saints.[482] Roman Catholicism, says H. J. Berry in his *Examining the Cults*, "rejects the Bible's teaching of salvation by grace through faith in Christ alone." "Such departures from the Scriptures . . . in the basic area of salvation blind the eyes of its followers to the grace of God which is in Christ Jesus."[483] One ex-Catholic ex-Mormon now-Protestant anti-Mormon, relating his story, says that, as a Catholic, he was "religious but unsaved." Catholicism is, he says, "a system of works." And, like Mormonism, it is strongly implied to be both non-Christian and Satanic.[484] Other writers are more direct. The Roman Catholic Church, Alex Dunlap declares, "has no relationship at all with Jesus Christ, my Saviour."[485] "I was a Roman Catholic," reports Stella Ciampa of her early life, "but not a Christian." Her onetime fellow Catholics, she laments, "are earnestly trying to merit eternal life through good works, but good works cannot save. . . . It is my desire to see them become true Christians."[486] Leave "the papal system," pleads Alex Dunlap. "Come to Christ."[487] Catholicism is sometimes described as representing a subtle and nuanced synergism.[488] By the standards anti-Mormons use on the Latter-day Saints, the Church of Rome must therefore fall outside the bounds of Christendom.

It may, of course, not bother some anti-Mormons to call Catholics non-Christians (although it most certainly will disturb

---

481 So Ridenour (1979): 27-51; cf. Zacchello (1984): 172.

482 Ironside (1982): 16-17; cf. 24, 32-40.

483 Berry (1979): 98, 99; cf. Zacchello (1984): 76, 86-90, 102-111; Spittler (1962): 109, 112, 116; Boettner (1986): 254-69.

484 Ed Kelly, in *The Utah Evangel* 33 (July/August 1986): 6.

485 Dunlap, "Alex Dunlap Answers Roman Catholic Priest," 8.

486 Ciampa, "Catholic or Christian?"

487 Dunlap, "Alex Dunlap Answers Roman Catholic Priest," 10-11.

488 For example, by Harvey (1964): 233.

most ordinary users of the word). But what will the anti-Mormons do with Luther's close associate, Philipp Melanchthon, one of the founding fathers of Protestantism? He, for one, was disturbed by some of the implications of Luther's extreme position on salvation by grace alone, and flirted with a doctrine of synergism, of works combining with faith in the attainment of salvation.[489] Was Melanchthon a Christian? We have found nobody who denies that he was. We cannot understand, therefore, how the Latter-day Saints can be purged from Christendom for holding a view rather similar to his.

Other believers in Jesus, besides the Catholics and leading reformers, are in danger of expulsion from Christendom for similar reasons. "Eastern Orthodox Christians," for instance, "emphasize a unity of faith and works. For the Orthodox, being conformed to the image of Christ . . . includes a response of our faith *and* works."[490] Where did they and the Catholics and Philipp Melanchthon get such a notion? To some, their position seems merely to represent the culmination of a historical trend toward ethical emphasis within Christianity, a regrettable tendency toward "moralism" and "legalism." The Protestant scholar Justo Gonzales, with considerable distaste, identifies that tendency already in the early postapostolic Church. The situation was worst in the Roman West, he says, but it was bad everywhere. The Apostolic Fathers just don't seem to have understood the Protestant doctrine of salvation by grace alone.[491] "It has often been remarked," writes F. F. Bruce, "that the Biblical doctrine of divine grace, God's favour shown to sinful humanity, so clearly (as we might think) expounded in the teaching of Christ and the writings of Paul, seems almost to go underground in the postapostolic age, to reappear only with Augustine. Certainly the majority of Christian writers who flourished between the apostles and Augustine do not seem to have

---

489 Brauer (1971); 799-800.

490 Rusch (1986): 12 (emphasis ours). This view is reminiscent of the Book of Mormon, at 2 Nephi 25:23.

491 Gonzales (1970): 1:94-96.

grasped what Paul was really getting at. . . . Marcion has been called the only one of these writers who understood Paul, and even he misunderstood him."[492]

Marcion!! Can this be the same heretic that Polycarp of Smyrna (d. A.D. 160) called "the first-born of Satan"? Yes, indeed it is.[493] Marcion was a second-century Gnostic Christian who distinguished between the God of the Old Testament—a mere demiurge, a kind of lesser supernatural craftsman—and the God of the New Testament, whom he termed "the Father." Thus, he rejected the Old Testament utterly, as well as any New Testament writings too much "tainted" with Old Testament ideas. He produced a canon of Scripture—the first—which recognized no apostle of Jesus except Paul. (The other apostles were considered falsifiers of the Gospel.) With his rejection of the Hebrew Bible and the law, and his fixation on Paul, one is tempted to see in Marcion the first Protestant. Certainly it is intriguing that an evangelical Protestant like F. F. Bruce would, on the issue of faith and works, feel more comfortable with Marcion than with the Apostolic Fathers. (It is especially striking since Augustine, Prof. Bruce's other authority, is now recognized by many scholars to have brought much of his own Manichaean—i.e., quasi-gnostic—background with him into Christianity.)[494]

If Protestants like Gonzales and Bruce have pictured Christian thought as degenerating from an early grace-alone position to a later focus on "works-righteousness," other scholarly observers, including Edwin Hatch, have identified the trend as leading in quite the opposite direction. To them, a growing emphasis on doctrine, on orthodoxy, came to supplant the ethical focus of earliest Christianity.[495] And it must be said that they have far better early examples

---

492 Bruce (1979): 334.

493 See Irenaeus, *Against Heresies* III, 3, 4. English translation in Roberts and Donaldson (1981): 1:416.

494 See Phipps (1980); also Teske (1986): 233-49.

495 See Hatch (1970): 1, cited above; cf. Brox (1983): 138.

for their position than Bruce's Marcion. The famous *Didache*, for instance, otherwise known as the *Teaching of the Twelve Apostles*, which dates back to before A.D. 70, is conspicuous for its "moralism and legalism."[496] That extremely early and important text found echo in the writers of the next century, who, knowingly or not, carried on its ethical emphasis. The second-century *Shepherd of Hermas* contains twelve commandments, which "are a summary of the duties of a Christian, and Hermas affirms that in obeying them there is eternal life." (This hardly sounds like salvation by grace alone.) Indeed, summarizes J. L. Gonzales, "it is possible to do more than the commandment requires, and thus to attain a greater glory." Ignatius of Antioch, that centrally important Father of the early second century, downplays Jesus' function as redeemer from sin, in order to emphasize the Son's role as revealer of God. "In fact, in the epistles of Ignatius the word 'sin' appears only once." On the other hand, Ignatius could advise Polycarp: "Let your works be your deposits, that you may receive the back-pay due to you."[497] Clearly, the saint was not a born-again saved-by-grace Protestant. Was he a Christian? The great Greek church fathers John Chrysostom and Gregory Nazianzen both seem to have advocated a synergistic doctrine in which man's effort to do good cooperates with God's assisting grace.[498]

According to the illustrious Werner Jaeger, "The oldest datable literary document of Christian religion soon after the time of the apostles is the letter of Clement of Rome to the Corinthians, written in the last decade of the first century." In it, "the special emphasis is on good works, as it is in the Epistle of James, which may belong to the same time and is so clearly polemical against

---

496 See Gonzales (1970): 1:69.

497 Ignatius of Antioch, *Epistle to Polycarp* 6:2. English translation in Lake (1970): 1:275.

498 Kelly (1978): 352. This, too, in the context of salvation understood as deification.

Paul."[499] Was Clement a Christian? Was James? The evangelical Protestant scholar James D. G. Dunn sees Jewish Christian loyalty to the Mosaic law, and thus to "works," throughout large portions of the New Testament.[500] And the prominent philosopher-theologian Frederick Sontag argues eloquently that Jesus himself was interested not in words, and not even in theological dogma, but in action. For the Jesus of Matthew, he says, "action is more important than definition."[501] Again we must ask, given the standards of the anti-Mormons, was Jesus a Christian?

One of the aspects of Mormonism which most upsets its critics in this regard is the insistence of the restored Gospel upon the ordinances of the priesthood as requirements for exaltation. Yet they have, in this regard, strong precedent in the beliefs of the ancient church. We will content ourselves with mentioning just one prominent Christian bishop, Cyril of Jerusalem (ca. A.D. 313-386), one of the so-called "Doctors of the Church." Cyril insisted strongly on the necessity of rituals.[502] "If any man receive not Baptism," he wrote, "he hath not salvation."[503] Intriguingly, too, Cyril wrote of an ordinance called "anointing," or "chrism." This ritual is of great interest, not only for the issue of faith and works but for the general subject of this essay, since, in connection with it, Cyril offers an unusually precise definition of what it takes to be

---

499 Jaeger (1961): 12, 15-16.

500 Dunn (1977): 245-52.

501 See Sontag (1986), especially 116-18. The quotation is from p. 116.

502 Not unlike the Catholic idea of "sacramental grace." Which is, itself, not altogether different from Mormon notions.

503 Cyril of Jerusalem, *Catechetical Lecture* III, 10. English translation in Schaff and Wace (1978): 7:16. He excepts "only Martyrs, who even without the water receive the Kingdom." Roman Catholics, too, hold that baptism is essential to salvation; cf. *This We Believe* (1962): 261; Zacchello (1984): 194; P. B. Smith (1970): 26-29, denounces Rome on this score. Irvine (1921): 29-33, inveighs against belief in "baptismal regeneration" as a "Roman heresy" which somehow has crept into the Church of England prayer book. He would be no fonder of Mormon beliefs on the subject.

a Christian. "Having been counted worthy of this Holy Chrism," he says, "ye are called Christians. . . . For before you were deemed worthy of this grace, ye had properly no right to this title."[504] The roughly contemporary Valentinian compilation known as *The Gospel According to Philip* lays down a similar rule: "Chrism has more authority than baptism. For because of chrism we are called Christians."[505] This definition of Christianity is significant not only because it seems to require a "work," but also because of the nature of that work. While the Latter-day Saints possess an ordinance called "anointing," their fundamentalist adversaries know nothing of any such ritual. By Cyril's standard, then, the Mormons have a chance of being Christians, but anti-Mormons seem to have no chance at all.

Sometime between November 1512 and July 1513, after an intense preoccupation with Paul's teaching in Romans 1:17, Martin Luther came to his doctrine of *sola gratia*, salvation by "grace alone." But we have seen that there is evidence that many earlier Christians did not at all hold to such a position. E. P. Sanders, among the foremost living authorities on the great apostle, points out that Luther's view "has often been shown to be an incorrect interpretation of Paul," and cautions that "we misunderstand [Paul] if we see him through Luther's eyes."[506] We could go further, in fact, and argue that the notion of salvation by grace alone hardly existed in early Christianity until, devoured by his own well-earned moral guilt and under the sway of his Manichaean past, Augustine introduced it. And it is clear thereafter that the vast majority of Christians continued to hold to the view that good works were

---

504 Cyril of Jerusalem, *Catechetical Lecture* XXI, 5. English translation in Schaff and Wace (1976): 7:150. On the anointing, see 1 John 2:20, 27. The words "chrism," "Christ," and "Christian" all derive from the Greek verb *chrio*, "to anoint."

505 *The Gospel According to Philip* 74:12-15. English translation in Layton (1987): 346.

506 J. O. Sanders (1991): 49; cf. 44, 48.

necessary to salvation. That, after all, is the position that Luther argued against, and that formed the background of his great "discovery."

However, we have shown clearly enough that important early Christian documents and personalities seem not to have shared the Protestant insistence on salvation by grace alone. Isn't it an odd use of the term "Christian" that might deny it to virtually all Christians before the sixteenth century, and to the great majority afterward? And does it seem that such a much-disputed question is a good one upon which to base the Mormons' summary excommunication from Christendom?[507]

Incidentally, since V. M. Bonniwell has compared the Latter-day Saints to the Galatians, it is worth noting that the eminent evangelical Protestant scholar F. F. Bruce refers to them as "Judaizing Christians."[508] We are aware of no authority who denies their Christianity. Are Mormons, then, who allegedly share in the heresy of Galatianism, to be termed non-Christians when the original "heretics" are not?

---

507 After all, the criticisms can go both ways. Mormons tend to suspect their adversaries of preaching what Dietrich Bonhoeffer called "cheap grace," or, in a phrase quoted by Pressau (1977): 38, "a theologically thin, no-sweat Christianity." But Mormons don't deny the Christianity of those who disagree. For a good summary of the Catholic position, see Pohle, "Grace," in Herbermann (1909): 6:689-714. It should perhaps be clear from these articles that there is more that could be said on this matter than the often simplistic presentations of fundamentalist anti-Mormons would seem to allow; cf. for example, Macquarrie (1973): 144-49, for a Protestant view in the Bultmannian tradition. (Would anti-Mormons call Bultmann Christian? He seems to agree fairly closely with them on this issue.) E. P. Sanders (1991): 37, 44-76, 84-116, 121-122, offers an analysis of Paul's thought on grace and works that will give little comfort to Protestant anti-Mormons. And, indeed, a recent article by Snodgrass (1986), entitled "Justification by Grace—to the Doers," argues for an interpretation of Paul that is quite close to the Mormon stance. Likewise, the prominent evangelical preacher John F. MacArthur, Jr., has cast doubt upon simplistic teachings of salvation by grace alone in a book which has lately been at the center of a notable controversy among conservative Protestants; cf. MacArthur (1989).

508 Bruce (1979): 108.

Claim 16. Mormonism is non-Christian because, having rejected justification by faith, its adherents cannot be confident of having salvation *now.*[509]

Response. But neither, apparently, could Ignatius.[510] Nor can Roman Catholics.[511] "Official RC dogma," complains Alex Dunlap, "declares a person who claims to know he is saved to be guilty of the sin of presumption."[512] "Most priests aren't saved!" exclaims Jimmy Swaggart. "The average priest has never met the Lord Jesus Christ as his own personal Saviour."[513] And while most Roman Catholic authorities would probably resist Swaggart's formulation, they would certainly reject the implication that grace, having once entered into a person's life, guarantees that person's salvation regardless of the sins he or she may later choose to commit. "There is no salvation," writes the Jesuit Father Hardon, "for those who, though incorporated in the Church by baptism, fail to persevere in sanctifying grace and die in the state of mortal sin."[514]

Actually, of course, members of The Church of Jesus Christ of Latter-day Saints believe that it is possible to have "the assurance that they [are] pursuing a course which [is] agreeable to the will of God." They are convinced that each individual saint can have "actual knowledge, realizing that when these sufferings are ended, he will enter into eternal rest and be a partaker of the glory of God." Such assurance is in fact the theme of the sixth Lecture on

---

509   See, as an example, Rowe (1985): 30-31; Decker (1979): 22; Fraser (1977): 14-15, 188. For Zacchello (1984): 108, this is one of the marks of "a true Christian." So, too, for Green (1984c) and Ransom, "It's Great to KNOW You're SAVED!"

510   This seems to be implied at Ignatius, *Romans* 3:2.

511   Ironside (1982): 14-15; Zacchello (1984): 108; Green (1984c); P. B. Smith (1970): 34-35; Boettner (1986): 264, 267-69.

512   Dunlap, "Alex Dunlap Answers Roman Catholic Priest," 9.

513   Swaggart (1985b): 39.

514   Hardon (1981): 98.

Faith, from which the preceding quotes have been taken.[515] Some anti-Mormons have sought to portray the Latter-day Saints as terrified of God's judgment, unsure of their standing before the Lord, desperately and vainly trying to pile up good works in order to buy off his arbitrary wrath, utterly lacking the peace that only born-again Protestantism can offer. This is not, however, a picture that most Latter-day Saints would recognize. Mormons worship a loving Father, who cares for and forgives his children, who has provided a Savior for them and deeply desires that all should be saved. It is mainstream "orthodox" Christianity, not Mormonism, that gave the world Dante's *Inferno* and the bottomless pit so luridly described by Jonathan Edwards.

Claim 17. "Christianity teaches Jesus is the only Son of God. But Mormonism proclaims that Jesus has a brother whose name is Lucifer."[516] Therefore, the Latter-day Saints cannot be considered Christian.

Response. This is a classic instance of how failure to supply the context of a belief—or, perhaps more to the point, refusal to do so—can make that belief seem horrific or bizarre, when in fact it is not strange at all. Karl Keating reports similar tactics among anti-Catholics: "It must be admitted," he writes, "they enjoy a certain tactical (if short-term) advantage in that they can get away with presenting bare-bones claims such as these; they wear out Catholicism's defenders by inundating them with short remarks that demand long explanations."[517]

Implicit in the anti-Mormon argument cited above is the assumption that it is impossible to affirm, at the same time, both the unique divine Sonship of Jesus Christ and Satan's kinship to both Jesus and ourselves as a spirit brother. But anyone who has studied Mormon doctrine can readily see that, given their theological

---

515 Lecture 6, paragraphs 3 and 5. The text is that given in Dahl and Tate (1990): 91-92.

516 *The Utah Evangel* 31 (January 1984): 12; cf. Decker, "Petition"; Decker and Hunt (1984): 199-201 (vs. Scharffs [1986]: 258).

517 Keating (1988): 75.

premises, Mormons can perfectly well affirm the latter statement while still agreeing with the former. Strictly speaking, there is no contradiction. Lucifer, Jesus, the angels, the entire human race—all are akin because all are the spirit children of God, our Heavenly Father. Thus, we are all brothers and sisters. But, in this world, Jesus Christ holds the utterly unique status of the Only Begotten Son of the Father in the flesh. The contradiction assumed by our anti-Mormon critics on this point simply does not exist when the doctrine of the Latter-day Saints is examined fairly and on its own terms.

Besides, a rather similar doctrine to that of the Mormons was taught by the Latin father, Lactantius (d. A.D. 320), whom all affirm to be Christian.[518] "According to Lactantius," as Giovanni Papini summarizes his position, "Lucifer would have been nothing less than the brother of the Logos. . . . The elder spirit, filled with every divine virtue and beloved by God above all other spirits, can easily be recognized as the Word, that is, the Son. But Lactantius's story leads one to think that the other spirit, also endowed with every grace, was the second son of the Father: the future Satan would be, no less, the younger brother of the future Christ."[519] If Lactantius could hold such a belief and still be a Christian, how can The Church of Jesus Christ of Latter-day Saints be driven from Christendom for teaching a similar doctrine?

The idea that Lucifer is a spirit child of God, gone wrong, seems to us no more obviously blasphemous, incidentally, than does the mainstream Christian notion that he is God's creation from nothing. Consider the following question: Who is more blameworthy—a loving father whose son, departing from the teachings of his youth, grows up to be a murderer? Or a brilliant inventor who,

---

518 See Lactantius, *Divine Institutes* II, 9. Among those who term Lactantius Christian are Brauer (1971): 481; Holzapfel (1925): 9; Cross and Livingstone (1983): 791; Brox (1983): 155; C. P. Williams, "Lactantius," in Douglas (1978): 575; Meagher, O'Brien, and Aherne (1979): 2:2018; Kraft (1966): 337-40.

519 Papini (1984): 81-82. Papini admits that he has found no similar belief in any other Christian theologian.

knowing full well what he is doing, deliberately creates a murderous robot? The answer seems clear enough to us. Yet the very people who denounce Latter-day Saints for saying that Lucifer is akin to God, although evil, seem to see no problem in affirming that an all-knowing, all-powerful, perfectly free God purposely created Satan out of nothing. We fail to see, however, in precisely what way such a view represents a vast improvement over Mormon teaching. Indeed, it seems to us that our critics' view involves God the Father in such matters as Auschwitz and the Cambodian massacres in a far more direct way than does that of the Latter-day Saints, just as the murderous robot's inventor is more directly implicated in its actions than is the disappointed father of a wayward son.

Bill Forrest offers yet another observation on this question, one worth noting here. Anti-Mormons, he points out, sometimes argue that Mormons have the wrong Jesus because their Jesus—unlike "the Jesus of the Bible"—has a spirit brother named Lucifer. But, Forrest points out, "it is just as logical to argue that Mormons have *the wrong Lucifer*, because *he* has a spirit brother named Jesus." And indeed, since "the Mormon Jesus" seems, as we have seen, to match in so many clear ways the characteristics of "the Jesus of the Bible," it would seem more plausible to say that the Latter-day Saints, if they are mistaken at all, have made their error in connection with the character of Satan rather than the person of Christ. But would such an error be weighty enough to expel millions of believers in Jesus from Christendom? Is Lucifer more important than God in the minds of some anti-Mormons?[520]

Claim 18. Mormons are not Christian. Instead, as Paul foretold in Galatians 1:6-9, they preach "another gospel."[521]

---

520 See Forrest, "The Wrong Jesus?" in *Mormon Issues* 1, p. 3.

521 See, for example, J. O. Sanders (1962): 120; "What Is a Cult?"; Decker, "To Moroni with Love," 21-22; "Questions and Answers"; "The Mormon Church and the African"; and "Mormonism: Christian or Cult?" The passage is quoted in the form-letter sent to all who request information from the Southern California chapter of Ex-Mormons for Jesus.

Response. But, obviously, this "argument" assumes what it is intended to prove—and so proves nothing. Besides, such passages can be applied to anyone the critic chooses. This particular one is often applied to Roman Catholics. ("Professional anti-Catholics," observes Karl Keating, "take the fundamentalist position as a given, the Catholic position as a usurpation, and their chief concern is to undermine the latter, not to justify the former.")[522] The Chick Publications pamphlet "Are Roman Catholics Christians?" informs its readers that "Roman Catholics trust in 'another gospel,' a gospel of works with no assurance of salvation."[523]

Latter-day Saints, too, can make use of this passage. After all, Protestant doctrine is precisely as far from Mormon doctrine, every bit as "different," as Mormon doctrine is from Protestant doctrine. Latter-day Saints see the prophecy fulfilled in the rise of apostate Christianity, including fundamentalist Protestantism.[524] (And we might incidentally add that, as historians of religion, the Mormon concept of a universal apostasy seems to us an entirely plausible model of Christian history.)

Claim 19. Mormonism is non-Christian because, in the nineteenth century, it practiced the hideous doctrine of blood atonement—killing heretics, adulterers, and the like.[525]

Response. This accusation was denied by nineteenth-century Mormon leaders, and it is rejected by every reputable historian of nineteenth-century Mormonism.[526] On the other hand, there is no

---

522   Keating (1988): 67.

523   Chick Publications February 1990 Retail Catalog, 8.

524   E.g., in W. Thompson, "What We Should Know about Roman Catholicism"; Breese et al. (1985): 49; Ironside (1982): 4; Irvine (1921): 144; Boettner (1986): 10. Note the title of the work by P. B. Smith, which covers Catholicism. (For a Catholic response, see Holzapfel [1925]: 22-23.)

525   See "Blood Atonement and the Mormon Church." Also Fraser (1977): 20; Whalen (1963): 170-71; Decker and Hunt (1984): 232-33 (vs. Scharffs [1986]: 334-36).

526   See, for example, Brigham Young's denial in his interview with Horace Greeley, 13 July 1859 (Greeley [1968]: 9:132-35). A sampling of historians:

doubt at all that burnings and inquisitions abound in the history of Christendom, in Calvinist Geneva and Elizabethan London and colonial Salem, in Zwingli's Zürich as well as in Rome. As the *Catholic Encyclopedia* remarks, "it is well known that belief in the justice of punishing heresy with death was so common among the sixteenth-century reformers—Luther, Zwingli, Calvin, and their adherents—that we may say their toleration began where their power ended."[527]

Latter-day Saints know very well how traditional Christianity— emphatically not excluding clergy—can treat heretics. Much of nineteenth-century Mormon history is a desperate attempt to get away from murderous "Christians."

Claim 20. Mormonism is non-Christian because it once advocated polygamy.[528]

Response. Frequently lurking behind such charges is a hostility among traditional Christian thinkers toward embodiment and sexuality—a hostility that reaches its most extreme form in such manifestations as anchorite asceticism and priestly celibacy, but which is certainly not limited to these. The great formulator of such Christian attitudes is Augustine, of whom Daniel Maguire states that, "On matters of sex and marriage . . . Augustine the Christian was never fully free of Mani."[529] "Does Augustine's understanding of sex and marriage," wonders Eugene Hillman, "perhaps owe more to his own pagan background, and particularly to his Mani-

---

Kimball (1981): 209-10; Arrington and Bitton (1979): 54, 353; Allen and Leonard (1976): 121-22; Sessions (1982): 124-30, 391; Arrington (1985): 250, 253; Bringhurst (1986): 36, 130. There is a strand of Latter-day Saint thought, it is true, that resembles something we might call "blood atonement," though it is light-years removed from the murderous fantasies ascribed to Mormons by some of their critics. E. P. Sanders (1991): 106-107 indicates that similar thinking underlies 1 Corinthians 5:4-5.

527 Blötzer, "Inquisition," in Herbermann et al. (1910): 8:35.

528 Martin (1955): 51; cf. van Baalen (1983): 152-60; Johnson (1983): 434. Johnson's brief treatment of Mormonism is a great disappointment in an otherwise superb book, and especially so to admirers of his *Modern Times.*

529 Maguire (1970): 8; cf. P. Brown (1969): 369; Feucht (1961): 51-53.

chaean experience, than to his Christian faith?" It would be ironic, would it not, if it turns out that anti-Mormons are using a standard derived from pagans—from Manichaeans and Platonists (or even, most amusingly, from Hindus)—to determine the limits of Christianity on this issue?[530]

In fact, Christian history demonstrates beyond question that polygamy cannot be used as a club with which to drive the Mormons from Christendom. It is too blunt an instrument, and would chase too many obvious Christians from the fold as well.[531] The sixth-century Arab Christian kings of Lakhm and Ghassan were polygamists, for instance, as were the contemporary Christians of Ethiopia.[532] Pope Clement VII, faced with the threat of a continent-dividing divorce, considered bigamy as a solution to the problem of Henry VIII. Was he, with such thoughts, flirting with becoming a non-Christian?[533] Did Martin Luther cease to be a Christian when he made the same suggestion, in September 1531, to King Henry's envoy, Robert Barnes?[534] Nearly a decade later, Luther counselled Philip of Hesse to take Margaret von der Sale as a second wife. He justified the idea from the Old Testament, as the Mormons would in a later century. Furthermore, he suggested public denial. (Generally, he had written in an earlier letter, he favored monogamy, remarking that "a Christian is not free to marry several wives *unless God commands him* to go beyond the liberty

---

530 Not a few scholars have argued for India as the ultimate source of Christian monasticism as well as Islamic Sūfism. Asceticism may well have its earliest recorded manifestation among the early non-Aryan populace of the Indian subcontinent.

531 For a somewhat similar argument to what follows, see S. E. Robinson (1991): 91-96.

532 Margoliouth (1905): 38, 160.

533 See Holst (1967): 212, n. 2.

534 For the Latin texts of two letters to Barnes related to this issue, with notes, see Enders (1903), 9:80-99.

which is conditioned by love.")[535] But when Philip actually did marry Margaret in March of 1540, he did so—contrary to Luther's counsel—publicly. Indeed, the marriage was performed by Philip's Lutheran chaplain and in the presence of Luther's chief lieutenants, Philipp Melanchthon and Martin Bucer. Needless to say, a storm of criticism broke out. Writing to John Frederick of Saxony on 10 June 1540, Luther declared, "I am not ashamed of the counsel I gave even if it should become known throughout the world. Because it is unpleasant, however, I should prefer, if possible, to have it kept quiet."[536] Was Luther a pagan? Did his associates, Bucer and Melanchthon, leave Christianity when they joined in Luther's advice?[537] Of course not. This was "Christian Polygamy in the Sixteenth Century," as Elder Orson Pratt termed it in a well-informed 1853 article.[538] Citing the statement by Luther, Melanchthon, and Bucer, to the effect that "the Gospel hath neither recalled nor forbid what was permitted in the law of Moses with respect to marriage," Elder Pratt quite correctly concluded that the case of Philip of Hesse "proves most conclusively, that those Divines did sincerely believe it to be just as legal and lawful for a Christian to have two wives as to have one only."[539]

Yet many Protestant Christians today are convinced that polygamy disqualifies Latter-day Saints from acceptance within Christendom. Why? "What is surprising," notes Manas Buthelezi,

---

535 From a letter of 1526, in Tappert (1955): 276 (emphasis ours). The parallel to Jacob 2:27-30 should be obvious.

536 An English translation of the letter is found in Tappert (1955): 288-91. For a brief account of the incident, see Bainton (1950): 373-75.

537 See the annotated German text of a letter from Luther, Melanchthon, and Bucer, given in Enders (1903), 12:319-28. Compare Stupperich (1960): 95; Holst (1967): 212, n. 2; Manschreck (1985): 261-70. Later, in the eighteenth century, Friedrich Wilhelm II of Prussia took plural wives on at least two occasions, citing Luther's counsel to Philip of Hesse as a precedent and with the approval of his own Lutheran court chaplain; cf. Heinrich (1981): 257.

538 Pratt (1853): 177-83.

539 Pratt (1853): 179, 182.

"is that the Christian Church has raised this essentially cultural matter to the level of a soteriological absolute."[540]

Many observers of Christianity in Africa, including the illustrious modern Jesuit theologian Karl Rahner, have raised serious questions about whether Indo-European marital custom really belongs to the essence of being Christian.[541] "Let it be publicly declared," writes H. W. Turner, "that a polygamous African church may still be classed as a Christian church."[542] But if a "polygamous African church" can be called Christian, why cannot a once-polygamous American church? Anti-Mormons would not, we assume, want to claim that the definition of "Christian" differs between Africa and North America. If so, they will have to pinpoint the precise longitude where the difference kicks in.

Claim 21. Mormonism is non-Christian because its theology is in error. Mormons are mistaken about the nature of salvation, and their prophets have sometimes misspoken.[543] "Mormonism is a cult [and, hence, not Christian] because it is wrong about God."[544] The Mormon doctrine of deity is "such a confusion and contradiction that Mormonism's view is seen as absolutely non-Christian."[545]

Response. But this is rather strange even if one were to grant, for the moment, that such accusations are merited. Has confusion become the unpardonable sin? Must Christians be theologically

---

540 Buthelezi (1969): 69.

541 See Hillman (1975), Buthelezi (1969), and Holst (1967).

542 Turner (1966): 321.

543 These views are stated, in an especially naive manner, in an April 1986 letter to one of the authors from a minister in Colorado.

544 *The Utah Evangel* 31 (March 1984): 8. "Christian" and "cult" are very frequently used by anti-Mormons as antonyms. (See, for example, Ed Decker's "The Mormon Dilemma: Christian or Cult?" which, incidentally, never really addresses the question it poses.) There is no justification in the lexicography of standard English for such a view.

545 Robertson (1983): 13.

error-free?[546] Does their Christianity depend upon adherence to Aristotle's principle of non-contradiction?

What, then, of such a character as the famous Calvinist preacher-theologian Jonathan Edwards? There are profound differences between the God of his sermons and the God of his theoretical treatises. Of Edwards, A. O. Lovejoy could write that he "did not differ from most of the great theologians in having many Gods under one name."[547] Do his inconsistencies expel him from Christendom? But we need not pick on Edwards, for the disagreements among the various denominations of Christendom (and, more and more, within them) are legendary. Is Arminianism correct, or strict Calvinism? They are mutually contradictory. Yet both are called Christian.

Similarly, the Quakers and Catholics cannot both be right. Quakers look to inner illumination for guidance, while Catholics rely on an infallible papacy. Protestantism, complains Father Holzapfel, is a "subjectivism, which recognized no infallible authority in religious things."[548] Catholicism is a strongly liturgical tradition, but the Quakers have no liturgy at all. Which group—if either—is Christian?

At what precise point do mistakes disqualify someone from being a Christian? Who set the standard? And who granted the authority to do so? In fact, of course, theological error is very much a matter of opinion. So varied have been Christian beliefs through the centuries that it is sometimes tempting to see Christianity as "largely a unity of name."[549] A Greek high school textbook notes that "extreme Protestant groups such as Evangelicals,

---

546 S. E. Robinson (1991): 59-60, offers a brief discussion of this issue.

547 Lovejoy (1964): 44.

548 Holzapfel (1925): 10. Fundamentalists will respond that they do indeed have an infallible authority—the Bible. But Holzapfel has some rather penetrating criticisms of that position. In any case, the important point here is that this is the Catholic position, a position quite contrary to the Protestant one.

549 As Lovejoy (1964): 6, in fact does.

Pentecostals and Mormons are the worst heretics."[550] The Catholic Konrad Algermissen sees in Mormonism "a religious syncretism of the most varied heresies," and cites among them a teaching on the sacrament supposedly derived from American Protestantism, a view of baptism purportedly taken from the Baptists, and a doctrine of repentance allegedly absorbed from Methodism.[551] (In fact, Catholics generally—including Pope John Paul II—tend to use the term "sect" to cover all non-Catholic groups, specifically including the Latter-day Saints, Jehovah's Witnesses, and evangelical Protestants.)[552]

The question at issue is not whether Mormonism is true, and not whether it is theologically adequate. The question is, Is Mormonism Christian? If the critics want to argue that these are really one and the same question, they must do more than merely assume their conclusion.

Claim 22. Joseph Smith's so-called "First Vision" utterly separates Mormonism from Christianity.[553] "For most of its 155 year history . . . Mormonism has denied being Christian."[554] In-

---

550 Cited by John Carr, in the *Wall Street Journal* (16 June 1986).

551 Algermissen (1962): 47: "einen religiösen Synkretismus verschiedenster Irrlehren." Cf. Heribert Holzapfel's Catholic critique of the Baptists, at Holzapfel (1925): 35-45. Significantly, though, Catholics tend not to label those who disagree with them "non-Christian," as Molland (1959): 355, notes. Neither do Mormons.

552 See Maust (1990): 60-61.

553 Decker, "To Moroni with Love," 4-5, 18-19. This passage is rather opaque; cf. also Tucker (1989): 49, 91; Decker and Hunt (1984): 125; contrast Scharffs (1986): 182.

554 *The Utah Evangel* 33 (April 1986): 8; *The Evangel* 38 (April 1991): 4; *The Evangel* 36 (December 1989): 3; cf. Scharffs (1986): 86-87, for the incoherence of a similar charge made by the authors of *The God Makers*. The basis of this accusation is usually to be found in some such passage as Orson Pratt's remarks in *JD* 6:167. Tope, "Who's Persecuting Who? [*sic*]," has assembled a number of allegedly damning Mormon comments about Christianity. It would require more space and time than we have available here to respond on this issue. Suffice it to say that the critics pull such statements utterly out of context, making no effort to put them in what the theologians like to call their *Sitz im Leben*. The misinterpretation is so profound that it is, frankly, difficult to imagine that it is not intentional.

deed, it has generally denounced Christianity.[555] Its "nationwide effort to be known as Christian" is a campaign of only recent vintage.[556] Even now, though, Mormons never call themselves Christians.[557]

Response. This is plainly untrue. What is more, it is inconsistent with other allegations made by anti-Mormons. At the very least, our "experts" would seem to be divided against themselves. For if, as we have seen above, they charge that even the Articles of Faith represent a "deliberate attempt to deceive," the alleged Mormon campaign to feign a belief in Christ must have begun already by 1842! "We believe in God, the Eternal Father," says the well-known first Article of Faith, "and in His Son, Jesus Christ."

But the accusation that Latter-day Saints do not claim to be Christians simply cannot be sustained. Any number of statements from leaders of the Church throughout its history tell quite a different story.[558] Joseph Smith's statement of 8 May 1838, already quoted more than once in this essay, deserves repetition yet again: "The fundamental principles of our religion are the testimony of the Apostles and Prophets, concerning Jesus Christ, that He died, was buried, and rose again the third day, and ascended into heaven; and all other things which pertain to our religion are only append-

---

555 Decker and Hunt (1984): 245-46. But see Scharffs (1986): 352-53.

556 *The Utah Evangel* 31 (January 1984): 9, 12; (May 1986): 5; Decker and Hunt (1984): 199; contrast Scharffs (1986): 257.

557 Decker and Hunt (1984): 40, 46; cf. Scharffs (1986): 86-89, 121.

558 Some examples, chosen at random: Brigham Young, *JD* 14:198; Lorenzo Snow (fifth president of the Church), *JD* 4:239-40 (1 March 1857); Joseph F. Smith (sixth president of the Church), *JD* 23:169-75 (18 June 1882). The pamphlet by Forrest, "Are Mormons Christians?", is very short but recommended and contains several useful and enlightening quotations. Forrest and his colleague, Van Hale, have also reprinted some statements about Christianity by early Mormons in their *Scrapbook of Mormon Polemics*, No. 1. In most of these, a claim to be Christian must be inferred. It was not an issue for these men; they knew they were Christians. But the claim is clearly implied.

ages to it."[559] This hardly sounds like a denial or a denunciation of Christianity. Nor does the account of Captain Moroni in the Book of Mormon, published in 1830, where that great Nephite hero "prayed mightily unto his God for the blessings of liberty to rest upon his brethren, so long as there should a band of Christians remain to possess the land—For thus were all the true believers of Christ, who belonged to the church of God, called by those who did not belong to the church; . . . yea, all those who were true believers in Christ took upon them, gladly, the name of Christ, or Christians as they were called, because of their belief in Christ. . . . And therefore, at this time, Moroni prayed that the cause of the Christians . . . might be favored" (Alma 46:13-16).

The Church's newspaper in Nauvoo, *Times and Seasons*, reported in 1845 that "an imperial edict has been issued in China, giving Christian missionaries liberty to preach, and the Chinese freedom to embrace Christianity. . . . This will open the door for the Elders of the Latter-day Saints."[560] Why, if the Mormons did not consider themselves Christians, would they have expected any benefits from such an edict? Furthermore, the *Times and Seasons* occasionally recorded the excommunication of members of the Church for "unchristian conduct."[561] Why would they do such a thing, if they did not think themselves Christians? (Are Catholics excommunicated for "unbuddhist conduct"? Are Muslims punished for "conduct unbecoming a Hindu"?)

Joseph Smith's successor in the presidency of The Church of Jesus Christ of Latter-day Saints was just as emphatic as the founding prophet had been. "The moment the atonement of the Savior is done away," said Brigham Young, "that moment, at one sweep, the hopes of salvation entertained by the Christian world are destroyed, the foundation of their faith is taken away, and there is

---

559 *HC* 3:30. This is reminiscent of the simple summaries of Christianity given by Paul and Ignatius, as well as the Apostles' Creed. *TPJS*, 314, records a discourse of 9 July 1843, in which Joseph Smith implies that Latter-day Saints are Christians.

560 *Times and Seasons* 6 (15 November 1845): 1031.

561 As in *Times and Seasons* 5 (15 September 1844): 655.

nothing left for them to stand upon. When this is gone all the revelations God ever gave to the Jewish nation, to the Gentiles and to us are rendered valueless, and all hope is taken from us at one sweep."[562] "We hold the doctrines of Christianity," President Young told Horace Greeley on 13 July 1859.[563] "We are Christians professedly," he said in 1876, "according to our religion."[564] Even in somewhat bitter remembrance of the martyrdom of Joseph and Hyrum, Brigham Young aligned himself and his people with Christianity, referring with black humor to "our brother Christians who have slain the Prophets and butchered and otherwise caused the death of thousands of Latter-day Saints."[565] It is this sense of injury at the hands of other Christians—well justified, it must be said—that misleads our critics into the supposition that Mormons denounce Christianity. However, positive evaluations of Christianity were also made in comments addressed to audiences of Latter-day Saints. "We call ourselves Christians," Elder John Taylor, soon to become the third president of the Church, said in an 1873 address to the Salt Lake City Fourteenth Ward. "That is, we Methodists, Baptists, Presbyterians, Congregationalists, Episcopalians and 'Mormons,' we all call ourselves Christians. Well, perhaps we are, and then, perhaps we are not; it is a matter that would bear investigation, I think." His own investigation, he reported, showed that the Latter-day Saints have received the ancient gospel as taught to the first Christians.[566] This was the religion that John Taylor and other early Latter-day Saint converts

---

562 *JD* 14:41. Note Brigham's implicit assignment of Mormonism to "the Christian world." Compare the remark of Joseph F. Smith, sixth Mormon prophet, that "without Christ, revelation would not avail" (Smith and Kenney [1981]: 87). This was in a personal letter dated 14 July 1905, to his missionary son, George C. Smith—hardly part of some cynical public relations campaign.

563 Greeley (1968): 9:132.

564 *JD* 18:231 (17 September 1876). Compare his implication at *JD* 15:82 (2 June 1872).

565 *JD* 7:289.

566 *JD* 16:305-12 (16 November 1873).

had long sought. "We want no religion," wrote Elder Parley P. Pratt in his 1840 pamphlet "Plain Facts," "but pure Christianity."[567] Louis Alphonse Bertrand, in his autobiography *Mémoires d'un Mormon*, published in Paris in 1862, agreed: "Mormonism, it cannot be overemphasized, is merely Christianity enhanced by additional, timely revelation."[568] Then as now, the Latter-day Saints were convinced they had found "pure Christianity." In the words of a pair of contemporary scholars, nineteenth-century Mormons "saw their church as quintessentially Christian."[569]

There seems to be no evidence that leaders or members of The Church of Jesus Christ of Latter-day Saints have ever preferred to think of themselves as strangers to Christianity. Rather, as historian Klaus Hansen observes, they "have always emphatically insisted . . . that they are indeed Christians."[570] Wilford Woodruff, who would succeed John Taylor in the presidency of the Church, gave a conference speech on 9 October 1874 at the tabernacle in Salt Lake City, in which he equated "Christianity" with "the work of the Lord."[571] George Q. Cannon, who served as a counselor in the First Presidency to Brigham Young, John Taylor, Wilford Woodruff, and Lorenzo Snow, spoke of the Church as promulgating "a code of moral law by which the modern world, under the light of Christian truth, may achieve social redemption and be forever purified." In the same work, originally written in 1888, Cannon was quite content to cite with approval a journalist who, among other things, termed the Latter-day Saints a "sect of Christians."[572] During the annual conference of April 1916, Elder

---

567 Pratt (1990): 80.

568 "Le 'mormonisme,' nous ne saurions trop le redire, n'est autre chose que le christianisme complété par un supplément de révélation venu à son heure"; Bertrand (1862): 310 (our translation).

569 Bunker and Bitton (1983): 3.

570 Hansen (1981): 84.

571 *JD* 17: 245.

572 Cannon (1986): 438, 378.

George F. Richards of the Council of the Twelve implicitly identified Mormonism as Christian.[573] In April conference of 1920, Anthon H. Lund of the First Presidency expressed surprise that some would consider the Latter-day Saints non-Christians.[574] Anthony W. Ivins of the First Presidency was indignant at the same accusation during the annual conference of 1926. "The Church of Jesus Christ of Latter-day Saints," he declared, "is a Christian Church in the fullest sense of the word."[575] This was echoed on the next day by Elder Rudger Clawson of the Twelve, who declared, "We are decidedly a Christian church; . . . we are Christians."[576] In 1931, the seventh president of the Church, Heber J. Grant, expressly condemned claims that Latter-day Saints are not Christians.[577] His successor, George Albert Smith, in a 1945 address in Washington, D.C., also identified Mormons as Christians.[578] Joseph Fielding Smith, the tenth president of the Church, taught that Mormonism was "true Christianity," or "Christianity, pure and undefiled," as did his predecessor, David O. McKay.[579] President McKay explicitly blamed denials of Mormon Christianity on "bigotry" and "prejudice," declaring that the goal of the Latter-day Saints was to "Christianize" the world. "It is my sincere belief and testimony," he said in 1927, "that the

---

573 Report of the Eighty-Sixth Annual Conference of the Church of Jesus Christ of Latter-day Saints (1916): 53-54.

574 Report of the Ninetieth Annual Conference of the Church of Jesus Christ of Latter-day Saints (1920): 16.

575 Report of the Ninety-Sixth Annual Conference of the Church of Jesus Christ of Latter-day Saints (1926): 20; cf., generally, pp. 14-24; cf. also Pres. Ivins's remarks during the October conference of 1923.

576 Report of the Ninety-Sixth Annual Conference of The Church of Jesus Christ of Latter-day Saints (1926): 139.

577 Grant (1941): 98.

578 G. A. Smith (1948): 194, 206.

579 McConkie (1956): 3:290-91 (April 1924); 2:80 (April 1943); D. McKay (1953): 66, 91, 105 (representing statements made, respectively, in 1923, 1927, and 1934).

Latter-day Saints commonly called Mormons are Christians in the truest and fullest sense of the term."[580] "We are Christians," he repeated in 1952.[581] Such affirmations have continued to issue from Latter-day Saint leaders in more recent years. "Mormons are Christians," the late Elder Bruce R. McConkie, of the Council of the Twelve Apostles, declared in 1970, "and they have the only pure and perfect Christianity now on earth. Indeed, Mormonism is pure, unadulterated Christianity, restored anew in all its grandeur and glory."[582] Elder Robert E. Wells of the Seventy wrote an entire book on the question, entitled *We Are Christians Because* . . ., in 1985.

As we noted above, some vocal anti-Mormons claim that "Mormonism has denied being Christian" for "most of its . . . history."[583] The anti-Mormon *Evangel* often informs its readers that Latter-day Saints rejected the title of Christian for more than a century.[584] When? Where, from 1830 to the present, is there room for this alleged century of denial? Where is there room for any denial at all?

But it is not merely an occasional quotation that serves to illustrate the devotion of leaders of The Church of Jesus Christ of Latter-day Saints to the founder of Christianity. While presiding over the Church, John Taylor chose as the title of his 1882 book on the *Mediation and Atonement of Our Lord and Savior Jesus Christ* a phrase that clearly indicates his feelings on the subject. Is there anything remotely un-Christian, or anti-Christian, evident here?

---

580 He also made statements to this effect in 1923 and 1927. D. McKay (1953): 112, 120, 520-22.

581 D. McKay (1953): 533. President McKay implied the Christianity of Latter-day Saints in statements made in 1910, 1920, 1944, and 1947; cf. D. McKay (1953): 337, 294, 63, 275.

582 McConkie (1970): 2:113. Compare the strong assertions that Mormons are Christians in McConkie (1966): 132; Kimball (1982): 434.

583 *The Utah Evangel* 33 (April 1986): 8.

584 See, for instance, *The Evangel* 38 (April 1991): 4; *The Evangel* 36 (December 1989): 3.

And such literary productions have continued to issue from leaders of the Latter-day Saints. Commissioned by the presiding officers of the Church, James E. Talmage, of the Council of the Twelve, published his study of the life of Christ in his book *Jesus the Christ* in 1915. It has gone through scores of editions, and is one of the most beloved books in Mormondom, enjoying an almost quasi-canonical status. J. Reuben Clark, Jr., a counselor in the First Presidency of the Church for twenty-eight years and one of the most powerful men in twentieth-century Mormondom, labored long to produce his harmony of the gospels and 3 Nephi, which was finally published in 1954 as *Our Lord of the Gospels*. In none of these books is there the slightest hint of a campaign to deceive.

Bruce R. McConkie expressed something of the reverence that true Latter-day Saints feel for the title of "Christian" in a 1978 book, *The Promised Messiah*, directed to members of the Church. "Family members bear the family name; by it they are known and called and identified; it sets them apart from all those of a different lineage and ancestry. Adopted children take upon themselves the name of their newfound parents and become in all respects as though they had been born in the family." Having set up that general principle, he continued on to make its specific application: "And so it is that the children of Christ, those who are born again, those who are spiritually begotten by their new Father, take upon themselves the name of Christ. By it they are known; in it they are called; it identifies and sets them apart from all others. They are now family members, Christians in the real and true sense of the word." They "carry his name and are obligated to bear it in decency and dignity. No taint of shame or disgrace, no sliver of dishonor must ever be permitted to attach itself to that name 'which is above every name,' for 'at the name of Jesus every knee should bow' (Philippians 2:9-10) and pay homage to him who is above all save the Father only. The saints of God must remember who they are and act accordingly."[585] Thus, although, like all human beings, they probably want to be liked and known for what they

---

585 McConkie (1978): 363.

are, Latter-day Saints do not care to be known as Christians merely
for the sake of association with other believers in Christ. It is to
prevent misunderstanding and denial of their allegiance to the Lord
Jesus Christ that they protest claims that they are not Christian.

Such quotations and examples could be multiplied as long as
patience and paper continue. But there is really little point in doing
so, since the claim that Mormons have only recently begun to
pretend that they are Christians is so manifestly without merit.
There has never been a period when The Church of Jesus Christ of
Latter-day Saints has declined to call itself Christian; there has been
no time when it has not declared the sovereignty of Christ. One
writer, in fact, could allege with mild amusement in 1897 that
Mormons seemed to think they were the *only* Christians. However
misguided such an idea might be, it certainly indicates—if he is
reporting accurately—that the Latter-day Saints he had spoken with
had a high opinion of the title of "Christian." Why else would they
want to claim it exclusively for themselves?[586]

In order to establish their assertion that the relationship between
Mormonism and Christianity is adversarial, anti-Mormons routinely
distort the message Joseph Smith was given in the grove in 1820.
Robert McKay serves nicely to illustrate such distortion. He speaks,
for example, of "many hateful denunciations of Christianity made
by past [Mormon] leaders, one of which has become canonized
scripture."[587] What the other "hateful denunciations" might be,
McKay does not tell us. On the other hand, it is almost certain that,
by "canonized scripture," he refers to the 1838 account of Joseph
Smith's First Vision. But is that account really "hateful"? (We find
it difficult to imagine a Latter-day Saint denunciation of Christianity
that could possibly exceed in hatefulness some of the statements
quoted at the beginning of this essay.) Most of the negative
statements in the First Vision appear to be quotations from biblical

---

586 Utter (1897): 13-32. It should be noted that such an exclusive claim to the title
of Christian is not, and has never been, the official position of The Church of Jesus
Christ of Latter-day Saints.

587 *The Evangel* 38 (October 1991): 3.

prophets—prophets venerated by Robert McKay no less than by the Latter-day Saints.[588] "In this official account of the First Vision," McKay tells his readers, "Joseph wrote that God told him that all Christian churches were wrong and all Christian beliefs 'were an abomination in his sight.' "[589] This is not true. Neither the 1838 nor any other account of the First Vision says that "all Christian beliefs" are an "abomination." No thinking Latter-day Saint, and certainly no Latter-day Saint leader, has ever claimed for a moment that all the beliefs of other Christians were completely wrong. How could we possibly hold to such a view, when we agree with our fellow Christians on so very much? "In reality and essence," said Joseph Smith, commenting on the relationship between Mormons and other Christians, "we do not differ so far in our religious views, but that we could all drink into one principle of love."[590] Have Latter-day Saints ever taught that Protestant or Catholic belief in Jesus as Redeemer was an abomination? Have we ever denounced their veneration of the New Testament? Do we find their belief in the existence of God abominable?

Quite the contrary. "The Catholics have many pieces of truth," noted John Taylor.[591] Joseph Smith felt the same way, and denounced anti-Catholic bigotry with both eloquence and passion.[592] Protestant anti-Catholics are illogical, he told his followers, and, to compound their error, they fail to recognize the great worth of "the old Catholic church traditions." "If the whole tree is corrupt," the Prophet demanded, "are not its branches corrupt? If the Catholic religion is a false religion, how can any true religion come out of it? If the Catholic church is bad, how can any good thing come out of it?" But, in fact, the Catholic church is neither entirely bad nor

---

588 Compare Joseph Smith—History 1:19 to Isaiah 29:13; Colossians 2:22; Titus 1:14; 2 Timothy 3:5.

589 *The Utah Evangel* 34 (May-June 1987): 6.

590 *HC* 5:499.

591 *JD* 1:154-156; 12 June 1853.

592 As at *HC* 2:465 and *TPJS*, 375, 313.

wholly false. "The character of the old churches [has] always been slandered by all apostates since the world began."[593]

But the respect of Mormon prophets and apostles is by no means confined to the Church of Rome. "Have the Presbyterians any truth?" asked the Prophet Joseph Smith. "Yes. Have the Baptists, Methodists, etc., any truth? Yes."[594] "The Latter-day Saints recognize and appreciate the great work accomplished by the Christian churches of the world since the Reformation," President Anthony W. Ivins said in April 1926. "For all the good which such an organization may accomplish the Lord will give them credit, and they will be rewarded for their efforts to establish faith in the hearts of people, I believe far beyond their expectations, for everything that is good, and persuadeth men to do good, cometh from God. The Latter-day Saints wish all people who are thus striving God-speed."[595] President Ivins was even willing to speak well of churches that oppose and denounce The Church of Jesus Christ of Latter-day Saints. "We encourage and bless them in their righteous efforts, and the Lord will bless them for all the good that they accomplish."[596] Thus, when Robert McKay announces that "Mormonism, to be completely honest, must either repudiate its claim to being Christian, or cease to attack Christianity," we can easily see that his announcement rests upon an untruth.[597]

For Mormonism does not attack Christianity as such, nor does it assert that other Christian churches are entirely wrong. When it criticizes other faiths at all, which is very rare, it laments only the corruptions that, it has been informed by the Lord, have crept into the churches that claim to follow Jesus of Nazareth. More typically,

---

593 *TPJS*, 375; cf. Ehat and Cook (1980): 381-82.

594 *HC* 5:517.

595 Report of the Ninety-Sixth Annual Conference of the Church of Jesus Christ of Latter-day Saints (1926): 23-24; 18-19.

596 Report of the Ninety-Seventh Semi-Annual Conference of the Church of Jesus Christ of Latter-day Saints (1926): 14.

597 See *The Utah Evangel* 34 (May-June 1987): 6.

the Latter-day Saints simply attempt to share the additional light that God has given them. "We are asking you," President George Albert Smith told a Presbyterian minister in England, "to keep all the truths you have acquired in your churches, from the scriptures and from your educational institutions. Keep also the fine characters you have developed and the love and beauty that are in your hearts. . . . Keep all this. It is a part of the gospel of Jesus Christ. Then let us sit down and share with you some of the things that have not yet come into your lives that have enriched our lives and made us happy. We offer you these things without money and without price. All we ask you to do is hear what we have to say, and if it appeals to you, accept it freely. If it does not, then we will go our way to somebody else that we hope will be more fortunate."[598] The Prophet Joseph Smith had made much the same point years earlier. "If I esteem mankind to be in error," he said, "shall I bear them down? No. I will lift them up, and in their own way too, if I cannot persuade them my way is better; and I will not seek to compel any man to believe as I do, only by the force of reasoning, for truth will cut its own way. . . . Christians should cease wrangling and contending with each other, and cultivate the principles of union and friendship in their midst."[599]

James K. Walker offers an interesting justification for the denial that Latter-day Saints are Christian.[600] "Traditional Christians," he observes, "say the Mormon Church is not truly a Christian church. Is that really so different from Mormons saying that the LDS Church is the only true Church?" As a matter of fact, it is. To say that The Church of Jesus Christ of Latter-day Saints is the only true church is quite a different proposition from saying that other churches are not Christian. Therefore, it is unlike the critics' claim that The Church of Jesus Christ of Latter-day Saints is not a Christian church. Consider a few analogies: If Fred the economist

---

598 Cited at Pusey (1981): 272.

599 *HC* 5:499.

600 Walker (1992).

claims that his theory is the only fully adequate or true theory of business cycles, is he thereby claiming that there are no other such theories? Hardly. And Fred's claim would scarcely justify rival economists in contending that his is not a theory of business cycles at all. Likewise, if Katharine the physicist says that her depiction of subatomic reality is true, and better than any alternative, is she asserting that nobody else has such a picture at all, or that competing theories are really about crop rotation or tennis? Certainly not. Should dissenting scientists claim that her theory is absolutely unrelated to subatomic physics? If they did, it would seem a rather strange response. And when Boris, blissfully hunched over his bowl of tomato soup, declares that tomato is the best of all soups, should his friend Ivan, who prefers clam chowder, seriously reply that tomato soup is not soup at all, but rather a form of ice cream or a type of salad?

Walker goes on to declare that there is "something wrong" with saying that "all Christian churches are wrong" while claiming, at the same time, to be a Christian church. "By its own claims Mormonism cannot be a Christian church *too*. If all professing Churches are false, Mormonism must be Christian *instead*. There is no middle ground. . . . Why is it wrong to say, 'Mormonism is Christian?' It is because to say Mormonism is a true Christian church is to admit that no other church is." And, truly, there would be "something wrong" with such a declaration. But Walker has provided no evidence that any Latter-day Saint has ever said such a thing. Nor has Robert McKay given us any reason to accept his cute syllogism, offered as a demonstration of alleged Latter-day Saint inconsistency on this issue: "1. Christian churches are false. 2. But Mormonism is Christian. 3. Therefore Mormonism is false."[601]

What the Lord told Joseph Smith in the grove was that the churches and creeds of 1820 were defective and distorted by error. He did not say that they were entirely and utterly wrong (since they preserved much truth), nor did he say that each and every Christian

---

601 *The Evangel* 38 (November 1991): 3.

church would always be wrong. Nor did he include the as-yet-unorganized Church of Jesus Christ of Latter-day Saints in his judgment. He did not say that Christianity, as such, is false. There is nothing logically wrong with saying that the churches of 1820 were incorrect on many important issues ("corrupt"), and then saying that The Church of Jesus Christ of Latter-day Saints (organized in 1830) is true. If such a statement were logically unacceptable, then so would be the assertion that Einstein's special theory of relativity is a superior theory in physics to, or "truer than," the Newtonian theory that preceded it. Yet historians of science routinely say precisely that, and Einsteinians never say that physics, as such, is false. Inadequate scientific theories can still be scientific, just as inadequate Christian theologies can still be Christian. The Copernican notion of the solar system is a more adequate astronomical theory than the Ptolemaic view, and Kepler's theory is even better. However, all three theories are theories of the solar system. They are all astronomical theories, just as Catholicism, Methodism, Russian Orthodoxy, and Mormonism are all Christian theologies.

To say that Mormonism is Christian is not, as such, to endorse its specific historical or doctrinal claims. Logically, as we have seen, it is quite possible for a denomination to be Christian while being, simultaneously, mistaken on one or more theological points. This is, in fact, presumably how various Protestant, Catholic, and Orthodox groups view each other. What is more, this is how Latter-day Saints have historically viewed the Christians who disagree with them. Mormons have not, generally if ever, seriously denied that other churches were Christian. "We have no need," Joseph F. Smith, sixth president of the Church, said in April 1917, "to tear down the houses of other people (using this expression as a symbol). We are perfectly willing that they should live in the homes they have erected for themselves, and we will try to show them a better way. While we will not condemn that which they love and cherish above all other things in the world, we will endeavor to show them a better way and build them a better house, and then invite them kindly, in the spirit of Christ, of true Christianity, to enter the better dwelling."[602] Thus, "to say Mormonism is a true Christian church" is *not* to say that "no other church is." Even to say that Mormonism is true in all its historical and doctrinal claims is not to make such a statement, for it is not a part of official Mormon doctrine to deny the Christianity of others. And, logically, it is quite conceivable that a fully adequate ("true") Christian denomination might be surrounded by other, less adequate ("true") Christian denominations.

Latter-day Saints have never regarded themselves as enemies of Christianity. If anything, theirs seems often to be a case of un-requited love.

Conclusion

So where do we stand? We have examined numerous arguments designed to show that The Church of Jesus Christ of Latter-day Saints stands beyond the limits of Christendom. We have, we hope, given them fairly and accurately. We have referred to various figures and documents from several periods across the history of Christianity. Where does this fairly complex and dense analysis leave us?

We have seen critics of Mormonism declare that the standard for denying the name "Christian" to Mormons is the Bible. Yet we have found that the Bible not only contains no definition of the word but, in fact, hardly mentions it. Nor does earliest Christianity provide any clear guidance. So, while they deny it, the critics are thrown back necessarily on extrabiblical criteria for judgment that they then attempt to read into the New Testament canon.[603] However, we have seen that these criteria, if consistently applied,

---

602 J. F. Smith (1949): 256.

603 We would, in fact, be more than willing to argue that many of these criteria are even opposed to biblical teaching. Unfortunately, treatment of this topic is beyond the scope of the present work. However, examples might include Platonic and Neoplatonic views of deity and of the material cosmos, as well as Augustine's Manichaean doctrine of "original sin," discussed above; cf., on the latter, Phipps (1980): 124-33.

would lead to results that most people—if perhaps not our "experts"—would recognize as absurd. But the criteria are not even consistently applied, and arbitrariness reigns. (In 1986, the Protestant magazine *The Christian Century* quoted television evangelist Jerry Falwell's criticism of former President Jimmy Carter for sponsoring the Salt II and Panama Canal treaties. Anyone who would do so, Fallwell declared, "is not a Christian.")[604] If there is any one constant, it can be formulated in the following rule: "If we don't believe it or do it, it isn't Christian." The *Evangel's* Robert McKay, at least, is refreshingly frank about his approach to the question. "Having assumed that what I believe is Christian doctrine," he remarks, "any doctrines which contradict mine are by definition not Christian."[605]

However, this is a far cry from the boast of the critics that they are conveying objective information by their refusal to grant Mormons the (pagan-invented) title of "Christian." All their refusal really seems to convey is how little they perceive Mormonism to resemble their own beliefs, which have somehow become the cosmic standard. It means that Mormons are not like them. Many anti-Mormons come, in fact, to sound very much like Henry Fielding's fictional Parson Thwackum: "When I mention religion," he says, "I mean the Christian religion; and not only the Christian religion, but the Protestant religion; and not only the Protestant religion, but the Church of England."[606]

Implicit in the refusal to admit that Mormons are Christians is an attempt to impose a bogus uniformity on what has historically gone under the name of "Christian." This attempt flies in the face of "the notorious fact that persons who have equally professed and

---

604 *The Christian Century* (1 October 1986): 833.

605 *The Evangel* 38 (September 1991): 8. Compare the characterization by Pressau (1977): 65, of what he refers to as the "conventional" mind-set: "A 'Biblical' church is one that thinks and therefore acts as we do." S. E. Robinson (1991): 1-7, offers a cogent Latter-day Saint response to this sort of thinking, which he terms "exclusion by definition."

606 Fielding (1952): 39.

called themselves Christians have, in the course of history, held all manner of distinct and conflicting beliefs under the one name."[607] "Christians have argued, often passionately, over every conceivable point of Christian doctrine from the *filioque* to the immaculate conception," observes David Steinmetz, Kearns Professor of the History of Christianity at Duke University. "There is scarcely an issue of worship, theology, ethics, and politics over which some Christians have not disagreed among themselves."[608] By what authority, then, does any single group arrogate to itself the right to bestow or deny the title of "Christian"? No informed observer would deny that there are striking differences between Mormonism and traditional Christianity. Mormons proclaim this themselves when they speak of "The Great Apostasy." But there is a vast difference between acknowledging differences, noting that Mormonism is "not really based upon the teaching of the Bible *as understood and interpreted by the historic Christian church*," and denying that Mormons are Christians at all.[609]

Yet such a denial, according to James Spencer, not only represents the consensus of informed orthodox Christians on Mormonism, but is their unanimous judgment.[610] Even if Spen-

---

607 Lovejoy (1964): 6; cf., too, E. P. Sanders (1991): 22, 26, who, having listed five "fundamental convictions" expressed in the early Christian message, notes that all but two of them "became the subject of debate or even hostile controversy *among Christians*" (emphasis ours).

608 As quoted by S. E. Robinson (1991): 36-37.

609 The quotation—emphasis ours—is from G. L. Archer's "Translator's Preface" to Ahmanson (1984): 8. G. L. Archer is one of those who make this leap. It is instructive to watch the (apparently unconscious) process in Burrell and Wright (1983), by which "mainstream Christianity" becomes first "orthodox Christianity" and then "Christianity" *simpliciter*. Rev. John L. Smith, writing in *The Utah Evangel* 34 (April 1987): 5, declares it "obvious . . . that in the traditional sense, Mormonism is not Christian." Of course, no intelligent Latter-day Saint would dispute for even a moment that Mormonism differs radically from "traditional" Christianity. But it seems, since Rev. Smith and *The Evangel* routinely deny Mormonism to be Christian in any sense at all, that he and his associates do not admit that anyone can be a Christian in anything *but* "the traditional sense."

610 Spencer (1984): 138.

cer's claim were true, of course, it would signify nothing in itself. "Informed opinion" in Salem knew that witchcraft was a serious community problem. "Informed opinion" in 1929 knew that prices on the stock exchange would continue to soar. "Informed" Roman opinion knew the early Christians to be a dangerous threat to society. Truth is not established by opinion polls, and not even by surveying "experts." As the great medieval rabbi Moses Maimonides expresses this point, "when something has been demonstrated, the correctness of the matter is not increased and certainty regarding it is not strengthened by the consensus of all men of knowledge with regard to it. Nor could its correctness be diminished and certainty regarding it be weakened even if all the people on earth disagreed with it."[611] Rather, it must be demonstrated by its intrinsic reasonableness and by its consistency with the evidence. Such is precisely the case here. We have seen that the standards by which Mormons are denied the title of "Christian" rest on illusion and lead to absurdity, so that even a unanimous verdict of experts would have to be characterized as simply wrong.

But there is no unanimous verdict of experts to the effect that The Church of Jesus Christ of Latter-day Saints is non-Christian. Spencer's claim is not true. Many authorities on Mormonism—even those who are most critical of it—acknowledge its Christianity.[612]

---

611 Maimonides (1963): 2:290.

612 See, e.g., Shipps (1985): 187, n. 24 (Shipps, a Methodist, is probably the leading non-Latter-day Saint authority on Mormonism); cf. the citation of Shipps in Oman (1982): 9-10; Siedenschnur, "Mormonen," in Brunotte and Weber (1958): 2:1453; McLoughlin (1978): 16-17; Charlesworth (1983), 1:xxiv; Heinerman and Shupe (1985): 96; Eble (1986): 116; Benz (1978): 215; Eggenberger (1969): 3; Beaver et al. (1982): 417, who are Evangelicals, term Mormonism an "unorthodox Christian sect"; Algermissen (1962), whose very hostile book ranks Mormons among "Juden und Nichtkatholische Christen"; McDannell and Lang (1990); Barley et al. (1987); E. K. Thompson (1957): 204-5; *Das Bertelsmann Lexikon*. D. J. Davies, a Church of England minister as well as an anthropologist, identifies Latter-day Saints as Christians on pp. 1, 23, 60, 71, and 99 of his study on *Mormon Spirituality*. The *Handbuch: Religiöse Gemeinschaften*, which, as its title implies, is a handbook for German clergymen, has always counted Mormonism as Christian, although its latest edition (p. 299) announces an intention to look at the question again. Mormons are classed as Christians by Brunkow (1983): 293-304; Coxill and

An even larger group of writers on Mormonism fails to address the question, almost certainly because—and rightly so—the issue never occurs to them.[613]

There is, after all, something rather peculiar about the assertion that The Church of Jesus Christ of Latter-day Saints is not Christian. It is not a self-evident truth, and would even seem to contradict obvious fact. (This is presumably why it is so frequently

---

Grubb (1967): 267, 300, 325; Gründler (1961): 1:328-36. To Holzapfel (1925): 9-10, 14-15, *all* of the *"Sekten"* are Christian; indeed, they are Protestant! Bartley (1989): 9, operating from a very hostile British Catholic position, locates the Latter-day Saints among "American fundamentalist sects." Rev. Roger R. Keller, a Presbyterian who had briefly been a Mormon in his youth, wrote a pamphlet arguing that Mormons are Christians. (Two Protestant journals refused to run the piece as an article.) Following that, Keller (1986b) wrote a book entitled *Reformed Christians and Mormon Christians: Let's Talk*, which obviously holds to the same opinion. (Shortly following the completion of his book, Dr. Keller was reconverted to The Church of Jesus Christ of Latter-day Saints. This does not lessen the value and relevance of his opinions, however. Quite the contrary. Coming as they do from a scholar who knows both Reformed Protestantism and Mormonism intimately, from within, Dr. Keller's views possess a unique authority.) A number of other sources strongly *imply* the Christianity of Mormonism, but without stating it explicitly. Among these are Crim (1981); Parrinder (1971), where the Baha'is are present but the Mormons are conspicuously absent; Mead (1985); Heyer (1977); Christie-Murray (1989); Douglas, Elwell, and Toone (1989): 257; the *Encyclopedia of World Religions* (1975); Sandeen and Hale (1978). Barrett (1982): 56-58, classes Mormons under *"marginal Protestantism* (para-Christian, quasi-Christian, or tangentially Christian deviations from mainline Protestantism)." It is difficult to see how he justifies such stand-offishness in the light of his own definition on p. 47.

613 Thus, a quick survey of encyclopedias finds no denial of Mormons' Christianity in the following: *World Book, Americana, Britannica, Collier's, Compton's, Chambers's* (which is very hostile), *Brockhaus Enzyklopaedie, Grosses Duden Lexikon*. Nor is there any denial to be found in the *Oxford English Dictionary*, nor in such standard reference works on Christianity and religion as those of Cross and Livingstone (1983); Brandon (1970); Weir (1982); Ferm (1945); Meagher, O'Brien, and Aherne (1979): vol. 2; Hinnells (1984); Campenhausen (1960). Even when Mormon divergence from traditional Christianity is explicitly noted, Mormon Christianity is tacitly acknowledged: Mead (1985): 135, is aware that "certain aspects of Latter-day Saints' theology depart from the traditional orthodoxy of Catholic and Protestant churches." Mormonism, writes Broderick (1976): 401, "is not a church in the mainstream of Protestant thought." Holzapfel (1925): 79-87, and Hutten (1953): 417-53, offer very sharp criticism, but somehow fail to notice that Mormons are not Christians.

announced with an air of breathless discovery.) Mormons declare themselves Christian, and are astonished to be told they are not. They belong to a Church in which every prayer is uttered, every sermon is given, and every ordinance is performed literally in the name of Jesus Christ. Their hymns—the devotional heart of their Sunday worship—sing of Christ and his atonement. At Christmas and Easter, they join with hundreds of millions of Christians around the world in a celebration of his life. In baptism and in the weekly communion they know as "the sacrament," they testify that they are willing to take upon themselves his name (D&C 20:37, 77).[614] Their first Article of Faith announces their belief in "God the Eternal Father, and in His son, Jesus Christ." The Book of Mormon closes with an exhortation to "come unto Christ, and be perfected in him" (Moroni 10:32). One of the high points of the Doctrine and Covenants is a stirring testimony of Jesus (D&C 76:22-24). Their story begins with the claim of a young boy to have seen the Father and the Son. That young boy later claimed to be a prophet, defining "the spirit of prophecy" as "the testimony of Jesus."[615] His successors, likewise regarded as prophets, are assisted by a presiding quorum of "Twelve Apostles, or special witnesses of the name of Christ in all the world" (D&C 107:23).

Is it plausible to describe such people as "non-Christian"? It would hardly seem so, unless one is prepared to follow the idiosyncratic usage of the term that permits statements like, "I have been an active and committed Lutheran since my earliest youth; I became a Christian last July."[616] But language is a social construct, and meaning must be shared to be intelligible. To use terms in extraordinary ways, almost solipsistically, without alerting an audience, is confusing at best, as it is in the dialogue—if it can be called that!—between Humpty Dumpty and Alice. As illustrated by

---

614 See numerous related references in the Index to the Latter-day Saint "Triple Combination."

615 Citing Revelation 19:10; cf. *HC* 3:38, 5:427.

616 A similar statement was made recently to the authors. Compare P. B. Smith (1970): 55.

the case of certain Islamic zealots—who, when they accuse a woman of being a prostitute, really mean that she goes out in public without a veil—it can be distinctly dangerous. Yet most (if not all) of the arguments that claim to demonstrate that Mormonism is not Christian have, as we have seen, relied on private understandings of common words.[617] Indeed, the denial that Mormons are Christians is, in and of itself, a massive instance of the elementary fallacy of equivocation, using—as it does—a very common word in a very peculiar sense.

Needless to say, if the current flood of anti-Mormon radio and television programs, films, pamphlets, casettes, and books were merely an inexhaustible source of quaint specimens for a class in practical reasoning, there would be no cause for concern. But they are not. Instead, they are often the vehicles of a religious intolerance that is genuinely frightening. A certain nationally-syndicated "Christian" radio talk show, for instance, devoted an entire program in August of 1990 to the question of whether witchcraft and occult movements should be constitutionally protected. It was the opinion of the show's host that, if American law were properly formulated, "false religions" would not be so protected.[618] And if some Mormons are tempted to shrug such discussions off as posing no conceivable threat to The Church of Jesus Christ of Latter-day Saints, dangerous only to real bad guys like Satanists, we would remind them that, to many vocal anti-Mormons, Mormonism *is* "Satanist witchcraft" and an "occult religion." There is abundant evidence, in fact, which we unfortunately cannot treat here, that

---

617 Anti-Mormons seem prone to jargonizing and equivocation even when such word games are not directly useful in mauling Mormons. Ed Kelly's use of "religion" and "Christianity" as lexical opposites is typical; cf. *The Utah Evangel* 33 (July/August 1986): 6. The same sort of thing goes in on anti-Catholicism; cf. Keating (1988): 89; Ciampa, "Catholic or Christian?"

618 Averill (1989): 124, speaking in an American context, notes fundamentalist Protestantism's "hostility toward some of our most basic political institutions, including judicial independence, constitutional liberties, social and religious pluralism, and the equal access to the political process that is promised to all citizens irrespective of ideology." See also Averill (1989): 97.

certain American anti-Mormons feel themselves unfairly restrained in their holy crusade by constitutional guarantees of freedom of religion. There is even evidence to suggest that, in countries where such freedom is not legally protected, enemies of the Church are quite willing to make use of government coercion to combat Mormonism.[619] *The Utah Evangel* has continuously suggested that Latter-day Saints should not hold political office, and that they should be deprived of academic employment and the privilege of speaking at certain college campuses solely because of their religious beliefs.

Of course, the threat to the Latter-day Saints is not primarily legal. The majority of us, presumably, and for the forseeable future, are quite safe behind constitutional guarantees of human rights and freedom of religion. However, Prof. Gordon Thomasson has written a sobering paper, as yet unpublished, describing the potential threat posed even to the *lives* of Mormons in the Third World, where principles of human rights are not always so well-established, by incendiary films like *The God Makers*. (In our opinion, the sequel, *Temples of the God Makers*—which Thomasson had evidently not seen—is even more dangerous. Perhaps deliberately so.) And even the history of the United States, including the not too distant past, has seen unpleasant ethnic and religious conflicts escape the bounds set by law.

More than one Latter-day Saint has attended an anti-Mormon rally only to emerge deeply shaken by the passions on display, by the fierce rhetoric of denunciation, by the frequently charismatic but also manipulative character of the orchestrators of these meetings,

---

619 Conversations with certain officials of the Church, as well as a close observation of anti-Mormon activities for many years, leave no doubt in our minds that this is so. Enemies of the Church have attempted to use government authority to block Latter-day Saint missionary activities in Kenya and Chile, for example. Furthermore, the enforced suspension of Church activities in Ghana, in June 1989, came because, as one well-placed observer puts it, senior officials of the government "had been misled by professional revilers of the Church into believing scurrilous lies about the Latter-day Saints and their beliefs." See Morrison (1990): 117; cf. remarks of Emmanuel Abu Kissi, in LeBaron (1990): 31-32. That suspension has since been lifted.

by the almost palpable hostility directed against Mormon beliefs and
—inescapably, if always denied by the fomenters of such emotions
—against the Mormons themselves. (We have already cited
mainstream Protestant writer and social worker Lloyd Averill's
perception of "frustration, outrage, desperation, and latent violence" in the rhetoric of anti-Mormonism.)[620] Dr. D. Brent
Collette, director of the Church's Institute of Religion adjacent to
the campus of the University of California at Berkeley, will serve
to illustrate the experience of not a few Latter-day Saints who could
tell similar stories: Seeing an anti-Mormon meeting advertised in a
local newspaper, he decided out of curiosity to attend. However,
instead of the fairly small gathering he had expected, he found
himself in the midst of a sizeable and distressingly hostile rally. As
the speakers went on and on about the Satanic character of
Mormonism, about its true conspiratorial nature, about its threat
even to the lives and property of those around it, he found himself
growing ever more upset. Finally, a woman sitting ahead of him
leaned over to her husband and whispered rather loudly that "this,"
by which she meant the treacherous Mormon conspiracy, "was just
like the Nazis." Brother Collette could no longer restrain himself.
"Yes," he said, leaning forward, "this *is* just like the Nazis. And
I'm the Jew."

It is not mere paranoia on the part of Latter-day Saints that
makes them fear the violence that anti-Mormon crusades can stir
up. One professional anti-Mormon based in South America, Dean
Helland, has recently expressed the opinion that Ed Decker's
sensationalistic campaigns there "may have been partially responsible for the continual bombings of Mormon churches by political
extremists in Chile." He thereby acknowledges that anti-Mormon
activity can place Latter-day Saint buildings, missionaries, and
members at serious physical risk. Helland's admission is an interesting one, however, for the manner in which it is phrased. He does
not criticize Decker's distortions and misrepresentations, nor his
inflammatory sensationalism. Indeed, in Helland's view, although

---

620 Averill (1989): 107.

their violent actions were wrong, the Chilean bombers were not fundamentally mistaken in their view of The Church of Jesus Christ of Latter-day Saints. He speaks gently of "this unanticipated participation by terrorists in combatting Mormonism"—almost as if they were simply overenthusiastic allies in a common cause. Indeed, the real fault here lies, as always, with the Latter-day Saints themselves. Decker's agitation in Chile had involved not inaccurate claims, not demagoguery of the worst kind, not the deliberate whipping up of hatred against the Latter-day Saints, but merely "the exposure of Mormon secrets." The terrorists were upset "at least in part by some of the things which were exposed in Decker's teachings." It was imprudent, Mr. Helland implies, to reveal these horrifying things. Perhaps, he suggests, to minimize death and destruction in the future, anti-Mormons should be more cautious in their disclosures of the sordid and appalling truth about the Latter-day Saints. Helland recommends that a more subtle procedure be used to combat Mormonism "in volatile parts of the world . . . where anti-American political sentiments have been manifested repeatedly in violent ways."[621] Presumably, though, the same old sensationalism, the same tired untruths and half-truths, will continue to serve just fine in areas where violence is less common. (We have no reason to suppose, by the way, that Ed Decker has agreed even to Mr. Helland's minimal moderation.)

Mainstream Christians and Christian organizations who stand by as The Church of Jesus Christ of Latter-day Saints is gang-assaulted by heresy hunters may well be, in Thomas Merton's memorable phrase, "guilty bystanders." Sometimes, by joining in or by making their facilities available to anti-Mormons—however uncomfortable they may feel with anti-Mormon "excesses," however ill at ease they may be with hatred as a spiritual tool—they think that they serve God. As one very prominent anti-Mormon put it, when confronted with irrefutable evidence of his own dishonesty, "When

---

621 Helland (1990): 2-3, and unpaginated abstract. This dissertation is, incidentally, a perfectly dreadful piece of work, and reflects no credit upon the school that, accepting it, granted its author a doctorate.

you're fighting the Devil, any means are fair."[622] But these fellow-traveling anti-Mormons may also be self-deceived, vainly imagining that militant fundamentalism will sate itself on the Latter-day Saints, and leave them alone. Instead, it may simply eat them last. Already, to be sure, it does not limit its appetite or its sometimes disreputable tactics to the Latter-day Saints. Karl Keating's experience suggests that, for some militant Protestants, the Church of Rome, too, is a victim whom no rules of fair play are to protect: "The claim of leading fundamentalists that their attacks on the Catholic religion are made out of love for individual Catholics loses much of its credibility because they are unwilling to decline the use of unfair tactics. One might say they are unwilling to wage a just war; they want to do battle, and they do not hesitate to use any weapon at hand, no matter how foul."[623]

Surely the experience of our sad century should have taught us the importance of rules of law and fairness. Constitutional guarantees of free speech and freedom of religion were not designed to protect *popular* opinions, but *unpopular* ones. But in so doing, they protect all opinions from the fickleness of majority fashions. It is in the interest even of popular thinkers and dominant religions to insist that laws and principles of fairness be impartially applied, for the rules that protect their adversaries may one day protect them. An exchange from Robert Bolt's famous screenplay, *A Man for All Seasons*, makes this point eloquently. It features Sir Thomas More and his zealously righteous son-in-law.

"*Roper*: So now you'd give the Devil benefit of law.

More: Yes. What would you do? Cut a great road through the law to get after the Devil?

Roper: I'd cut down every law in England to do that!

More: (Roused and excited) Oh? (Advances on Roper) And when the last law was down—and the Devil turned round on you—where would you hide—Roper, the laws all being flat? . . .

---

622 The remark was made in conversation with an acquaintance of ours.

623 Keating (1988): 59.

Yes, I'd give the Devil benefit of law, for my own safety's sake."[624]

We have in mind here not only the sorts of laws enacted by legislatures and enforced by police. Surely, it is also in the interest of all to ensure that discussions of religious issues are carried out fairly and without misrepresentation, that words are not arbitrarily redefined in order to exclude and victimize less powerful and less popular groups, that Christian history is not distorted in order to banish those who choose not to conform to the consensus of the hour. Surely even non-"cultists" should see that it is in their interest to speak up when they see those rules trampled upon in a zealous attempt to combat "false religion." "In Germany they came first for the Communists," Pastor Martin Niemoeller is reported to have said, "and I didn't speak up because I wasn't a Communist. Then they came for the Jews, and I didn't speak up because I wasn't a Jew. Then they came for the trade unionists, and I didn't speak up because I wasn't a trade unionist. Then they came for the Catholics, and I didn't speak up because I was a Protestant. Then they came for me, and by that time no one was left to speak up."[625]

If Mormons are banished from Christendom, will other denominations and individuals long be absent from the agenda of triumphant fundamentalism? Will all Christians be pressured to toe the extreme Protestant line? Robert McKay serves notice that groups besides the Latter-day Saints could become his prey, when he casually speaks of "other churches, both Christian and non-Christian."[626] (Mosques we know, and synagogues we know. Even *stupas*. But what is a non-Christian *church?*) Loraine Boettner, using language sadly familiar to Mormons, calls Roman

---

624 Bolt (1962): 56 (act 1, scene 6).

625 This famous passage is attributed to Niemoeller, a hero in the German Christian resistance to Hitler, but the source is unclear.

626 In *The Utah Evangel* 33 (July/August 1986): 1. Bellah and Greenspahn (1987) offer useful perspectives on historic and contemporary interreligious hostility in American society.

Catholicism "anti-Christian."[627] Already, Dave Hunt, co-author of *The God Makers*, has moved on to attack his fellow Evangelicals in volumes bearing such titles as *The Seduction of Christianity*. The theological bloodlust visible in much anti-Mormonism is not easily controlled, and will not easily be channeled. In a recent book entitled *Witch Hunt*, Bob and Gretchen Passantino plead with their fellow conservative Protestants to recognize that "different" is not "wrong." But their plea is unlikely to calm the supercharged, inquisitorial atmosphere that they themselves, as vocal anti-"cultists," have most assuredly helped to create.[628]

Humpty Dumpty was right: It really is a question of power. And in the struggle of ideas, as George Orwell knew, control of the dictionary is no small thing.[629]

So how are we to determine who is Christian and who is not? It is not altogether clear that we have any responsibility, or any right, to make such a determination. "For any one branch of the church to claim that those within its fold alone constitute the body of true Christians," writes Loraine Boettner "is both crude and impudent, and is inconsistent with the principles of love and charity so clearly commanded in the Scriptures."[630] Christendom has known (and rejected) such claims in the past: Lucifer of Cagliari, the fourth-century bishop of that Sardinian city, was fond of calling his opponent "pagans," and of describing their meeting places as "camps of the devil." Luciferians, sounding much like Dave Hunt and his language of "seduction," denounced those whose doctrines differed from theirs by charging that, because of dogmatic deviations, "the Church has become a brothel." As W. H. C. Frend

---

627 Boettner (1986): 458; cf. 459. On p. 71, he cites Lucien Vinet to the same effect.

628 Passantino and Passantino (1990).

629 Keating (1988): 81: "As in so many matters, fundamentalists and Catholics are at loggerheads because they define terms differently."

630 Boettner (1986): 26.

notes, Lucifer's view reduced the church to "the real salt of the earth, namely Lucifer and his followers."[631]

The Christian world as a whole has never felt comfortable with such an intolerant and exclusive view, and should not. Probably the best way to deal with the question of who is and who is not Christian is simply to believe what people say when they claim to be Christians.[632] The Lord will judge their hearts.

If anyone claims to see in Jesus of Nazareth a personage of unique and preeminent authority, that individual should be considered Christian. Such is the consensus of both scholarly and everyday usage. It is the only understanding of the term that accounts for the way it has actually been used, as well as the way it continues to be used by most speakers of English and other languages today. (This does not mean, of course, that we must recognize every Christian theology as accurate and adequate. Debates can and probably should continue on such issues.) Only this understanding of the term can make sense of the fact that, through history, such disparate groups as the Ebionites, the Marcionites, and the Mormons, have been classed under it. And—an added demonstration of its ability to account for the data—this understanding clearly excludes movements such as Islam and Manichaeism, which, while viewing Jesus as a prophet, regard him as neither unique nor preeminent—and whose adherents do not in any case aspire to be known as Christians.[633]

---

631 On the aptly named Lucifer, see Frend (1981): 557-58.

632 This is one of the definitions proposed by D. B. Barrett, who was faced with the vexing task of generating global statistics on Christianity: " 'Christians' means all those who profess to be Christians in government censuses or public-opinion polls, i.e., who declare or identify themselves as Christians, who say 'I am a Christian,' 'We are Christians,' when asked the question 'What is your religion?' " He sees biblical support for this in Matthew 10:32 and Romans 10:9; cf. Barrett (1982): 47. The Society of Christian Philosophers uses the same method: "Membership is open to any person who classifies himself/herself as both a philosopher and a Christian," says the inside back cover of *Faith and Philosophy: The Journal of the Society of Christian Philosophers* 9 (January 1992).

633 Some idea of the broad sense which a *real* expert, like the eminent Peter Brown, is willing to give to the term "Christianity" is apparent in the fact that he

" 'What think ye of Christ?' (Matthew 22:42) is still the supreme test of orthodox Christianity," writes G. H. Fraser in his book, *Is Mormonism Christian?* "The Lord accepted Peter's confession, 'Thou art the Christ, the Son of the living God,' and on the basis of this confession, the structure of the Church is built (Matthew 16:15-18)."[634] This is precisely the confession made by Mormons in testimony meetings and missionary lessons every day around the world. Why, then, having acknowledged that Peter's confession was good enough for Jesus, does Fraser demand yet more of the Latter-day Saints? And from whom do he and his allies receive their authority to do so?

Einar Molland, having surveyed the difficulties in defining the term "Christian," concludes that, "There is really only one characteristic that must be present in any community which should be recognized as Christian: belief in Jesus Christ as the son of God, as Lord and Saviour. Any faith which rests upon and is permeated by this belief must be said to lie within the limits of Christendom, while any faith which rejects or is inconsistent with the Divinity of Christ is beyond the pale."[635] Mormonism unabashedly "rests upon and is permeated by" belief in Jesus Christ as the son of God, as Lord and Savior. Why, then does Einar Molland deny that

---

describes even the Manichaeans as "radical Christians." See P. Brown (1969): 43-44, 55, 58. Prof. Brown possibly follows St. Augustine on this point, for that great Christian-turned-Manichaean-turned-Manichaean-Christian apparently regarded Manichaeaism as Christian too; cf. Teske (1986): 236 n. 5, 237, 240 n. 20, 242 n. 23. We are little inclined to go so far, but Prof. Brown's view does clearly imply how little support anti-Mormons are likely to get from genuine scholars in their effort to monopolize the word "Christian" for fundamentalist Protestantism. Similarly, Julian Baldick's ingenious contention that Islam is really a form of Christianity is stimulating, but must ultimately be rejected; cf. Baldick (1989): 2, 169.

634 Fraser (1977): 55.

635 Molland (1959): 356-57. He continues, asserting without any evidence whatsoever, that "The doctrine of the Holy Trinity is organically related to the Divinity of Christ." Does he intend to say that one must accept fourth-century Hellenistic metaphysics to be a Christian?

Mormons are Christian?[636] What powerful extrabiblical force makes even some otherwise reputable scholars violate their own clearly enunciated principles, in order to banish The Church of Jesus Christ of Latter-day Saints from Christendom?

Protestant thinker Frederick Sontag argues that "perhaps the most authentic definition of 'Christian' would be: 'One who feels himself called to serve Jesus or to follow him as master.' " Anti-Mormons, however, refuse to accept this definition, at least when it comes to the Latter-day Saints. No matter how devoted to the Savior he or she may be, it seems that no Latter-day Saint can satisfy the inquisitors of anti-Mormonism. Why? Professor Sontag may be able to suggest a reason: "Although both simple and biblical, the problem with this definition—and perhaps the reason both church officials and theologians have been unwilling to settle for it—is that it is subjective and non-exclusive."[637]

The problem, in other words, is that the simple definition of a Christian as someone who "feels . . . called to serve Jesus or to follow him as master" is of little use in excluding people who do not wish to be excluded. It cannot serve the interests of those whose own sense of value derives wholly or in part from their delicious awareness of the valuelessness of others. But this is to deprive fallen humanity of one of its acutest and least Christ-like pleasures, for in-groups define themselves largely by those whom they exclude. In this game of one-upmanship, of which C. S. Lewis spoke so insightfully in his essay, "The Inner Ring," for someone to win, it is essential that someone else must lose.[638] Sadly, such considerations may have particular relevance to the conservative Christians who make up the overwhelming majority of vocal anti-Mormons. Lloyd Averill has lamented the fact that, "in fundamentalist hands, being 'saved' or 'born again' is . . . often seized as a mark of spiritual and moral superiority over the 'unsaved,' that is,

---

636 At Molland (1959): 355.

637 Sontag (1986): 113-14.

638 See C. S. Lewis (1965): 55-66.

those—whether nonfundamentalist Christians or non-Christians—whose experience differs from that of the fundamentalists. Indeed, for some fundamentalists, being 'saved' confers legitimacy on the use of the most violent and unloving rhetoric in denouncing and damning the 'unsaved' and on taking delight in contemplating the destruction that is presumed to await them in the providence of an irreconcilable fundamentalist God."[639] Averill points to what he terms fundamentalism's "apparent eagerness for schism." Indeed, he calls the movement "inherently schismatic."[640] "Its tests for Christian fellowship become so severe," says Edward J. Carnell, former president of the evangelical Fuller Theological Seminary, "that divisions in the Church are considered a sign of virtue." And this, notes Carnell, seems essential to fundamentalist identity. "Status by negation must be maintained," he observes, "or the *raison d'être* of fundamentalism is lost."[641]

Yet Frederick Sontag's simple definition is probably the only one that can account for the way the word "Christian" is actually used.[642] We have seen that the oldest and probably the original

---

639 Averill (1989): 165. Of course, in reading of the obvious failings of some of their critics, Latter-day Saints must resist the strong temptation to commit the same smug error. On p. 123, Averill quotes Christopher Lasch, who describes fundamentalist religiosity as "self-righteous and idolatrous. It perceives no virtue in its opponents and magnifies its own."

640 Averill (1989): 10, 39; cf. 98, 110-18.

641 Averill (1989): 52. Keating (1988): 25, cites Peggy L. Shriver, assistant secretary general of the National Council of Churches of Christ in the United States, as saying that "because an insecure ego can be supported by the scaffolding of a fundamentalist faith, it is not surprising that many people who are 'marginal' to society are drawn to fundamentalism." However, Keating prudently rejects this as a potentially dangerous argument.

642 In *The Evangel* 38 (October 1991): 4, Robert McKay attacks the notion that anyone who believes in Christ is a Christian as "a very shallow definition of what a Christian is." "Going by this definition," he points out, "Moslems could almost be called Christians. By this definition, Jews could almost be called Christians." However, McKay's use of the word "almost" is extraordinarily important, for even he can't quite bring himself to the full measure of what he seems to want to imply. In fact, Muslims are *not* referred to as Christians. Jews are *not* referred to as

meaning of *Christianoi* was nothing more complicated than "Christ's people," or perhaps "partisans of Christ." And "Christ's people" describes precisely what members of The Church of Jesus Christ of Latter-day Saints feel themselves called to be.

It is a pity that the common loyalty implied in the term "Christian" seems unable to unify the followers of Christ in a struggle against the powerful foes who menace them all. In a world of violence and hatred and hunger and wretched addiction, it is tragic that "Christ's partisans" often prefer to regard each other as the enemy. Surrounded by materialism and immorality and unbelief, many Christians have their guns trained on one another. Yet, in a world where most still do not know Christ, the common love that his people feel toward him as their Redeemer surely should weigh at least as heavily in the scales as their doctrinal differences. "The Kingdom of God," said Martin Luther, "is like a besieged city surrounded on all sides by death. Each man has his place on the wall to defend and no one can stand where another stands, but nothing prevents us from calling encouragement to one another."[643]

Doctrinal disagreements, we hasten to point out, are not unimportant. "A" and "not-A" are unlikely to be simultaneously true, and it is important that we devote our attention to sifting truth from error. Debate and discussion are not of themselves evil. If they are conducted fairly, without anger and evil contention, with an eye to truth rather than to self-gratifying "victory," they can serve important and indeed vital ends. Followers of Christ can profit from differing experiences and insights. But dogmatic disputes should be kept in their proper perspective. "There is every evidence," states Professor Sontag, "that Jesus was primarily

---

Christians. McKay goes on to contrast the views of Christ held by Jehovah's Witnesses, New Agers, and the Worldwide Church of God (Armstrongites), and then asks if they can all be considered Christian. "The idea is ridiculous," he says. But is it? Excepting only the New Agers—for the simple reason that they probably would not describe themselves as Christians—we think not.

643 Cited by England (1984): 185-86.

interested in one's sense of calling and gave little attention to theological debates."[644]

Who should be our model? Jesus? Or Lucifer of Cagliari? Eugene England's admonition deserves consideration: "It would be tragic," he writes, "if we Christians, standing each in our different places, were to desert our place on the wall against death—against our true enemies, the world, the flesh, and the devil—and, accepting spectral evidence from the father of lies, were to turn on each other. We have no business but to call encouragement to each other."[645] Latter-day Saints would do well—on grounds of history and theology, as well as for reasons of simple tolerance and good human relations—to take the advice Karl Keating gives to Catholics facing a fundamentalist. "Allow him the title of Christian," says Keating, "even if he will not return the favor."[646]

In the 1980s, a committee of scholars and teachers from the Graduate Theological Union in Berkeley, Harvard Divinity School, and the Divinity School of the University of Chicago carried out a five-year examination of the role of religion classes in the undergraduate college curriculum. Among the products of that collaboration was a pamphlet posing questions and offering suggestions for introductory courses in religious studies. Certain of the questions posed (and left unanswered, for the reader's reflection) are directly relevant to our concerns in this essay: "Is a religion," the pamphlet asks, "presented from the perspective of a privileged elite? Are there unexamined decisions made about what is orthodox and what is not? The Mormons, for example, wish to be called Christians. . . . Are [they] labeled Christian because they say they are, or is there another criterion used to exclude them? Are the criteria for such judgements clearly articulated and consistently applied?"[647]

---

644 Sontag (1986): 114.

645 England (1984): 186.

646 Keating (1988): 316.

647 K. M. Brown, "Thinking about the Introductory Course: Some Preliminary Questions," in Juergensmeyer (1988): 9.

We are now in a position to answer these questions. Our survey of the arguments and the evidence has, we believe, shown that anti-Mormon arguments on this subject have rarely if ever been clearly articulated, and that consistent application of them leads to absurd and unacceptable results. We have discovered that anti-Mormon denials of Latter-day Saint Christianity are indeed tangled up with "unexamined decisions . . . about what is orthodox and what is not," and that those decisions do not, in fact, bear close examination on historical and logical grounds. We conclude that there is no "privileged elite" to whose judgment we must defer on this question. There is only the broad and deep stream of common usage, reflecting the judgment of millions, if not billions, of ordinary people since the time of Christ, including scholars and peasants, theologians, insiders and outsiders, believers and unbelievers. This stream can, of course, be turned. New meanings and new usages can be created by forceful thinkers and clever poets. But the stream has not yet been turned, and it will take more than the weak and inconsistent arguments offered so far to change the meaning of the term "Christian" and thrust the Latter-day Saints outside its confines. In point of fact, the Mormons are Christians precisely because they sincerely say they are. No other criterion is needed—for the Latter-day Saints or for anyone else. No other coherent criterion has been offered, and it is doubtful that any other can be.

"It is not necessarily theology which makes us Christian," Rev. Roger Keller reminded us some years ago, "but rather our common confession of Jesus Christ as Lord. That confession in the early Church preceded all sophisticated theological discussions, and it is that same confession today that identifies us as Christian. The confession that Jesus is Lord is as central to the Mormon faith as it is to that of the Presbyterians, Methodists, Catholics, or Baptists."[648]

---

648 Keller (1986a): 9; cf. Sontag (1986): 114. As noted, Dr. Keller is now a member of The Church of Jesus Christ of Latter-day Saints.

▲

Mormonism as a "Cult":
The Limits of Lexical Polemics

▲

As MISSIONARIES IN Switzerland, we were frequently met at the door with the question, "Kommen Sie von einer Sekte?" ("Are you from a *Sekte*?"). *Sekte*, we soon learned, was the popular and even official label for our denomination, as well as for all others not recognized as *Landeskirchen*, or state churches.[1] The technical distinction between the two groups was simple: State churches could collect the "church tax" through a state tax office—somewhat like tithes being withheld by the Internal Revenue Service.[2] But the difference in the popular mind made by this distinction was far weightier. Members of a *Sekte* were effectively relegated to second-class citizenship in a land of state churches. Because of the word's negative connotations, to be affiliated with a *Sekte* required a

---

1 In certain cantons of Switzerland (e.g., Zürich), the official term for *Sekte* is *Verein* ("society, association"). In day-to-day conversation, however, this term is not used.

2 Some social services are provided through the *Landeskirchen*. This makes adoption, for example, much more difficult—and sometimes impossible—for those who are not affiliated with state churches.

quality of courage, conviction, and indifference to the opinions of one's neighbors that is hard for most Americans to imagine. Despite occasional protestations of the innocuousness of the term, the looks of horror that were elicited when *we* (in mock innocence) asked someone if he or she belonged to a *Sekte* suggested that the word did indeed have a strong—and strongly negative—emotional charge to it.[3]

Perhaps it was this use of the word *Sekte* in the service of religious polemics that has made us more keenly aware, since our missions, of a similar use of the term "cult" (particularly by fundamentalist Christians) to describe a large number of religious groups, representing a very wide range of teaching and practice from Eckankar to Mormons, from the Healthy Happy Holy Organization to Christian Scientists. In at least two important ways, the terms "cult" and "*Sekte*" are alike: both words maintain an "in-group-out-group" division, and both pack a strong negative charge. On one side are mainline Protestant churches and sometimes Catholics; on the other, groups like Jehovah's Witnesses, The Way International, the Church Universal and Triumphant, Jonestown, the Divine Light Mission, and the Mormons. (There is no mistaking the implied guilt by association: after all, Jonestown was a cult, and look what it did!)

The powerful emotional impact of the four-letter word "cult"—carried even in its short, explosive, violent sound[4]—is illustrated by two recent letters to the *Biblical Archaeology Review*, in which the magazine is taken to task for having referred to the presumed

---

3 In English, on the other hand, the progression from "sect" to "denomination" has frequently been seen as a decline. H. Richard Niebuhr provides a good example of this. For a negative evaluation of the idea, see Mullett (1984): 168-191. It is currently fashionable to recognize such a decline in Mormonism. Thomas F. O'Dea, however, saw Mormonism as having avoided "sectarian stagnation"; see O'Dea (1954): 285-293. O'Dea rejects the label "sect" for Mormonism, and questions the church-sect distinction in any case.

4 Wesley Walters, in the title of his article, "From Occult to Cult with Joseph Smith, Jr.," uses the word only for the sound and the bad overtones that it shares with "occult"; it plays little if any role in the article proper; see Walters (1977): 121-37.

site of Joshua's temple as a "cultic center." One reader objects: "Cult conjures up images of evil men deceiving people and leading them off into foolish error. When I read about the Mt. Ebal altar, I don't want Jim Jones jumping out at me." Complains another: "When you worship the true and the living God, you are not engaged in a cultic ritual." (Ironically, of course, these readers protest a use of the term that goes back to at least the seventeenth century, and which is precisely that of the Latin *cultus*. It is the polemical use of the word "cult" that finds no sanction in the *Oxford English Dictionary*.)[5] The term's impact is further illustrated in a classified advertisement that ran for several years in the respected evangelical publication, *Christianity Today*. "Mormonism is a cult!" it proclaimed. "See why." Those curious to discover why were sent *The Utah Evangel*, an anti-Mormon tabloid. (Would the impact of the advertisement have been as great had it read, "Mormonism is a religious denomination! See why"?)[6] A recent letter to *The Evangel* (successor to *The Utah Evangel*) leaves little doubt about the word's connotations: "I refuse to capitalize the word, mormon, for to us, this is nothing but a cult, and not worthy of being honored in this manner."[7]

The term "cult" often appears with other words carrying a negative connotation. Recent publications like *Walter Martin Confronts the Cults*, *Confronting the Cults*, and *Confronting Cults: Old and New* share with the French *L'Offensive des Sectes* a rhetoric of conflict.[8] The opening lines of L. D. Streiker's *Cults:*

---

5 Cf. the more traditional use of the term "cult" and "cultic" in J. Neusner, ed. *Christianity, Judaism and Other Greco-Roman Cults: Studies for Morton Smith at Sixty* (1975); and J. Milgrom, *Studies in Cultic Theology and Terminology* (1983).

6 More recently, however, *Christianity Today* made UMI, the publisher of the *Utah Evangel* (now *The Evangel*), change its ad on Mormonism to read "false religion" instead of "cult." Perhaps *Christianity Today* recognized the unalloyedly pejorative—and potentially actionable—connotations of the term.

7 *The Evangel* 38 (November 1991): 2.

8 G. R. Lewis (1966); Starkes (1984); Chéry (1954): 31: "'Offensive actuelle des sectes? Le mot n'est pas trop fort." ("A current offensive by the cults? The word is not too strong.")

The Continuing Threat are reminiscent of Joe McCarthy: "The cults are coming to your city—to your neighborhood—to the family next door—to your family—to your life! An invasion is underway. Beachheads have already been established in communities throughout America." (Bob Larson imagines "the war of the cults versus Christianity"; Walter Martin conjures up "the shock troops of cultism.")

Also to be noted is the language of dehumanization and devaluation. "A cult is a perversion," opens one book on the subject. We read of *The Chaos of Cults*, *The Cult Explosion*, where Walter Martin grimly warns his readers that "a virulent cultic . . . revival is sweeping our country." "Cultists" are said to "feed on" nominal Christians. The Mormon Church is a "wolf-pack." 1983 saw publication of *The Lure of the Cults* by the sociologist and devoted "cult"-watcher, Ronald Enroth, as of H. L. Bussell's *Unholy Devotion: Why Cults Lure Christians*. Notice here the language of seduction. (Can we imagine *The Lure of the Denominations?*)

An interview with Enroth in *Christianity Today* bears the sinister and inflammatory title: "The Dimensions of the Cult Conspiracy." Jim Jones, Sun Myung Moon, and the mysterious L. Ron Hubbard are involved—of course. But there is more: "It is not unusual," reveals Enroth, "for me to find students . . . who are surprised to learn that the Mormons are a cult."[9] Such naive folk are, no doubt, soon made to see the light. "Mormonism can be best understood," according to the book, *The God Makers*, "in relation to the larger occult conspiracy, of which it is a part."[10]

But if Mormons and others are to be classed as "cults," the word must be defined. The term *Sekte* has, in Switzerland at least, a kernel of official meaning. However, in the absence of an estab-

---

9 "The Dimensions of the Cult Conspiracy" (1981): 27; cf. Matrisciana (1985). On the cover of Matrisciana's book can be found the statement: "There is an unparalleled mystical conspiracy threatening today's world." (This strange use of mysticism as a hobgoblin is surprisingly common among anti-"cultists.")

10 Decker and Hunt (1984): 254.

lished church in America, users of the term "cult" must provide their own definition for it. Some, following the sociologists, define a cult as a group that lives in tension with the larger community, demands a high level of commitment from its members, and tends to be authoritarian and exclusivistic.[11] But if, by this definition, Mormonism is a cult, other groups, too, may be so classified. Early Quakerism is a good example,[12] as are the Amish. Atwood and Flowers, in their recent study of "Early Christianity as a Cult Movement," demonstrate that the primitive Church itself reflected the same (ostensibly "cultic") characteristics.[13] Early Christians lived in varying degrees of tension with both the values of Jewish society and of the wider Roman world. Origen of Alexandria exhorted third-century Christians "to despise the life that is eagerly sought after by the multitude," and "to be earnest in living the life that resembles that of God."[14] And the costs of discipleship in early Christianity were potentially high: the prospect of rejection, persecution, and even martyrdom was real—but did not seem too great a price to pay. Indeed, to suffer for Christ was often viewed

---

11 This description is most applicable to the "cult movement," which is distinguished by Stark and Bainbridge from the "audience cult" (a group that has almost no organization or structure, such as astrology or Theosophy) and the "client cult" (where there is only slightly greater organization than in the audience cult), Stark and Bainbridge (1979): 127-28. It should be stressed that the work of sociologists in defining the terms "Church," "Sect," and "Cult"—quite unlike the usage of most of the writers considered in this paper—is descriptive, and not evaluative.

12 See Mullet (1984): 168-91.

13 Atwood and Flowers (1983): 245-61. This would come as a shock to "Ex-Mormons for Jesus" and their like. An advertisement that their Los Angeles area chapter used to run in local newspapers asked, rhetorically, "Is Mormonism Christian or Cult?"—mistakenly assuming the two categories to be mutually exclusive, as do McKay and Smith (1985): 9, 10, 23, 29.

14 Origen, *Contra Celsum* II, 45. English translation in Roberts and Donaldson (1979): 4:449. Interestingly, Catholics since the Second Vatican Council have begun to reapply to themselves names such as "das wandernde Gottesvolk" ("the wandering people of God"), an epithet that echoes Hebrews 11 in suggesting conflict with the values of society.

as a privilege. The whole *Epistle to the Romans* by Ignatius of Antioch is a plea that they not pray that he escape the death of a martyr, but that he endure it nobly. If he can die in Christ, writes Ignatius, he has no desire to live: "Though I am alive while I write to you, yet I am eager to die. My love (i.e., Christ) has been crucified, and there is no fire in me desiring to be fed."[15] Further, as Graham Shaw has argued forcefully and in detail, there is an emerging strain of authoritarianism already present in the New Testament—particularly in Paul.[16] And as for exclusivism: To the early believer, there was no salvation outside of the Christian community, as is indicated by the *logion* ascribed to Jesus: "He that believeth and is baptized shall be saved; but he that believeth not shall be damned" (Mark 16:16).[17] (Walter Martin adds to these "cult characteristics" the lack of professional clergymen[18]—but here, too, he merely describes early Christianity.)[19] For Latter-day Saints, at least, who view their church as a restoration of ancient patterns, any classification that places them with the primitive Church cannot be considered a slight.

---

15 Ignatius of Antioch, *Epistle to the Romans* 7:2. English translation in Roberts and Donaldson (1981): 1:76; on this desire to achieve a "martyr's crown" among the early Christians see Nibley (1987b): 172-81; Droge and Tabor (1992): 128-65.

16 Shaw (1983): 1-23.

17 There has been considerable discussion lately as to whether this saying originates with Jesus. But whether it does or not, it certainly reflects the exclusivistic tendencies that characterized the early Christian community.

18 Martin (1984): 17-21. Unfortunately, "Dr." Martin's definitions cannot be treated here in their entirety. They are most instructive. In *The New Cults*, 17-21, he offers a number of characteristics: (1) strong leaders; (2) additional scriptures; (3) rigid standards for membership; (4) transient membership; (5) active proselyting; (6) no professional clergy; (7) claims of exclusive truth; and (8) "cultic vocabulary." Martin (1983): 25 yields only nine signs of culthood: (1) exclusivism; (2) blinding of followers to the truth; (3) threats of imminent Armageddon; (4) false promises of instant spiritual, emotional, and material help; (5) boasts of exclusive revelations; (6) claims of extrabiblical authority; (7) demands of complete obedience to leaders; (8) deceptive terminology that insulates them from the Bible; and (9) alienation of followers from the rest of the world and from Christ.

19 And early Quakers; see Mullett (1984): 174-75, for some rather strong Quaker language on the issue.

More often than by sociological definition, however, "cults" are identified by their conformity to or deviation from a presumed standard of Christian orthodoxy.[20] It is typical of "cults," writes Walter Martin, that they "blind their followers to the truth" and alienate them from a "saving relationship with Jesus Christ."[21] Earl Schipper defines a cult as a group that reinterprets or denies the divinity of Christ, offers an unbiblical basis for salvation, and claims a new revelation from God that either restores a lost biblical gospel or teaches truth in addition to the Bible.[22] The anti-Mormon *Evangel* raises many of these same charges against the Latter-day Saints: thus, in their view, Mormonism is a cult because it is excessively devoted to one person,[23] because it adds to the word of God,[24] because it requires works in addition to grace,[25] because it uses "unethically manipulative techniques of persuasion and control,"[26] because it tells its members that it and they are good while the outside world is evil,[27] and because such usage is generally accepted: "practically everyone who writes on the American cults includes Mormonism as a cult."[28]

---

20 See, for example, McKay and Smith (1985): 13-28. Oswald Eggenberger admits the utility of sociological analysis, but he insists that theological considerations come first in identifying *Sekten*; see Eggenberger (1969): 4. "If the world only knew the Mormon doctrine of a God-Mother," asserts *The Utah Evangel* (July 1985), "there would be no question but that Mormonism is a cult."

21 Martin (1983): 25.

22 Schipper (1982): 14-18.22 fe

23 *The Evangel* 38 (September 1991): 4.

24 *The Evangel* 38 (December 1991): 5.

25 Ibid.

26 *The Evangel* 38 (September 1991): 4. This unusually literate comment is actually quoted from *PTA Today* (November 1989): 24, which evidently makes no reference whatever to Mormonism.

27 Ibid.

28 *The Evangel* 37 (November 1990): 1. Of course, virtually every expert on the Bermuda Triangle believes in *it*. People who devote their lives or careers to illusory

Schippers's definition might have been crafted to describe Islam, yet he passes by the Muslims to attack only such groups as Mormons, Jehovah's Witnesses, Christian Science, the Unification Church, and The Way International. His title, *Cults of North America*, betrays the weakness of his definition: If mainstream Christianity is applied as the standard, all religions that deviate from or reject that standard have to be classed as "cults," including (besides Islam) Buddhism, Hinduism, and Judaism. Recognizing that so inclusive a definition renders it almost meaningless, many (including Schipper) arbitrarily apply the term "cult" only to groups active in the United States.[29] But even here the net is cast wide. Walter Martin puts the number of "cultists" at 30 million in the United States alone![30]

The hesitancy of our heresiographers to label major world faiths "cults" probably does not stem from principle.[31] Gordon Lewis, it is true, defines a cult as "any religious movement that claims the backing of Christ or the Bible, but distorts the central message of Christianity."[32] But this could apply to Judaism! Further, the most recent edition of Walter Martin's popular work, *The Kingdom of the Cults*, includes Islam, and, although unwilling to call it a cult, treats it in much the same fashion as other entries. (Also covered is something called "Eastern Religions," which seems to mean Hinduism.) And, after labeling spiritualism the most ancient, Martin tells us that "the second oldest of all the cult systems considered in

---

crusades are likely to be true believers! ("Don Quixote, the acknowledged expert on such giants, certainly counts that windmill among them.")

29 Compare, for example, the attempted definition of Starkes (1984): 4.

30 See Martin (1981): 1; also Martin (1983): 15.

31 Ed Decker and Dave Hunt equate Hinduism with the occult, and can speak of "Hindu-Buddhist occultism"; see Decker and Hunt (1984): 29, 254.

32 G. R. Lewis (1966): 4. Islam would probably fit this definition. Persistent medieval legends made of Muhammad a renegade cardinal, disappointed in his bid for the papacy. Thus, to medieval minds not altogether unlike those of our own heresiographers, Islam was simply an unusually obnoxious schism.

this book is . . . Zen Buddhism."[33] Nicheren Shoshu, a Buddhist movement dating from the thirteenth century, is condemned by Martin among *The New Cults*—a title that clearly betrays his parochial North American orientation.[34] Such groups are included despite Martin's own declaration that a cult is "a group of people gathered about a specific person or person's misinterpretation of the Bible,"[35] and despite his statement elsewhere that cults represent "major deviations" that yet claim to be Christian.[36] And where in Zen Buddhism are we to find the threats of imminent Armageddon that Mr. Martin lists among the characteristics of the "cult?"[37] Virtually all the "experts" agree that Baha'ism, a syncretistic offspring of Shi'ite Islam, is a "cult," and all take the International Society of Krishna Consciousness to be a model of the type.[38] Yet Josh McDowell and Don Stewart define a "cult" as "a perversion, a distortion of biblical Christianity"[39]—which neither Baha'ism nor Shi'ism nor the veneration of Krishna can possibly be thought to be.

---

33 Martin (1985): 261. In 1985 *Kingdom of the Cults* was fourth on the bestseller list of the Christian Booksellers Association; see also Lyons (1985): 65-66.

34 Martin (1984).

35 Martin (1985): 11.

36 Martin (1983): 17.

37 Martin (1983): 25.

38 On the Baha'is, see, for example, Larson (1983); McElveen, (1979): 169; Robertson (1983); Starkes (1984). Walter Martin's one-year program in "Christian Apologetics" recently awarded a master's degree for a thesis refuting Baha'ism. This represents a remarkable achievement, for the student apparently knows neither Arabic nor Persian.

39 McDowell and Stewart (1983): 17. H. F. Beck generously offers to consider as a cult any twisting of any major world religion (his is a different kind of voice, quasi-officially Lutheran); see Beck (1977). But do Christian scholars really have any competence to referee disputes in Buddhist doctrine or Islamic law? None of the usual anti-"cult" specialists seems to be interested in following Beck's lead. They have little if any concern, say, for Hindu orthodoxy.

Why all the contradiction? Perhaps merely for tactical purposes. To be called a "cult," a religion must be small. Major religions may be spared the word for reasons of decorum, while being judged just as harshly. Merrill F. Unger, a prominent evangelical scholar, is merely more explicit than most when he pronounces not only "cults" but also non-Christian world religions to be, literally, demonic.[40] (The authors of *The God Makers* argue that Mormonism is just like Hinduism—that is, it is a system of Satan worship.) "The sociological considerations of cult activity," asserts Bob Larson, "must mirror the standard that Christ is the source of determining error and truth. . . . Even established world religions which do not bear the sociological earmarks of a cult will be included (in my book) because of their departure from Christian theology."[41]

Fritz Ridenour reserves the title of "cult" for people like Mormons and Jehovah's Witnesses, but also ("biblically") condemns Judaism, Islam, Hinduism, Buddhism, and Roman Catholicism.[42] There is, in fact, a marked tendency to anti-Catholicism on the part of many self-proclaimed "cult" experts. J. K. van Baalen, for example, while declining to call Roman Catholicism an "unchristian cult," declares nevertheless that "it is a corrupt and exceedingly dangerous political machine, and it is a religious body full of doctrinal error and superstition."[43] Others are less hesitant. Anti-Catholic Bill Jackson writes, "It is difficult to come up with

---

40 Unger (1984). J. K. van Baalen—an unecumenical mind, to put it mildly—refused to acknowledge any significant areas of commonality shared by Christianity with other religions; see van Baalen (1983).

41 Larson (1983): 26-27. Floyd McElveen approvingly cites a division of the religions of the world into two groups: Christian fundamentalists (good), and everyone else (bad). But only "bad" groups are specifically named—including Atheists, Mormons, Spiritualists, and Baha'is; see McElveen (1979): 169-70; cf. 132-33.

42 Ridenour (1979).

43 Van Baalen (1983): 5.

any modern definition of what is a cult and include Jehovah's Witnesses, Mormons, and a host of others and omit the largest false religious system of all—Roman Catholicism."[44] Similarly, Donald Spitz asserts that Jehovah's Witnesses and Mormons are cultists, as are Roman Catholics.[45] Karl Keating, a Catholic writer, has probably put his finger on the nub of the matter when he states that "a cult is any religion that is not fundamentalism."[46] Some Roman Catholics have returned the favor, characterizing a variety of non-Catholic groups—including Baptists and Pentecostals—as "sectarian," because they represent groups that set themselves "apart from the world and . . . judge everyone else who fails to conform to [their] set of beliefs."[47] Attempting to refute Mormon belief in an ancient apostasy, *The Utah Evangel* declares that "any objective study of Catholicism will reveal a small but courageous group of Christians who never bowed to Rome. Though perhaps 50,000,000 of these died martyr's [*sic*] deaths, they never ceased to exist. . . . They rejected the papacy. . . . They rejected baptismal regeneration. They believed in salvation by grace. . . . They relied upon the Bible as their only rule of faith and practice. . . . They believed in

---

44 Keating (1988): 83.

45 Keating (1988): 105. The anti-Catholic writer Keith Green says much the same thing: Catholics are not Christians, but cultists; see Keating (1988): 101.

46 Keating (1988): 81.

47 According to Raymond K. DeHainaut (1987): 33-34, "The Roman Catholic book on sects [*Las Sectas en America Latina*, published by the Conference of the Latin American Episcopacy of the Roman Catholic Church, or CELAM] defines a sect as a group that sets itself apart from the world and tends to judge everyone else who fails to conform to its narrow set of beliefs. . . . Protestants and Roman Catholics differ somewhat as to which groups they would label sectarian. The Catholic book places Baptists, as well as Mormons, Jehovah's Witnesses, Pentecostals, Theosophy, and Masonry in its list of sects. . . . Some Protestant theologians contend that the Roman Catholic Church itself functions like a sect because of the disproportionate emphasis it places on the veneration of the Virgin Mary. José Miguez Bonino, a Methodist theologian in Buenos Aires, argues in a 1960 article, *Iglesia y Secta: revision de un vocabulario*, that the cult of Mary contains all the characteristics of a sect."

the priesthood of every believer. . . . The church did not cease to exist."[48]

"The hallmarks of cultic conversion," writes Ronald Enroth, "usually include the abandonment of a familiar life style; severing of ties with friends and families; a radical and sometimes sudden change in personality; the relinquishing of possessions; introduction of a new set of values, goals, and beliefs; the assuming of a totally new identity, including for some a new name; the acquisition of a new 'spiritual' family; unquestioned submission to leaders and group priorities; isolation from the 'outside world' with its attendant evil; subversion of the will; thought reform; the adoption of new sociocultural and spiritual insignia; and a host of other less dramatic though equally significant characteristics."[49] However, while the definition was undoubtedly framed with Krishna Consciousness and the "Moonies" in mind, it is quite as evocative of Catholic monasticism and religious orders, and is no less applicable to Thomas Merton and St. Francis of Assisi than to the Buddha and Jim Jones.

The arbitrary and *ad hoc* character of such attempts at definition is clear in an article by the German Catholic authority on *Sekten*, Konrad Algermissen. Citing two Protestant theologians who describe a *Sekte* as a group accepting an extrabiblical source of authority and denying the doctrine of justification by grace alone,

---

48 *The Utah Evangel* 31 (November 1984); cf. McElveen (1979): 127-129. Not surprisingly, they sound just like born-again Protestants. After interrogation by an author of this paper, one dedicated anti-Mormon reluctantly conceded that a person could not be a Catholic and a Christian at the same time. This is perhaps not the majority view; it is unlikely in any event to be given much publicity during campaigns to convince the general populace—which is comprised of Catholic as well as Protestant—that Mormonism is a "non-Christian cult." The question seems to be one of tactics; the mindset is the same as that nineteenth-century one treated by Davis (1960): 205-24. (Martin Marty and others have studied the present Protestant dream of a "Christian America.") After Salt Lake City is disposed of, do we move on to Rome?

49 Enroth (1977): 12. Some of this definitely applies to early Quakers.

a description paralleled in many anti-"cult" polemics,[50] Algermissen is appalled, and notes that, by such a definition, Catholics
would be categorized as a *Sekte*. So he simply reformulates the
definition to apply to Mormons and Seventh-Day Adventists, but
not to Catholics.[51]

Some, such as Walter Martin, define as a cult any group "which
differs significantly in some one or more respects as to belief or
practice, from those religious groups which are regarded as the
normative expression of religion in our total culture."[52] (In a move
that Kierkegaard might have appreciated, the average becomes the
ideal!) However, this definition is of little use in a pluralistic
society. Is cult status dependent upon statistics? Are America's Jews
a cult? Is Sikhism a cult here, but a legitimate religion in India's
Punjab? Or is "Dr." Martin's norm, Western culture, the standard
for all the planet? What of the growing Muslim minority in North
America? A major world religion in Africa, Asia, and part of
Europe, is Islam a cult here? At what numerical level will Islam—or
Mormonism—cease to be a cult?

The second-century Church father Tertullian felt that many non-
Christians in his day desired no closer investigation of Christianity
"in case things they prefer to have believed should be proved

---

50 See McKay and Smith (1985): 23-27.

51 Algermissen (1964): 735-36. H.-Ch. Chéry responds in precisely the same way
to the charge of one "Pastor Hoff" that the Roman Catholic Church is "sectaire";
see Chéry (1954): 37. The sarcasm of Prof. Dr. Algermissen's prose is characteristic of this genre in German; see especially Algermissen (1964): 741-47. No pretense
of value neutrality here! Mormonism is discussed at some length, as "Der Typ einer
neuzeitlichen Sekte," Algermissen (1964): 744-747. The two Protestant theologians
are Kurt Hutten and F. Blanke. A. A. Hoekema's standard treatment is also
dependent upon Hutten's definition, given in *Die Glaubenswelt der Sektierer*; see
Hoekema (1984): 377-88. (Mormons will not be surprised to learn they are among
"the four major cults.")

52 Martin (1985): 11. Martin has taken this particular definition—one of several
(not always compatible) which occur in his books—from Charles Braden, a liberal
Protestant historian of religions.

untrue."[53] In the same way, one suspects that some who use the term "cult" do so to warn people away from further investigation.

"How to cope with the cults?" asks the cover of a book entitled *Know the Marks of a Cult*. "There are so many of them . . . all different. Who has time to study all their weird doctrines in order to refute them? Here is a better way. No need to get bogged down in the details of this or that cult. No need to debate fine points in the original Greek or Hebrew. No need to fight over the interpretation of obscure passages of scripture."[54] After all, as Ronald Enroth observes, there is some diversity, but "in a real sense the familiar expression, once you've seen one, you've seen them all, is applicable to current cult groups."[55] (This of a category that purportedly includes Ezra Taft Benson, the Maharishi, Seventh-Day Adventists, Jonestown, and the Rajneesh commune in Oregon!) "Strange as it may seem," asserts Dave Hunt with astonishing understatement, "most cults are basically the same. Even apparent differences are generally only skin deep."[56] Bob Larson knows something called "cultic philosophy," although he acknowledges some variations.[57] Walter Martin can speak of "cultic vocabulary,"[58] and the title of his most ambitious book, *The Kingdom of the Cults*, suggests a monolithic enemy.

The emotional impact and consequences of the term are implied in a story related approvingly by Ronald Enroth: "In a Midwestern suburb a religious organization called Eckankar had scheduled an information meeting for the public in the community room of a local bank. Following the publication of a story in a major local

---

53 Tertullian, *Apologeticus adversus Gentes pro Christianis* II, 19. English translation in Glover (1966): 17.

54 Breese (1984).

55 Enroth (1977): 12.

56 Hunt (1980): 19.

57 Larson (1983): 27.

58 Martin (1984): 17-21.

newspaper describing Eckankar as a 'religious cult,' the bank changed its mind and withdrew its approval of the use of the room by the group. 'We weren't aware they were considered a cult,' explained the bank's branch manager."[59]

The mere mention of the word "cult" by the local newspaper, with no consideration of the actual teachings of the group, was enough to persuade the bank manager to rescind permission to use the bank's facilities. "Any cult," proclaims Bob Larson, "which places itself in opposition to historic Christianity should not be allowed to hide behind a cloak of religious good will or misleading terminology."[60]

Jews for Jesus, a group "widely respected among evangelicals . . . was listed as a cult alongside Moonies and Hare Krishnas" on the dustjacket of *Mindbending.*[61] Moishe Rosen, the national coordinator of Jews for Jesus, laments that, since his group has begun to be referred to as a "cult," many pulpits that had previously been available have been closed.[62]

But if polemics about "cults" inhibit an understanding of groups so designated, and close doors to them, such words occasionally turn against their own masters. According to *Newsweek,* a new organization called "Fundamentalists Anonymous" now exists to aid those "struggling to shake fundamentalism's cultlike grip."[63] Evangelical Christians, who often describe the aggressive proselyting methods of certain "cults" as "brainwashing,"[64] have had the same charge leveled against them. Flo Conway and Jim Siegelmann, in *Snapping: America's Epidemic of Sudden Personality*

---

59 Enroth (1981): 1.

60 Larson (1983): 26.

61 "Jewish Leaders Attempt to Fight Effects of Evangelism," (1984): 40.

62 Ibid., 42.

63 See the fascinating article by Woodward, Anderson, and Springen (1985): 63.

64 Cf., e.g., Enroth (1977).

Change, compare evangelical conversion to joining the "Moonies."[65] According to Lawrence Foster, "the deprogrammer Ted Patrick . . . refers to Billy Graham as a dangerous cultist."[66] Likewise, while some Christians have lauded "deprogramming" as a necessary and acceptable response to the indoctrination techniques of "cults," Jewish parents and community leaders have used and defended similar methods (which they call "counseling") for Jewish young people who have converted to Christianity, frequently of an evangelical type. Lawrence Foster recounts: "I remember my amusement, for example, listening to a militant rabbi from the Hassidic movement (which some might characterize as a Jewish fringe or cultic group) harangue a respectable middle-aged Jewish audience about the dread dangers of the 'cults.' His primary concern was not with the Moonies or Hare Krishnas, but mainstream Protestant groups that he felt were attracting Jewish converts. Similarly, I was somewhat taken aback in talking with an East Asian student who expressed his repugnance at the 'cultic' character of Christianity, especially its periodic 'ritual cannibalism' of its founder. For a moment, I failed to realize that he was referring to the Eucharist or Lord's Supper. Beliefs or rituals that appear similarly bizarre to an outsider can be found in all the major world religions—Judaism, Christianity, Islam, Hinduism, and Buddhism alike. In effect, the only popular meaning of the word 'cult' is, 'a religious group that someone else doesn't like.' Such definitions are less than useful as analytical tools."[67]

In the recent celebrated Catherine Crowell Webb rape case, prosecutors were wary of Mrs. Webb's withdrawal of her accusation against Gary Dotson, a withdrawal occasioned, she testified, by guilty conscience upon her being "born again." "Sources close to the investigation," the Chicago *Tribune* reported, "say authorities remain unconvinced because the woman is associated with a

---

65 Conway and Siegelmann (1978).

66 Foster (1987): 186.

67 Foster (1987): 187-88.

religious cult and living in an emotionally charged atmosphere."
Mrs. Webb is a Baptist.[68]

J. K. van Baalen long bewailed society's tolerance for "anti-Christian cults" such as Mormonism and Christian Science.[69]
More recently, certain anti-Mormons have sought to enlist the authoritarian regimes of Chile and Kenya against the Church. But the hue and cry about "cults," "brainwashing," and "deprogramming" have brought in their wake a potential threat to the freedom of all religious groups. "Religious movements, and perhaps ultimately religion itself," remarks sociologist Thomas Robbins, "are increasingly being viewed as social problems."[70] Laws have been proposed in Germany, Great Britain, Canada, and several states in the United States that, though ostensibly designed to protect against methods of "brainwashing" used by the "Moonies," are in fact so ambiguous that they could be construed to prohibit any sort of proselyting that might lead to a change in lifestyle.[71] Predicts Prof. Robbins: "As the hostility to the 'abuse' of cults . . . mounts, the general privileges and tax exemptions of churches per se will likely come under the gun."[72] But even now, the result of the campaign against alleged "cult excesses"—led, to a large extent, by devout Christians—has been, as the evangelical scholar Irving Hexham points out, that "secularists are able to urge the acceptance of laws which replace religious freedom by a grudgingly granted religious toleration."[73] Given the hazards of the term "cult," we suggest that its pejorative use be abandoned.

---

68 Cited by O'Sullivan (1985): 22.

69 See, for example, van Baalen (1983): 6.

70 Robbins (1985): 2:172. Robbins fears that the "era of detente" in religious studies may be coming to an end, and that value-neutrality is on its way out.

71 Cf. the Lasher Amendment, State of New York in Assembly 11122-A (25 March 1980); cited in Irving Hexham, "Cults," in Elwell (1983): 289.

72 Robbins (1985): 177.

73 Robbins (1985): 177.

Even in social science usage, notes A. W. Eister, the word remains "vague and unsatisfactory." "Numerous variations and extensions of these concepts exist in the literature," he writes, "many of them devised without solid empirical grounding, sometimes merely rehearsing 'armchair definitions' made decades ago and seldom tested against actual cases or even rigorously examined for their logical (or sociological) consistency."[74] What, then, of those whose aim is less to understand than to condemn, whose goal is more to obscure than to illumine?

Those polemicists who use the term "cult" seem—and like to seem—to be conveying by its use hard, objective information about the groups they so designate. "Perhaps the best method of determining that Mormonism is a cult," asserts *The Utah Evangel*, "would be to consult recognized authorities in the field. . . . We did not let the tobacco industry determine the danger in its use. We called in experts. Mormonism is incapable of assessing whether or not it is a cult. Almost all the experts say it is."[75] Yet it is not at all clear that the information conveyed by use of the term goes beyond telling us that the group in question is one of which these alleged "experts" disapprove. What else can yoga, Unitarians, the Esalen Institute, and the "martial arts"—all, incredibly, listed in Larson's *Book of Cults*—possibly have in common? (If any other criterion is operative, it seems to be that the group under discussion must be small, weak, or passive enough that insults are without risk.)

"Apart from theological considerations," writes Bob Larson, "what classifies a certain group as a 'cult'? The designation obviously requires a subjective value judgment."[76] Significantly, our polemical "cult experts"—with no known exception—avoid

---

74 Eister (1972): 320.

75 *The Utah Evangel* 31 (March 1984). It's all as straightforward as a chemical test; cf. McKay and Smith (1985): 41. "We believe 'Why Mormonism Is a Cult' has proven without a doubt that Mormonism is a cult. Little more need be said. Our arguments are conclusive. . . . Facts speak for themselves"; McKay and Smith (1985): 43.

76 Larson (1983): 27.

publishing on the subject for a scholarly audience, before which they might be held to rigorous account. "It is possible," as Paul Hedengren observes, "to use language in such away as to appear superficially to be making assertions, when in fact the language use is logically equivalent to growling."[77]

Instead of the abused, and abusive, term "cult," we propose more neutral terminology, such as "religious movement," "religious group," or "church." According to Lawrence Foster, "there is no analytical substance to the popular definition of a cult as a danger- ous group with bizarre religious beliefs that follows a deranged or cynically opportunistic leader. One person's 'cult' is another person's 'true faith.' . . . In effect, the only popular meaning of the word 'cult' is, 'a religious group that someone else doesn't like.' Such definitions are less than useful as analytical tools. . . . Since 'cult' is essentially a pejorative term without analytical precision, I shall henceforth refer to such groups as 'new religious move- ments' or 'new religions.' "[78] Perhaps the best approach would be to apply to each group the name that its adherents use in referring to themselves.[79] This action alone would practically eliminate the term "cult" from religious discourse. (Further, no false uniformity would be imposed upon widely differing faiths.)[80]

---

77 Hedengren (1985): 41.

78 Foster (1987): 187, 188, 189. Among the "Guidelines and Suggestions for Writing Critical Notes for *Religious Studies Review*," handed out to all reviewers for this publication of the Council of Societies for the Study of Religion—currently headquartered at Mercer University, in Macon, Georgia—is the advice to "avoid pejorative terminology." The first example given of such "pejorative terminology" is the word "cult."

79 This is unlikely to happen, alas. As W. C. Smith has pointed out, religions are rarely known by names that they themselves have chosen; cf. Smith (1963): 80, 273.

80 Paul Heclas has shown that even a threefold classification of just those religious groups stemming from the 1960s and 1970s fails adequately to represent their variety; see Heclas (1985): 81-97; Chéry (1954): 31-35. What value, then, can reside in a classification that puts not only these groups, but also Mormonism, a thirteenth-century faction of Japanese Buddhism, and a nineteenth century offshoot of Iranian Shiʿism, into one catch-all category?

As Tertullian insisted, truth requests only "that she not be condemned without a hearing."[81] Latter-day Saints and doubtless others currently stigmatized as "cultists" ask little more than that their doctrines and teachings be granted a fair hearing, with the way cleared of impediments, lexical or otherwise.

---

81 Tertullian, *Apologeticus* I, 2.

▲

Bibliography

▲

Ahmanson, John. *Secret History: An Eyewitness Account of the Rise of Mormonism*, translated by Gleason L. Archer. Chicago: Moody, 1984.

Alexander, David, and Pat Alexander. *Eerdmans Handbook to the Bible*. Grand Rapids: Eerdmans, 1977.

Algermissen, Konrad. *Das Sektenwesen der Gegenwart*. 2nd ed. Aschaffenburg: Pattloch Verlag, 1962.

———. "Der Grundirrtum der modernen Sekten." In Michael Schmauss and Alfred Laepple, *Wahrheit and Zeugnis*. Düsseldorf: Patmos, 1964.

Allen, James B., and Glen M. Leonard. *The Story of the Latter-day Saints*. Salt Lake City: Deseret Book, 1976.

Althaus, Paul. *The Theology of Martin Luther*, translated by Robert C. Schultz. Philadelphia: Fortress, 1966.

Anderson, Richard L. *Understanding Paul*. Salt Lake City: Deseret Book, 1983.

Arrington, Leonard J. *Brigham Young: American Moses*. New York: Knopf, 1985.

Arrington, Leonard J., and Davis Bitton. *The Mormon Experience: A History of the Latter-day Saints*. New York: Knopf, 1979.

Atwood, James D., and Ronald B. Flowers. "Early Christianity as a Cult Movement." *Encounter* 4:3 (1983): 245-61.

Aune, D. E. "The Problem of the Messianic Secret." *Novum Testamentum* 11 (1969): 1-31.

Averill, Lloyd J. *Religious Right, Religious Wrong: A Critique of the Fundamentalist Phenomenon.* New York: Pilgrim, 1989.

Bainton, Roland. *Here I Stand: A Life of Martin Luther.* Nashville: Abingdon, 1950.

Baldick, Julian. *Mystical Islam: An Introduction to Sufism.* New York: New York University Press, 1989.

"Baptism for the Dead." La Mesa, CA: Utah Christian Tract Society, n.d.

Barker, Kenneth, ed. *The NIV Study Bible: New International Version.* Grand Rapids: Zondervan, 1985.

Barley, L.M., C.D. Field, B.A. Kosmin, and J.D. Nielsen, eds. *Religion.* Oxford: Pergamon, 1987.

Barlow, Philip. "Unorthodox Orthodoxy: The Idea of Deification in Christian History." *Sunstone* 8 (September-October 1983): 13-18.

Barrett, David B. *World Christian Encyclopedia.* Nairobi: Oxford University Press, 1982.

Barth, Karl. *The Doctrine of the Word of God. Church Dogmatics*, 1:1. New York: Scribner's Sons, 1936.

Bartley, Peter. *Mormonism: The Prophet, the Book and the Cult.* Dublin: Veritas, 1989.

Bauer, Walter. *A Greek-English Lexicon of the New Testament and Other Early Christian Literature*, translated and edited by William F. Arndt and F. Wilbur Gingrich. Chicago: University of Chicago Press, 1957.

Beaver, R. Pierce, et al., eds. *Eerdman's Handbook to the World's Religions.* Grand Rapids: Eerdmans, 1982.

Beck, Hubert F. *How to Respond to the Cults.* St. Louis: Concordia, 1977.

Beggiani, Seely J. *Early Syriac Theology.* Lanham, MD: University Press of America, 1983.

Bellah, Robert N., and Frederick E. Greenspahn, eds. *Uncivil Religion: Interreligious Hostility in America.* New York: Crossroad, 1987.

Benko, Stephen. *Pagan Rome and the Early Christians.* Bloomington, IN: Indiana University Press, 1986.

Benz, Ernst W. "Imago Dei: Man in the Image of God." In *Reflections on Mormonism: Judaeo-Christian Parallels*, edited by Truman G. Madsen. Provo: Religious Studies Center, Brigham Young University, 1978.

Berry, Harold J. *Mormonism: Latter-day Confusion*. Lincoln, NB: Back to the Bible, 1973.

————. *Examining the Cults*. Lincoln, NB: Back to the Bible, 1979.

Bertrand, Louis A. *Mémoires d'un Mormon*. Paris: Dentu, 1862.

Blair, Edward P. *Abingdon Bible Handbook*. Nashville: Abingdon, 1975.

Blevins, B. L. *The Messianic Secret in Markan Research, 1901-76*. Washington, DC: University Press of America, 1981.

"Blood Atonement and the Mormon Church." Phoenix, AZ: Alpha and Omega Ministries, n.d.

Boa, Kenneth. *Cults, World Religions, and You*. Wheaton, IL: Victor Books, 1984.

Boettner, Loraine. *Roman Catholicism*. Phillipsburg, NJ: Presbyterian and Reformed Publishing, 1986.

Bolle, Kees W. *Secrecy in Religions*. Leiden: Brill, 1987.

Bolt, Robert. *A Man for All Seasons*. London: French, 1962.

Bonwetsch, N. "Wesen, Entstehung und Fortgang der Arcandisciplin." *Zeitschrift für die historische Theologie* 43 (1873): 203-99.

Boobyer, G. H. "The Secrecy Motif in St Mark's Gospel." *New Testament Studies* 6 (1959): 225-35.

Bouzignac, Guillaume, "Noé, Noé! Pastores, Cantate Domino," edited by Steven Sametz. New York: Broude Brothers, 1986.

Brandon, S. G. F., ed. *A Dictionary of Comparative Religion*. New York: Scribner's Sons, 1970.

Brauer, Jerald C., ed. *The Westminster Dictionary of Church History*. Philadelphia: Westminster, 1971.

Breese, Dave. *Know the Marks of Cults*. Wheaton: Victor Books, 1984.

Breese, Dave, et al. *Exposing the Deceivers: Nine Cults and What They Teach*. Lincoln, NB: Back to the Bible Correspondence School, 1985.

Brennan, Joseph. *A Handbook of Logic*. 2nd ed. New York: Harper & Row, 1961.

Bringhurst, Newell G. *Brigham Young and the Expanding American Frontier*. Boston: Little, Brown, 1986.

Broderick, Robert C. *The Catholic Encyclopedia*. Nashville: Nelson, 1976.

Brown, Peter. *Augustine of Hippo*. Berkeley: University of California Press, 1969.

Brown, Raymond E., Joseph A. Fitzmyer, and Roland E. Murphy, eds. *The Jerome Biblical Commentary*. 2 vols. in one. Englewood Cliffs, NJ: Prentice-Hall, 1968.

Brown, Raymond E., and John P. Meier. *Antioch and Rome*. New York: Paulist Press, 1983.

Brown, Robert L., and Rosemary Brown. *They Lie in Wait to Deceive: A Study of Anti-Mormon Deception*. Vol. 2. Mesa, AZ: Braunsworth, 1984.

Brox, Norbert. *Kirchengeschichte des Altertums*. Düsseldorf: Patmos, 1983.

Bruce, F. F. *New Testament History*. Garden City, NY: Doubleday, 1972.

———. *The Spreading Flame*. Grand Rapids: Wm. B. Eerdmans Publishing Company, 1979.

———, ed. *The International Bible Commentary*. Rev. ed. Grand Rapids: Zondervan, 1986.

Brunkow, Robert deV., ed. *Religion and Society in North America*. Santa Barbara, CA: American Bibliographical Center, 1983.

Brunotte, Heinz, and Otto Weber, eds. *Evangelisches Kirchenlexikon: Kirchlich-theologisches Handwörterbuch*. 3 vols. 2nd ed. Göttingen: Vandenhoeck and Ruprecht, 1956-59

Bunker, Gary L., and Davis Bitton. *The Mormon Graphic Image, 1834-1914: Cartoons, Caricatures, and Illustrations*. Salt Lake City: University of Utah Press, 1983.

Burrell, Maurice C., and J. Stafford Wright. *Today's Sects*. 2nd ed. Grand Rapids: Baker, 1983.

Buthelezi, Manas. "Polygyny in the Light of the New Testament." *Africa Theological Journal* 2 (February 1969): 58-70.

Butterworth, G. W. "The Deification of Man in Clement of Alexandria." *Journal of Theological Studies* 17 (1916): 157-69.

Buttrick, George A. *The Interpreter's Dictionary of the Bible.* 4 vols. and a supplement. Nashville: Abingdon, 1962-76.

Campenhausen, Hans Freiherr von, ed. *Die Religion in Geschichte und Gegenwart.* 3rd ed., fully revised. 7 vols. Tübingen: Mohr, 1957-65.

Cannon, George Q. *Life of Joseph Smith the Prophet.* Salt Lake City: Deseret Book, 1986.

Carroll, Lewis. *The Annotated Alice.* New York: New American Library, 1963.

Carver, James A. "Answering an Ex-Mormon Critic." Sandy, UT: Mormon Miscellaneous, 1983.

Casel, Odo. "Antike und christliche Mysterien." *Bayrische Blätter für die Gymnasialwissenschaft* 63 (1927): 329-40.

Cattau, Daniel. "What's All This Talk about Justification?" *The Lutheran* (19 February 1986): 8-10.

Celsus. *On the True Doctrine: A Discourse against the Christians,* translated by R. Joseph Hoffmann. New York: Oxford University Press, 1987.

Charlesworth, James H., ed. *The Old Testament Pseudepigrapha.* 2 vols. Garden City, NY: Doubleday, 1983-85.

Cherbonnier, Edmond LaB. "In Defense of Anthropomorphism." In *Reflections on Mormonism: Judaeo-Christian Parallels,* edited by Truman G. Madsen. Provo, UT: Brigham Young University, Religious Studies Center, 1978.

Chéry, H.-Ch. *L'Offensive des Sectes.* Paris: Les Éditions du Cerf, 1954.

Child, Heather, and Dorothy Colles. *Christian Symbols: Ancient and Modern.* London: Bell and Sons, 1971.

Christie-Murray, David. *A History of Heresy.* Oxford: Oxford University Press, 1989.

Ciampa, Stella. "Catholic or Christian?" Havertown, PA: The Conversion Center, n.d.

Coe, Jolene, and Greg Coe. *The Mormon Experience.* Eugene, OR: Harvest House, 1985.

Compton, Todd M. "The Handclasp and Embrace as Tokens of Recognition." In *By Study and Also By Faith*, edited by John M. Lundquist and Stephen D. Ricks. 2 vols. Salt Lake City: Deseret Book and F.A.R.M.S., 1990.

Conway, Flo, and Jim Siegelmann. *Snapping: America's Epidemic of Sudden Personality Change*. Philadelphia: Lippincott, 1978.

Conzelmann, Hans. *1 Corinthians: A Commentary on the First Epistle to the Corinthians*, translated by James W. Leitch. Philadelphia: Fortress, 1975.

Couliano, Ioan P. *The Tree of Gnosis: Gnostic Mythology from Early Christianity to Modern Nihilism*, translated by H. S. Wiesner and I. P. Couliano. San Francisco: Harper Collins, 1992.

Coxill, H. Wakelin, and Kenneth Grubb. *World Christian Handbook 1968*. London: Lutterworth, 1967.

Crim, Keith, ed. *Abingdon Dictionary of Living Religions*. Nashville: Abingdon, 1981.

Cross, F. L., and E. A. Livingstone, eds. *The Oxford Dictionary of the Christian Church*. 2nd ed. Oxford: Oxford University Press, 1983.

Dahl, Larry E., and Charles D. Tate, Jr., eds. *The Lectures on Faith in Historical Perspective*. Provo: Religious Studies Center, Brigham Young University, 1990.

Davies, Douglas J. *Mormon Spirituality: Latter Day Saints in Wales and Zion*. Nottingham, England: University of Nottingham, n.d.

Davis, David B. "Some Themes of Counter-Subversion: An Analysis of Anti-Masonic, Anti-Catholic, and Anti-Mormon Literature." *The Mississippi Valley Historical Review 47* (September 1960): 205-24.

Davis, H. Francis, Aidan Williams, Ivo Thomas, and Joseph Crehan, eds. *A Catholic Dictionary of Theology*. 3 vols. London: Nelson and Sons. 1962-71.

Decker, J. Edward. "The Mormon Dilemma: Christian or Cult?" Typed transcript of an address given "in a Seattle church, early in 1979." In BYU Special Collections Library.

———. "Petition."

———. "The Question of Freemasonry." Issaquah, Washington: Saints Alive in Jesus, n.d.

——. "Those Plain and Precious Things." Issaquah, WA: Saints Alive in Jesus, n.d.

——. "To Moroni with Love." 2nd ed. Seattle: Life Messengers, n.d.

Decker, J. Edward, and Dave Hunt. *The God Makers*. Eugene, OR: Harvest House Publishers, 1984.

DeHainaut, Raymond K. "Sects and Religious Corporations Invade Latin America." *International Christian Digest* 1 (November 1987): 33-34.

De la Croix, Horst, and Richard G. Tansey. *Gardner's Art through the Ages*. 7th ed. New York: Harcourt Brace Jovanovich, 1980.

"The Dimensions of the Cult Conspiracy" (interview with Ronald Enroth). *Christianity Today* 25:18 (23 October 1981): 26-27.

Douglas, J. D., ed. *The New International Dictionary of the Christian Church*. Rev. ed. Grand Rapids: Zondervan, 1978.

Douglas, J. D., Walter A. Elwell, and Peter Toon, eds. *The Concise Dictionary of the Christian Tradition*. Grand Rapids: Zondervan, 1989.

Draper, James T., Jr. *Authority: The Critical Issue for Southern Baptists*. Old Tappan, NJ: Revell, 1984.

Dummelow, J. R. *Commentary on the Holy Bible*. New York: Macmillan, 1920.

Dunlap, Alex O. "Alex Dunlap Answers Roman Catholic Priest." Havertown, PA: The Conversion Center, n.d.

Dunn, James D. G. *Unity and Diversity in the New Testament: An Inquiry into the Character of Earliest Christianity*. London: SCM, 1977.

Eble, Kenneth E. "Among the Mormons." *Dialogue: A Journal of Mormon Thought* 19 (Summer 1986): 101-18.

Edwards, Paul, ed. *The Encyclopedia of Philosophy*. 8 vols. New York: Macmillan, 1967.

Edwards, Rem B. "The Pagan Dogma of the Absolute Unchangeableness of God." *Religious Studies* 14 (September 1978): 305-13.

Eggenberger, Oswald. *Die Kirchen, Sondergruppen und religiösen Vereinigungen: Ein Handbuch*. Zürich: EVZ-Verlag, 1969.

Ehat, Andrew F., and Lyndon W. Cook. *The Words of Joseph Smith*. Provo, UT: Religious Studies Center, Brigham Young University, 1980.

Eister, Allan W. "An Outline of a Structural Theory of Cults." *Journal for the Scientific Study of Religion* 11:4 (December 1972): 320.

Elwell, Walter. *Evangelical Dictionary of Theology*. Grand Rapids: Baker, 1983.

Encyclopedia of World Religions. London: Octopus Books, 1975.

Enders, Ernst L., ed. *Dr. Martin Luther's Briefwechsel*. 17 vols. Stuttgart: Verein der Verlagsbuchhandlung, 1884-1915.

England, Eugene. *Dialogues with Myself: Personal Essays on Mormon Experience*. Midvale, UT: Orion Books, 1984.

Enroth, Ronald. *Youth, Brainwashing, and the Extremist Cults*. Grand Rapids: Zondervan, 1977.

———. *What Is a Cult?* Downers Grove, IL: InterVarsity, 1981.

Fahlbusch, Erwin, ed. *Taschenlexikon Religion und Theologie*. 5 vols. 4th ed. Göttingen: Vandenhoeck & Ruprecht, 1983.

Farah, Caesar E. *Islam: Beliefs and Observances*. Woodbury, NY: Barron's, 1970.

Fee, Gordon D. *The First Epistle to the Corinthians*. Grand Rapids: Eerdmans, 1987.

Ferguson, Everett, et al., eds. *Encyclopedia of Early Christianity*. New York and London: Garland, 1990.

Ferm, Virgilius, ed. *An Encyclopedia of Religion*. New York: The Philosophical Library, 1945.

Feucht, Oscar E., ed. *Sex and the Church: A Sociological, Historical, and Theological Investigation of Sex Attitudes*. St. Louis: Concordia, 1961.

Fielding, Henry. *The History of Tom Jones, A Foundling*. Chicago: Encylopaedia Britannica, 1952.

Forrest, Bill. "Are Mormons Christian?" Salt Lake City: Mormon Miscellaneous, n.d.

Foster, Lawrence. "Cults in Conflict: New Religious Movements and the Mainstream Religious Tradition in America." In *Uncivil Religion: Interreligious Hostility in America*, edited by Robert N. Bellah and Frederick E. Greenspahn. New York: Crossroad, 1987.

Fraser, Gordon H. *Is Mormonism Christian?* Chicago: Moody, 1977.

Frend, W. H. C. *Martyrdom and Persecution in the Early Church.* Grand Rapids: Baker, 1981.

Fuller, Reginald C., Leonard Johnston, and Conleth Kearns, eds. *A New Catholic Commentary on Holy Scripture.* Nashville: Nelson, 1975.

Gaster, Theodor H. *The Dead Sea Scriptures in English Translation.* 2d ed., revised and enlarged. Garden City: Doubleday Anchor, 1964.

Geer, Thelma. "Who Is This Man . . . and Why Did He Marry 19 Times?" Safety Harbor, FL: Ex-Mormons for Jesus, n.d.

Glover, T. R., tr. *Tertullian: Apology, De Spectaculis.* Cambridge, MA: Harvard University Press, 1966.

Goldstein, Jonathan A. "The Origins of the Doctrine of Creation Ex Nihilo." *Journal of Jewish Studies* 35 (Autumn 1984): 127-35.

Gonzales, Justo L. *A History of Christian Thought.* 3 vols. Nahsville: Abingdon, 1970.

Grant, Heber J. *Gospel Standards.* Salt Lake City: The Improvement Era, 1941.

Gravel, Heinrich. *Die Arcandisciplin I: Geschichte und Stand der Frage.* Lingen: van Asken, 1902.

Greeley, Horace. "Interview with Brigham Young." In *The Annals of America.* Chicago: Encyclopaedia Britannica, 1968.

Green, Keith. "The Holy Eucharist." Catholic Chronicles 1. Lindale, Texas: Last Days Ministries, 1984a.

———. "The Sacrifice of the Mass." Catholic Chronicles 2. Lindale, Texas: Last Days Ministries, 1984b.

———. "Salvation according to Rome." Catholic Chronicles 3. Lindale, TX: Last Days Ministries, 1984c.

———. "What Did Vatican II Really Change?" Catholic Chronicles 4. Lindale, TX: Last Days Ministries, 1984d.

Gründler, Johannes. *Lexikon der christlichen Kirchen und Sekten.* 2 vols. Vienna: Herder, 1961.

Gruss, Edmond C. *What Every Mormon Should Know.* Denver: Accent Books, 1976.

———. *Cults and the Occult.* Phillipsburg, NJ: Presbyterian and Reformed Publishing, 1980.

Gunkel, Hermann, and Leopold Zscharnack, eds., *Religion in Geschichte und Gegenwart*, 5 vols. Tübingen: Mohr, 1927.

Haag, Herbert. *Is Original Sin in Scripture?*, translated by Dorothy Thompson. New York: Sheed and Ward, 1969.

Hamblin, William J. "Aspects of an Early Christian Initiation Ritual." In *By Study and Also By Faith*, edited by John M. Lundquist and Stephen D. Ricks. 2 vols. Salt Lake City: Deseret Book and F.A.R.M.S., 1990.

Hamilton, J. G. de Roulhac, ed. *The Best Letters of Thomas Jefferson*. Boston: Houghton Mifflin, 1926.

Handbuch: Religiöse Gemeinschaften. Gütersloh: Mohn, 1985.

Hansen, Klaus J. *Mormonism and the American Experience*. Chicago: University of Chicago Press, 1981.

Hanson, R. P. C. *Tradition in the Early Church*. Philadelphia: Westminster, 1962.

Hardon, John A. *The Question and Answer Catholic Catechism*. New York: Doubleday Image, 1981.

Harrison, F. F., G. W. Bromiley, and C. F. H. Henry. *Baker Dictionary of Theology*. Grand Rapids: Baker, 1960.

Harvey, Van A. *A Handbook of Theological Terms*. New York: Macmillan, 1964.

Hastings, James, ed. *Encyclopaedia of Religion and Ethics*. 12 vols. New York: Scribner's Sons, 1951.

Hatch, Edwin. *The Influence of Greek Ideas on Christianity*. Gloucester, MA: Smith, 1970.

Hayman, Peter. "Monotheism—A Misused Word in Jewish Studies?" *Journal of Jewish Studies* 42 (Spring 1991): 1-15.

Hedengren, Paul. *In Defense of Faith: Assessing Arguments against Latter-day Saint Belief*. Provo, UT: Bradford & Wilson, 1985.

Heiler, Freidrich. *Erscheinungsformen und Wesen der Religion*. Stuttgart: Kohlhammer, 1961.

Heinerman, John, and Anson Shupe. *The Mormon Corporate Empire*. Boston: Beacon, 1985.

Heinrich, Gerd. *Geschichte Preussens: Staat und Dynastie*. Frankfurt am Main: Propyläen, 1981.

Helland, Dean M. "Meeting the Book of Mormon Challenge in Chile." Ph.D. diss., Oral Roberts University, 1990.

Herbermann, Charles G., et al., eds. *The Catholic Encyclopedia*. 16 vols. New York: Appleton, 1907-14.

Heyer, Friedrich. *Konfessionskunde*. Berlin: de Gruyter, 1977.

Hill, William J. *The Three-Personed God: The Trinity as a Mystery of Salvation*. Washington, D.C.: Catholic University of America, 1982.

Hillman, Eugene. *Polygamy Reconsidered*. Maryknoll, NY: Orbis, 1975.

Hinnells, John R., ed. *The Penguin Dictionary of Religion*. London: Penguin Books, 1984.

Hoekema, A. A. *The Four Major Cults*. Grand Rapids: Eerdmans, 1984.

Holst, Robert. "Polygamy and the Bible." *International Review of Missions* 56 (April 1967): 205-13.

Holzapfel, Heribert. *Die Sekten in Deutschland*. Regensburg: Koesel & Pustet, 1925.

Hunt, Dave. *The Cult Explosion*. Eugene, OR: Harvest House, 1980.

Husik, Isaac. *A History of Mediaeval Jewish Philosophy*. Philadelphia: The Jewish Publication Society of America, 1970.

Hutten, Kurt. *Seher, Grübler, Enthusiasten*. Stuttgart: Quell-Verlag der Evangelischen Gesellschaft, 1953.

"Introducing Ex-Mormons for Jesus." Monrovia, CA: Ex-Mormons for Jesus, n.d.

Ironside, H. A. *Letters to a Roman Catholic Priest*. Neptune, NJ: Loizeaux Brothers, 1982.

Irvine, Wm. C., ed. *Heresies Exposed*. 3rd ed. Neptune, NJ: Loizeaux Brothers, reprint of 1921 ed.

"Is Mormonism Christian?" Torch Light Series. Grand Rapids: Gospel Truths Ministries, 1989.

Jackson, Samuel M, ed. *The New Schaff-Herzog Encyclopedia of Religious Knowledge*. 13 vols. Grand Rapids: Baker, 1977.

Jacob, Christoph. *"Arkandisziplin," Allegorese, Mystagogie: Ein neuer Zugang zur Theologie des Ambrosius von Mailand.* Frankfurt: Hain, 1990.

Jaeger, Werner. *Early Christianity and Greek Paideia.* Cambridge: Harvard University Press, 1961.

Janson, H. W. *History of Art.* Rev. and enlarged. New York: Abrams, 1969.

Jeremias, Joachim. *The Eucharistic Words of Jesus.* New York: Scribner's, 1966.

"Jesus Is Sufficient!" Phoenix: Alpha and Omega Ministries, 1986.

"Jewish Leaders Attempt to Fight Effects of Evangelism." *Christianity Today* 28:17 (23 November 1984): 42.

Johnson, Paul. *A History of Christianity.* New York: Atheneum, 1983.

Jonas, Hans. *The Gnostic Religion.* 2nd ed., enlarged. Boston: Beacon, 1963.

Juergensmeyer, Mark, ed. *A Handbook for Teaching the Introductory Course in Religious Studies.* Berkeley: Office for Programs in Comparative Religion, Graduate Theological Union, 1988.

Keating, Karl. *Catholicism and Fundamentalism: The Attack on "Romanism" by "Bible Christians."* San Francisco: Ignatius, 1988.

Keller, Roger R. "The Mormons: Facts Versus Fiction." Sandy, UT: Mormon Miscellaneous, 1986a.

———. *Reformed Christians and Mormon Christians: Let's Talk.* N.p.: Pryor Pettengill, 1986b.

Kelly, J. N. D. *Early Christian Doctrines.* Rev. ed. San Francisco: Harper and Row, 1978.

Kimball, Edward L., ed. *The Teachings of Spencer W. Kimball.* Salt Lake City: Bookcraft, 1982.

Kimball, Stanley B. *Heber C. Kimball: Mormon Patriarch and Pioneer.* Urbana: University of Illinois Press, 1981.

Kirschbaum, Engelbert. *Lexikon der christlichen Ikonographie.* 8 vols. 2nd ed. Freiburg: Herder, 1970.

Kittel, Gerhard, and Gerhard Friedrich, eds. *Theological Dictionary of the New Testament*. 10 vols., translated by Geoffrey W. Bromiley. Grand Rapids: Eerdmans, 1964-76.

Klauser, Theodor, ed. *Reallexikon für Antike und Christentum*. Stuttgart: Hiersemann, 1950.

Kollek, Teddy, with Shulamith Eisner. *My Jerusalem*. New York: Summit Books, 1990.

Kraft, Heinrich. *Kirchenväter Lexikon*. Munich: Kösel, 1966.

Krause, Gerhard, and Gerhard Müller. *Theologische Realenzyklopädie*. Berlin: de Gruyter, 1979.

Küng, Hans. *Christ sein*. Munich: Deutscher Taschenbuchverlag, 1980.

Lackmann, Max. *Sola Fide: Eine exegetische Studie über Jakobus 2 zur reformatorischen Rechtfertigungslehre*. Gütersloh: Bertelsmann, 1949.

Lake, Kirsopp, trans. *The Apostolic Fathers*. 2 vols. Cambridge, MA: Harvard University Press, 1970.

Lanczkowski, Günter. *Geschichte der Religionen*. Frankfurt am Main: Fischer Taschenbuchverlag, 1972.

Larson, Bob. *Larson's Book of Cults*. Wheaton: Tyndale House, 1983.

Layton, Bentley. *The Gnostic Scriptures*. Garden City: Doubleday, 1987.

LeBaron, E. Dale, ed. *"All Are Alike Unto God."* Salt Lake City: Bookcraft, 1990.

Lewis, C. S. *Mere Christianity*. New York: Macmillan Company, 1960a.

―――. *The World's Last Night and Other* ͬ *says*. New York: Harcourt Brace Jovanovich, 1960b.

―――. *A Grief Observed*. New York: Bantam Books, 1963.

―――. *The Weight of Glory*. Grand Rapids: Eerdmans, 1965.

―――. *The Screwtape Letters*. New York: Macmillan Company, 1973.

Lewis, Gordon R. *Confronting the Cults*. Grand Rapids: Baker, 1966.

Lindsell, Harold. *The New Paganism*. San Francisco: Harper and Row, 1987.

Lovejoy, Arthur O. *The Great Chain of Being*. Cambridge: Harvard University Press, 1964.

Ludlow, Daniel H., ed. *Encyclopedia of Mormonism*. 4 vols. New York: Macmillan, 1992.

Luther, Martin. *D. Martin Luthers Werke*. 57 vols. Weimar: Hermann Böhlaus Nachfolger, 1883-1939.

———. *Die gantze Heilige Schrifft Deudsch* [1545], edited by Hans Volz and Heinz Blanke. 2 vols. Munich: Rogner and Bernhard, 1972.

MacArthur, John F., Jr. *The Gospel According to Jesus*. Grand Rapids: Zondervan, 1989.

McBrien, Richard P. *Catholicism*. Minneapolis: Winston, 1980.

McConkie, Bruce R., ed. *Doctrines of Salvation: Sermons and Writings of Joseph Fielding Smith*. 3 vols. Salt Lake City: Bookcraft, 1956.

———. *Doctrinal New Testament Commentary*. 3 vols. Salt Lake City: Deseret Book, 1965-73.

———. *Mormon Doctrine*. 2d ed. Salt Lake City: Bookcraft, 1966.

———. *The Promised Messiah: The First Coming of Christ*. Salt Lake City: Deseret Book, 1978.

———. "Our Relationship with the Lord." In *BYU 1981-82 Fireside and Devotional Speeches*. Provo, UT: BYU University Publications, 1982.

McCurry, Bob. "The Truth about Halloween." East Point, Georgia: Temple. Pamphlet, n.d.

McDannell, Colleen, and Bernhard Lang. *Heaven: A History*. New York: Vintage Books, 1990.

McDowell, Josh, and Don Stewart. *Understanding the Cults*. San Bernardino: Campus Crusade for Christ, 1983.

McElveen, Floyd C. *The Mormon Illusion: What the Bible Says about Latter-day Saints*. Ventura, CA: Regal Books, 1979.

McKay, David O. *Gospel Ideals*. Salt Lake City: The Improvement Era, 1952.

McKay, Robert A., and John L. Smith. *Why Mormonism Is a Cult*. Marlow, OK: Utah Missions, 1985.

McKeever, Bill. "Behind Temple Doors." Santa Fe Springs, CA: Ex-Mormons for Jesus, n.d.

McLoughlin, William G. *Revivals, Awakenings, and Reform*. Chicago: University of Chicago Press, 1978.

McMurrin, Sterling M. *The Theological Foundations of the Mormon Religion*. Salt Lake City: University of Utah Press, 1965.

Macquarrie, John. *An Existentialist Theology*. Harmondsworth, UK: Penguin Books, 1973.

Madsen, Truman G., ed. *Reflections on Mormonism: Judaeo-Christian Parallels*. Provo, UT: Brigham Young University, Religious Studies Center, 1978.

Maguire, D. *Moral Absolutes and the Magisterium*. Washington: Corpus, 1970.

Maimonides, Moses. *The Guide of the Perplexed*, translated by Shlomo Pines. 2 vols. Chicago: University of Chicago Press, 1963.

Manschreck, Clyde L. *A History of Christianity in the World*. 2nd ed. Englewood Cliffs, NJ: Prentice-Hall, 1985.

Mantzaridis, Georgios I. *The Deification of Man: Saint Gregory Palamas and Orthodox Tradition*, translated by Liadain Sherrard. Cresswood, NY: St. Vladimir's Seminary, 1984.

Margoliouth, D. S. *Mohammed and the Rise of Islam*. New York: Putnam's Sons, 1905.

Martin, Walter. *The Rise of the Cults*. Grand Rapids: Zondervan Publishing House, 1955.

———. *Mormonism*. Minneapolis: Bethany House Publishers, 1976.

———. *Walter Martin's Cults Reference Bible*. Santa Ana: Vision House, 1981.

———. *Walter Martin Speaks out on the Cults*. Ventura: Vision House, 1983.

———. *The New Cults*. Ventura, California: Vision House, 1984.

———. *The Kingdom of the Cults*. Rev. and expanded. Minneapolis: Bethany House, 1985.

Matrisciana, Caryl. *Gods of the New Age*. Eugene, Oregeon: Harvest House, 1985.

Maust, John. "Pope Voices Concern over Catholic Defection." *Christianity Today* 34 (18 June 1990): 60-61.

Mays, James L., ed. *Harper's Bible Commentary*. San Francisco: Harper and Row, 1988.

M'Clintock, John, and James Strong, eds. *Cyclopaedia of Biblical, Theological, and Ecclesiastical Literature*. 12 vols. New York: Harper & Brothers, 1867-91.

Mead, Frank S., ed. *Handbook of Denominations in the United States*. Rev. by Samuel S. Hill. 8th ed. Nashville: Abingdon, 1985.

Meagher, Paul K., Thomas C. O'Brien, and Consuelo M. Aherne. *Encyclopedic Dictionary of Religion*. 3 vols. Washington, D.C.: Corpus, 1979.

Mensching, G. *Das heilige Schweigen*. Giessen: Töpelmann, 1926.

Metzger, Bruce M. *A Textual Commentary on the Greek New Testament*. New York: United Bible Societies, 1971.

Meyer, Marvin W., trans. *The Secret Teachings of Jesus: Four Gnostic Gospels*. New York: Random House, 1986.

Milgrom, Jacob. *Studies in Cultic Theology and Terminology*. Leiden: Brill, 1983.

Miller, Madeleine S. *A Treasury of the Cross*. New York: Harper & Brothers, 1956.

Molland, Einar. *Christendom*. New York: Philosophical Library, 1959.

Morey, Robert A. *How to Answer a Mormon*. Minneapolis: Bethany House, 1983.

"The Mormon Church and the African." San Juan Capistrano, CA: Christian Research Institute, n.d.

"Mormonism: Christian or Cult?" Rowland Heights, CA: Ex-Mormons for Jesus, n.d.

Morrison, Alexander B. *The Dawning of a Brighter Day: The Church in Black Africa*. Salt Lake City: Deseret Book, 1990.

Moyer, Elgin. *Wycliffe Biographical Dictionary of the Church*. Chicago: Moody, 1982.

Mullett, Michael. "From Sect to Denomination? Social Developments in Eighteen-Century English Quakerism." *The Journal of Religious History* 13:2 (December 1984): 168-91.

Munch, Johannes. *The Acts of the Apostles*. Garden City, NY: Doubleday, 1967.

Nash, Ronald. *The Concept of God*. Grand Rapids: Zondervan, 1983.

Nellas, Panayiotis. *Deification in Christ: The Nature of the Human Person*, translated by Norman Russell. Crestwood, NY: St. Vladimir's Seminary, 1987.

Neusner, Jacob, ed. *Christianity, Judaism, and Other Greco-Roman Cults: Studies for Morton Smith at Sixty*. 4 vols. Leiden: Brill, 1975.

Nibley, Hugh W. *Mormonism and Early Christianity*. Salt Lake City: Deseret Book and F.A.R.M.S., 1987.

———. *Since Cumorah*. 2d ed. Salt Lake City: Deseret Book and F.A.R.M.S., 1988.

———. *Tinkling Cymbals and Sounding Brass*. Salt Lake City: Deseret Book and F.A.R.M.S., 1991.

Nock, Arthur D. "The Christian *Sacramentum* in Pliny and a Pagan Counterpart," *The Classical Review* 38 (1924): 58-59.

Norman, Keith E. "Divinization: The Forgotten Teaching of Early Christianity." *Sunstone* 1 (Winter 1975): 14-19.

———. "Deification: The Content of Athanasian Soteriology." Ph.D. diss., Duke University, 1980.

Nygren, Anders. *Agape and Eros*, translated by Philip S. Watson. Chicago: University of Chicago Press, 1982.

O'Brien, T. C., ed. *Corpus Dictionary of Western Churches*. Washington, D.C.: Corpus, 1970.

O'Dea, Thomas F. "Mormonism and the Avoidance of Sectarian Stagnation: A Study of Church, Sect, and Incipient Nationality." *The American Journal of Sociology* 60:3 (November 1954): 285-93.

Oman, Susan S. "Are Mormons Christian?" *The Sunstone Review* 2:8 (August 1982): 9-10.

"One God: A Response to Mormon Apologists." Info Sheet #3. Phoenix: Alpha and Omega Ministries, n.d.

Orr, William F., and James A. Walther. *I Corinthians*. Garden City, NY: Doubleday, 1976.

O'Sullivan, John. "Rape in the New Age." *The American Spectator* 18 (August 1985): 22-23, 46.

Pagels, Elaine. *The Gnostic Gospels*. New York: Random House, 1981.

Palmer, Edwin H., ed. *The Encyclopedia of Christianity*. Wilmington, DE: National Foundation for Christian Education, 1964.

Papini, Giovanni. *The Devil*. New York: Dutton, 1984.

Parrinder, Geoffrey. *Dictionary of Non-Christian Religions*. Amersham, UK: Hulton, 1971.

Passantino, Bob, and Gretchen Passantino. *Witch Hunt*. Nashville: Nelson, 1990.

Paulsen, David L. "Early Christian Belief in a Corporeal Deity: Origen and Augustine as Reluctant Witnesses." *Harvard Theological Review* 83 (1990): 105-16.

Pelikan, Jaroslav. *The Emergence of the Catholic Tradition (100-600)*. *The Christian Tradition, vol. 1*. Chicago: University of Chicago Press, 1971.

———. *The Spirit of Eastern Christendom (600-1700)*. *The Christian Tradition, vol. 2*. Chicago: University of Chicago Press, 1974.

Peters, F. E. *Aristotle and the Arabs*. New York: New York University Press, 1968.

———. *Allah's Commonwealth*. New York: Simon and Schuster, 1973.

Peterson, Daniel C. "Does the Qur'an Teach Creation *Ex Nihilo*?" In *By Study and Also by Faith*, edited by John M. Lundquist and Stephen D. Ricks. 2 vols. Salt Lake City: Deseret Book and F.A.R.M.S., 1989, 1:584-610.

———. Review of Loftes Tryk, *The Best-Kept Secrets in the Book of Mormon*, in *Review of Books on the Book of Mormon* 3 (1991): 231-60.

Pétrement, Simone. *A Separate God: The Christian Origins of Gnosticism*, translated by Carol Harrison. San Francisco: Harper Collins, 1990.

Phipps, William E. "The Heresiarch: Pelagius or Augustine?" *Anglican Theological Review* 62 (1980): 124-33.

Placher, William C. *A History of Christian Theology*. Philadelphia: Westminster, 1983.

Powell, B. G. "The Purpose of the Messianic Secret: A Brief Survey." *Expository Times* 80 (1969): 308-10.

Pratt, Orson. "Christian Polygamy in the Sixteenth Century." *The Seer* 1 (December 1853): 177-83.

Pratt, Parley P. *The Essential Parley P. Pratt*. Salt Lake City: Signature, 1990.

Pressau, Jack R. *I'm Saved, You're Saved . . . Maybe*. Atlanta: Knox, 1977.

Prestige, G. L. *Fathers and Heretics*. London: SPCK, 1940.

"Questions and Answers: Is Mormonism Christian?" Garden Grove, CA: Ex-Mormons for Jesus, n.d.

"Questions for Your Temple Tour." Issaquah, WA: Saints Alive in Jesus, n.d.

Rahner, Karl, et al., eds. *Sacramentum Mundi: An Encyclopedia of Theology*. 6 vols. London: Burns & Oates, 1968-70.

Ransom, Ira T. "It's Great to KNOW You're SAVED!" Sacramento, CA: United Missionary Fellowship, n.d.

Reicke, Bo. *The Epistles of James, Peter, and Jude*. Garden City, NY: Doubleday, 1964.

Richardson, Alan. *Creeds in the Making: A Short Introduction to the History of Christian Doctrine*. London: SCM, 1990.

Ridenour, Fritz. *So What's the Difference?* Rev. ed. Ventura, CA: Regal Books, 1979.

Robbins, Thomas. "Nuts, Sluts and Converts: Studying Religious Groups as Social Problems: A Comment." *Sociological Analysis: A Journal in the Sociology of Religion* 46:2 (Summer 1985): 172.

Roberts, Alexander, and James Donaldson, eds. *The Ante-Nicene Fathers*. 10 vols. Grand Rapids: Eerdmans, 1987.

Robertson, Irvine. *What Cults Believe*. 4th ed. Chicago: Moody, 1983.

Robinson, James M., ed. *The Nag Hammadi Library*. San Francisco: Harper & Row, 1978.

Robinson, John A. T. *Can We Trust the New Testament?* Grand Rapids: Eerdmans, 1977.

Robinson, Stephen E. *Are Mormons Christians?* Salt Lake City: Bookcraft, 1991.

Rowe, David. "Trouble in Camelot." *World Christian* 4 (July-August 1985): 26-31.

Rudolph, Kurt. *Gnosis: The Nature and History of Gnosticism*, translated by Robert M. Wilson. San Francisco: Harper & Row, 1983.

Rusch, William G. "Getting to Know the Orthodox." *The Lutheran* (2 April 1986): 10-12.

Russell, Jeffrey B. *Medieval Civilization*. New York: Wiley & Sons, 1968.

Ryle, Bishop. "The Only True Church." Issaquah, WA: Saints Alive in Jesus, n.d.

Sackett, Charles. "A Mormon Temple Worker Asks Some Questions." Issaquah, WA: Saints Alive in Jesus, n.d.

Sandeen, Ernest R., and Frederick Hale. *American Religion and Philosophy*. Detroit: Gale Research, 1978.

Sanders, Alain L. "Tilting at 'Secular Humanism.' " *Time* 128 (28 July 1986): 68.

Sanders, E. P. *Paul*. Oxford: Oxford University Press, 1991.

Sanders, J. Oswald. *Cults & Isms: Ancient and Modern*. Rev. and enlarged. Grand Rapids: Zondervan, 1962.

Schaff, Philip, ed. *The Creeds of Christendom*. 3 vols. 6th ed. Grand Rapids: Baker, 1983.

Schaff, Philip, and Henry Wace, eds. *A Select Library of Nicene and Post-Nicene Fathers of the Christian Church*. 14 vols. Grand Rapids: Eerdmans, 1978-79.

Scharffs, Gilbert. *The Truth about "The God Makers."* Salt Lake City: Horizon, 1986.

Scheel, Otto. *Luthers Stellung zur heiligen Schrift*. Tübingen: Mohr, 1902.

Schindler, Laurenz. *Die altchristliche Arkandisziplin und die antiken Mysterien*. Tetschen a. E.: Programm, 1911.

Schweizer, Eduard. "Zur Frage des Messiasgeheimnis bei Markus." *Zeitschrift für die Neutestamentliche Wissenschaft* 56 (1965): 1-8.

Schipper, Earl. *Cults in North America*. Grand Rapids: Baker, 1982.

Scott, Latayne C. *The Mormon Mirage*. Grand Rapids: Zondervan 1979.

Seale, Morris S. *Muslim Theology: A Study of Origins with Reference to the Church Fathers*. London: Luzac, 1964.

Segal, Alan F. *Paul the Convert: The Apostolate and Apostasy of Saul the Pharisee*. New Haven: Yale, 1990.

Sessions, Gene A. *Mormon Thunder: A Documentary History of Jedediah Morgan Grant.* Urbana: University of Illinois Press, 1982.

Shaw, Graham. *The Cost of Authority.* Philadelphia: Fortress, 1983.

Shipps, Jan. *Mormonism: The Story of a New Religious Tradition.* Urbana: University of Illinois Press, 1985.

Smith, George Albert. *Sharing the Gospel with Others.* Salt Lake City: Deseret Book, 1948.

Smith, Hyrum M., III, and Scott G. Kenney, eds. *From Prophet to Son: Advice of Joseph F. Smith to His Missionary Sons.* Salt Lake City: Deseret Book, 1981.

Smith, John L. *Witnessing Effectively to Mormons.* Marlow, OK: Utah Missions, 1975.

———. *Hope or Despair?* Rev. and enlarged. Marlow, OK: Utah Missions, 1976.

———. "Is Mormonism Christian?"

———. "Mormonism: Christian or Cult?"

———. "Mormonism Has Another Jesus." Lebanon, OH: Fellowship Tract League, n.d.

Smith, Joseph F. *Gospel Doctrine.* 8th ed. Salt Lake City: Deseret Book, 1949.

Smith, Morton. *Clement of Alexandria and a Secret Gospel of Mark.* Cambridge, MA: Harvard University Press, 1973.

———. *The Secret Gospel.* Clearlake, CA: Dawn Horse, 1983.

Smith, Oswald J. "Which Church Saves?" Westchester, IL: Good News, n.d.

Smith, Paul B. *Other Gospels.* London: Marshall, Morgan & Scott, 1970.

Smith, Wilfred C. *The Meaning and End of Religion.* New York: Macmillan, 1963.

Snodgrass, Klyne R. "Justification by Grace—to the Doers: An Analysis of the Place of Romans 2 in the Theology of Paul." *New Testament Studies* 32 (1986): 72-93.

Sontag, Frederick. "The Once and Future Christian." *International Journal for the Philosophy of Religion* 19 (1986): 113-21.

Spencer, James R. *Beyond Mormonism: An Elder's Story*. Grand Rapids: Chosen Books, 1984.

Spittler, Russell P. *Cults and Isms*. Grand Rapids: Baker, 1962.

Stark, Rodney, and William S. Bainbridge. "Of Churches, Sects and Cults: Preliminary Concepts for a Theory of Religious Movements." *Journal for the Scientific Study of Religion* 18:2 (1979): 127-28.

Starkes, Thomas M. *Confronting Cults: Old and New*. Chattanooga: AMG, 1984.

Stendahl, Krister. "The Sermon on the Mount and Third Nephi." In *Reflections on Mormonism: Judaeo-Christian Parallels*, edited by Truman G. Madsen. Provo, UT: Brigham Young University, Religious Studies Center, 1978.

Stephens, W. P. *The Theology of Huldrych Zwingli*. Oxford: Clarendon, 1986.

Stewart, George R. *Names on the Globe*. New York: Oxford University Press, 1975.

Stupperich, Robert. *Melanchthon*. Berlin: de Gruyter, 1960.

Swaggart, Jimmy. "The Catholic Confessional." *The Evangelist* (November 1985a): 37-41.

———. "Christianity and Catholicism." *The Evangelist* (July 1985b): 35-40.

———. "What is Meant by the Trinity? And When We Get to Heaven Will We See Three Gods?" Typed, undated paper.

Tanner, Jerald, and Sandra Tanner. *The Lucifer-God Doctrine*. Salt Lake City: Utah Lighthouse Ministry, 1988.

Tappert, Theodore G., ed. and trans. *Luther: Letters of Spiritual Counsel*. Philadelphia: Westminster, 1955.

"Temple Marriage: Eternal Commitment or Eternal Damnation?" Issaquah, WA: Saints Alive in Jesus, n.d.

Teske, Roland J. "Divine Immutability in Saint Augustine." *The Modern Schoolman* 63 (May 1986): 233-49.

This We Believe; By This We Live. Rev. ed. of the Baltimore Catechism. Paterson, NJ: St. Anthony Guild, 1962.

Thompson, Edward K. *The World's Great Religions*. New York: Time, 1957.

Thompson, Wes. "What We Should Know about Roman Catholicism: Focus on the Mass." Huntington Beach, CA: Concerned Christians for Catholics, n.d.

Tope, Wally. "Are You REALLY Good Enough to Go to Celestial Glory?" La Canada Flintridge, CA: Wally Tope, n.d.

––––––. "But I Have a Testimony of the Holy Ghost That . . ." La Canada, CA: W. Tope, n.d.

––––––. "Can the Mormon Jesus Save You?" La Canada Flintridge, CA: Wally Tope, n.d.

––––––. "Faith without Works Is Dead . . ." La Canada, CA: Wally Tope, n.d.

––––––. "The Trinity: Nonsense or Good Sense?" La Canada Flintridge, CA: Wally Tope, n.d.

––––––. "Who's Persecuting Who [*sic*]?" La Canada Flintridge, CA: Wally Tope, n.d.

––––––. "Why Should I Pray about the Book of Mormon When . . .?" La Canada Flintridge, CA: Wally Tope, n.d.

––––––. "Would You Risk Eternal Life for These Men?" La Canada Flintridge, CA: Wally Tope, n.d.

Treadgold, Donald W. *A History of Christianity*. Belmont, MA: Nordland, 1979.

Tucker, Ruth A. "Nonorthodox Sects Report Global Membership Gains." *Christianity Today* 30 (13 June 1986): 48-51.

––––––. *Another Gospel: Alternative Religions and the New Age Movement*. Grand Rapids: Zondervan, 1989.

Tuckett, C. M., ed. *The Messianic Secret*. Philadelphia: Fortress, 1983.

Turner, H. W. "Monogamy: A Mark of the Church?" *International Review of Missions* 55 (July 1966): 313-21.

Unger, Merril F. *Demons in the World Today*. Wheaton: Tyndale House, 1984.

Utter, David. "Mormonism To-Day." *The New World* 6 (1897): 13-32.

Vacant, A., and E. Mangenot, eds., *Dictionnaire de Théologie Catholique*, 15 vols. Göttingen: Vandenhoeck & Ruprecht, 1894.

van Baalen, J. K. *The Chaos of Cults*. 4th ed. Rev. and enlarged. Grand Rapids: Eerdmans, 1983.

Vroom, Hendrik M. "Do All Religious Traditions Worship the Same God?" *Religious Studies* 26 (March 1990): 73-90.

Walker, James K. "A Response to Stephen E. Robinson's *Are Mormons Christians?*" An unpublished paper presented at the Christian Institute of Mormon Studies, Salt Lake City, Utah, June 1992.

Walters, Wesley, "From Occult to Cult with Joseph Smith Jr." *The Journal of Pastoral Practice* 1 (1977): 121-37.

Weir, Robert F. *The Religious World*. New York: Macmillan, 1982.

Welch, John W. *The Sermon at the Temple and the Sermon on the Mount: A Latter-day Saint Approach*. Salt Lake City: Deseret Book and F.A.R.M.S., 1990.

Wells, Robert E. *We Are Christians Because* . . . Salt Lake City: Deseret Book, 1985.

Wewers, Gerd A. *Geheimnis und Geheimhaltung im rabbinischen Judentum*. Berlin: de Gruyter, 1975.

Weyland, Jack. "When Nonmembers Say We're Not Christians, What Is the Best Way to Respond?" *Ensign* 15 (January 1985): 43-45.

Whalen, William J. *Separated Brethren: A Survey of Non-Catholic Christian Denominations in the United States*. Rev. ed. Milwaukee: Bruce. 1963.

"What Is a Cult?" Santa Fe Springs, CA: Ex-Mormons for Jesus, n.d.

"What the Mormon Church Teaches about Jesus Christ." Phoenix: Alpha and Omega Ministries, n.d.

"What the Mormons Think of Christ REALLY . . ." Wolcott, NY: Berean Christian Ministries, n.d.

Whealon, John F. Letter: "Catholics Concerned about Fundamentalism: Why Is the Catholic Hierarchy Afraid to Let Catholics Study the Bible on Their Own?" *Faith for the Family* 14:4 (April 1986): 16-17.

"Which Will You Believe? The Holy Scriptures, God's Unchangeable Word or The Human Traditions of Men [*sic*]." Havertown, PA: Conversion Center, n.d.

Widtsoe, John A., ed. *Discourses of Brigham Young*. Salt Lake City: Deseret, 1943.

Wilken, Robert L. *The Christians as the Romans Saw Them.* New Haven and London: Yale University Press, 1984.

Williams, Clyde J. *The Teachings of Lorenzo Snow.* Salt Lake City: Bookcraft, 1984.

Winston, David. "Creation Ex Nihilo Revisited: A Reply to Jonathan Goldstein." *Journal of Jewish Studies* 37 (Spring 1986): 88-91.

Witte, Bob. "And It Came to Pass." Safety Harbor, FL: Ex-Mormons for Jesus, n.d.

Woodward, Kenneth, L. "Bible-Belt Confrontation." *Newsweek* (4 March 1985): 65.

Woodward, Kenneth L., Monroe Anderson, and Karen Springen. "Is Fundamentalism Addictive?" *Newsweek* (5 August 1985): 63.

Wrede, William. *The Messianic Secret*, translated by J. C. G. Greig. Cambridge: Clarke, 1971.

Young, Frances. " 'Creatio Ex Nihilo: A Context for the Emergence of the Christian Doctrine of Creation." *Scottish Journal of Theology* 44 (1991): 139-151.

Yount, John H. "Black Brother, Black Sister, Can You Believe . . .?" Mission Viego, CA: Mission to Utah, n.d.

Zacchello, Joseph. *Secrets of Romanism.* Neptune, NJ: Loizeaux Brothers, 1984.

Scripture Citation Index

BOOK OF MORMON

Index of Early Christian Writings

▲

Subject Index

▲